THE SENSE OF FORM
IN LITERATURE AND LANGUAGE

MICHAEL AND MARIANNE SHAPIRO

SECOND, EXPANDED EDITION

SCOTTS VALLEY, CALIFORNIA

Shapiro, Michael, 1939–; Shapiro, Marianne, 1940–2003
   The sense of form in literature and language / by Michael and
   Marianne Shapiro
   p. cm.
   Versions of parts of this book were previously published in
various sources.
Includes bibliographical references and index.

Second, Expanded Edition, 2009,
   Scotts Valley, CA
First Edition, 1998, published by St. Martin's Press, New York, NY
ISBN 1449515738

Book design by Carol Pentleton

Or you survive when I in earth am rotten,
Or I shall live your epitaph to make,
From hence your memory death cannot take,
Although in me each part will be forgotten.
Your name from hence immortal life shall have,
Though I, once gone, to all the world must die:
The earth can yield me but a common grave,
When you entombed in men's eyes shall lie.
Your monument shall be my gentle verse,
Which eyes not yet created shall o'er-read;
And tongues to be, your being shall rehearse,
When all the breathers of this world are dead;
   You still shall live, such virtue hath my pen,
   Where breath most breathes, even in the mouths of men.

William Shakespeare, Sonnet 81

CONTENTS

PREFACE

More than a decade has passed since the first edition of this book (1998), during which the coauthor of many of the chapters, my wife and lifelong collaborator, the comparatist, medievalist, and Renaissance scholar Marianne Shapiro, met her untimely death. Emblematic of her modesty and generosity of spirit, she had chosen at the time of original publication to limit the recognition of her contribution to an acknowledgment in the final paragraph of the Preface.

The main impetus behind this second, expanded edition is my desire to make Marianne's coauthorship explicit, thereby making it a kind of sequel to our *Figuration in Verbal Art* (1988). I also wanted to add two chapters, "Literary-Historical Consequences of the Russian Non-Renaissance in a Comparative Context" and "Rereading Dostoevsky's *The Double.*" The first was written by us jointly—indeed, Marianne's very much the lion's share. The second existed as a manuscript in torso. She had struggled to finish it though gravely ill. In 2004, I completed her draft and prepared it for publication in the journal *Russian Literature* (*LVI* [2004]). In a letter to me describing his reaction to the article, the late dean of American Dostoevsky scholars, Victor Terras, judged it the most profound and most comprehensive analysis of *The Double* ever written.

Besides the addition of these two chapters, the only major changes from the first edition are the elimination of the division into three parts ("Prose," "Poetry," "Language") and the imposition of a new order of chapters based on their presumed importance to students and advanced readers. Minor changes, necessitated by these major ones, as well as others (corrections, especially in appendices 1–3 in chapter 1) have been introduced silently.

While she was alive and still far from her peak as a scholar, it was already remarked of Marianne by a fellow critic of the first rank that for intelligence, intellectual imagination, and productivity she had no peers in the field of Romance philology; and that to find her equals one would have to turn to such giants of two generations ago as Leo Spitzer and Erich Auerbach.

In this light, her characteristically unassuming self-assessment, dated two years before her death, is worth reproducing here:

> I have always been and continue to be involved in research and teaching in my original areas of specialization, the works of Dante and Renaissance epic (Ariosto and Tasso), and my current research has broadened and deepened into an involvement with cultural studies. I have consistently brought an interdisciplinary perspective to teaching and writing, as well as a strong belief in practical criticism and in the importance of versatility.
>
> My first book, *Woman Earthly and Divine in the Comedy of Dante*, was also the first modern work on the poem's female characters as such. I continued this line of research by publishing the first American study of the female troubadours of the 12th century, which stimulated a considerable body of research. These publications, predating the feminist wave in the United

States, have recently enjoyed a surge of renewed interest.

The book I published in 1990, *De vulgari eloquentia, Dante's Book of Exile*, contains the only English translation of the treatise based on original scholarship and is routinely cited as a source of information and explication of Dante's language theory. I have also made permanent contributions to the store of general knowledge of the *Comedy* in a number of my forty-odd articles on the subject. My latest book, *Dante and the Knot of Body and Soul* (St. Martin's Press, 1998) will, I believe, open entirely new vistas for Dante studies.

The scholarship summarized on my vita involves poetics and mythology as well as literary history. Over time it has drawn nearer to the concerns of Latinists and teachers of classics. *The Poetics of Ariosto*, for example, examines Renaissance rewritings of mythological narratives, and the Dante research reevaluates the crucial structural impact of the *Aeneid* on the *Comedy* in a consistently analytical perspective. I try to stay clear of the twin pitfalls of literature being either self-referential or solely a cultural document.

I have worked across disciplinary boundaries on such apparently disparate topics as ballet and television (the situation comedy *All in the Family*). *Figuration in Verbal Art* contains some of those pieces. In sum, they seek to establish a common interpretative language by which to examine the production of different arts within one compass.

My current project is a book called *Constructing Leonardo*, based on a course I gave at Brown in 1991. It will study the cultural image of Leonardo da Vinci (man and work) as it has been fashioned and elaborated from his lifetime to the present day. Leonardo's own writings will figure among the data. Of special relevance will be an exploration of the relationship between art and science, including a section on the spiroform "hand" of Leonardo the draftsman. Most of the book will deal with the Leonardo "myth" (including androgyny) built up over centuries and composed of a mélange of legend, art history, Freudian diagnosis, fictional reconstruction, modernist manifesto, and popular culture including film (such as *Mona Lisa*).

My distinguishing trait as a teacher is versatility. I have wide experience of and a deep attachment to teaching at every level, and I hope to continue exploring new areas of research and offering courses aimed at a variety of student audiences, including undergraduates with little university experience in humanistic studies. Two of the Ph.D.s whose doctoral dissertations I directed had little or no acquaintance with Italian literature or Provençal when they became my students; I saw them through their entire course of study. At the other end of the spectrum, it has been especially satisfying to watch the progress of language students, all the more so because English, not Italian, was my first language, and my approach benefits from an experience analogous to theirs. An ability to adjust to changing circumstances is, I believe, essential to success in teaching, as is a problem-solving attitude.

Marianne Shapiro died on June 3, 2003.

*This book is dedicated to the undying memory
of my wife the metaphysician.*

M. S.
Los Angeles, Calif.

PREFACE TO THE FIRST EDITION

This book is intended to continue the general line of research on language and literature under the aegis of Charles Peirce's theory of signs (his semeiotic) which I began in *The Sense of Grammar: Language as Semeiotic* and *The Sense of Change: Language as History*. While in these earlier books I was primarily concerned with establishing a semiotic linguistics, the present effort is devoted mainly to the analysis of verbal art, particularly of Russian prose fiction and poetry of the nineteenth and twentieth centuries. In this respect as well as others, this book is a natural continuation of *Figuration in Verbal Art:* both exemplify what a Peircean approach can contribute to the cognitive study of language and literature, and to the exploration of the semiotic nature of verbal creativity.

I began the serious study of language and literature some 40 years ago. In retrospect, I now realize that my early choice of Slavic linguistics as a home field equipped me with a special outlook which has determined the curve of my research ever since.

First, I am the beneficiary of a long and stable tradition of Slavic philological scholarship which regards the study of literature to be inseparable from the study of language. In the case of poetry, this orientation necessarily entails seeing verse as a structure, of which the building blocks are primarily linguistic; and taking the form of these building blocks to be part of the content. In the case of prose, it means paying close attention to levels of discourse, semantic stratification, and matters of style. Analysis of verse and analysis of prose fiction, while taking account of the differences in approach necessitated by differences in form and genre, join hands in the broader context of humanistic research because each must ultimately give its due to language as the only sure repository of meaning.

Second, as a practitioner of scholarship with Slavic as its focus, I have followed in the tradition of involving oneself immediately in research with a theoretical and universalizing significance while being simultaneously immersed in linguistic and literary analysis at its most practical microcosmic level. This kind of work routinely assumes a viable reconciliation between (1) languages and texts as general human phenomena to be studied without regard to time or place and (2) the attitude that every language and every text is the unique product of human creativity, inseparable from its temporal and cultural locus. Criticism rises above its ancillary role when its object presents difficulties—linguistic, conceptual, cultural, ideological.

Because art belongs squarely to the aesthetic realm it is only partially amenable to rational analysis. A fundamental asymmetry obtains between aesthetic objects as they are experienced and our ability to talk about them intelligibly. There is (then) no automatic gain in understanding from analysis, quite irrespective of its quality. If interpretation wishes to be of service, it must acknowledge that its epistemological locus is somewhere in the void between art and knowledge, in a mental no-man's-land where indeterminacy is the order of the day. Under these circumstances, the best a literary analysis aware of its inherent limitations can hope to achieve is to see texts in the round, using bits and pieces as evidence to form a representation of the work of verbal art that does justice to how the form shapes the content—and thereby our experience of it.

Versions of parts of this book, some coauthored by my wife, Marianne Shapiro, have appeared in *Language* 74: 1 (chapter 1), *Elementa* 2: 2 (chapter 3), *Alexander Lipson In Memoriam* (chapter 6), *University of Toronto Quarterly* 61: 3 (chapter 7), *Words and Images: Essays in Honour of Professor (Emeritus) Dennis Ward* (chapter 8), *American Contributions to the Eleventh International Congress of Slavists* (chapter 8), *Russian Verse Theory* (chapter 9); *American Speech* 68: 3, 65: 3, and 72: 4 (chapter 10); and *The American Journal of Semiotics* 10: 3–4 (chapter 11).

M.S.

New York, NY

INTRODUCTION

The following chapters collectively argue that the formal and conceptual are organically inseparable.

We open with "Sound and Meaning in Shakespeare's Sonnets," which seeks to explicate the long-intuited and long-debated relationship between the two fundamental linguistic categories as they determine the structure of Shakespeare's poems in methodologically viable and consistent terms. Nothing in this book better illustrates its guiding principle: that the formal and the conceptual aspects are not merely copresent but systematically intertwined. The argument asks readers to subordinate matters such as alliteration to a more rigorous means of sound differentiation, pleads for an analogical form of understanding rather than "one-to-one" links, and demonstrates the mutual impact of the phonological and the semantic matter of the poems.

One of the formal differences between verse and prose in the modern period is the higher degree of semiotic asymmetry between mimesis and allegoresis that prose countenances, indeed invites. "Rereading Dostoevsky's *The Double*" reanalyzes a particular conundrum of criticism on this pathbreaking early novel. Its complexities have created an obstacle to the paean it deserves through Dostoevsky's blurring—indeed his erasure—

of the boundaries between literal and figural meanings, between the senses of doubling that the author plumbs by a rich variety of means, among them a free use of repetition, irony, and intersecting self-deceptions—all forms of doubling. There follows no reunification, no explication in a nutshell of the wellsprings of action and feeling; no reintegration of personality. Dostoevsky himself thought, when looking back 30 years after *The Double*'s first publication, that he had failed to give the novel's form its due, but on the way to that self-appraisal he also saw his hero, Goliadkin, as the rendering of "a very great type in its social significance." In keeping with the latter judgment, this chapter argues that the work is a masterpiece of tragicomic mimesis instancing a foresighted, inspirational literary logic; that the social corollaries to Goliadkin and *The Double* are replete with significance; and that the psychological rendering of the Goliadkinist pathology is equal if not superior to that of Dostoevsky's great novels.

Readers of Dostoevsky have long recognized that far more than the cognition of meaning is involved in their experience of him, that their own open relationship with his work so forcefully compels a reconsideration of their own lives and actions as to render intelligible the (often extreme) subjectivity of the characters. "Dostoevsky's Modes of Signifying" probes the implications of interpretation and self-knowledge or ignorance among the characters themselves. Paradoxically, no process more actively exemplifies the "formal" or aesthetic aspect once the latter is understood to be sensible awareness itself, as literally opposed to the "anaesthetic," which involves a loss or deadening of feeling.

While the absence of a Renaissance in Russia has been taken for granted, the implications of this fact have not been exploited in seeking to understand the general trajectory of Russia's literary development. "Literary-Historical Consequences of the Russian Non-Renaissance in a Comparative Context" adopts a pan-Slavic and European perspective that refracts it in the light of a key concomitant, the absence of a rationalizing theology, and concludes with a semiotic characterization of the three main modes of representation—iconic, deictic, and symbolic—that seeks to explain the special features of Russian literary production.

"Interpreting Bulgakov's *The Master and Margarita*" relies on a prior emotional response to the work and an ensuing desire to solve its mysteries. Critical attempts at theologically based parallels or substitutions for characters and events notoriously yield no interpretative "key," yet the persistence of the Christ story amounts to more than an expensive prank, as readers intuitively recognize. To demonstrate this, however, means to take leave of literary speech, appreciation, and the rhetoric of praise. The close formal argument of this chapter, which touches upon the formal semiotics of the Trinity, strives beyond Bulgakov's shadowy representations of related matters to shed light on what the implied rules of this novel exclude from overt discussion: the "absenting" of God from the world.

Our approach to Sologub's grotesque and expressionistic novel *The Petty Demon*, on the other hand, takes its departure from a text-specific but arbitrary and confusing array of literary reference to Russian "monuments" like Pushkin—all too often a mere pretext for non-signifying catalogues. But allusion, with all of its implications for those rooted in the common culture mourned by this novel, is part of its very flesh and bone, the twist on literature more than a clue to the distortions throughout. From the mocking flashes of intertext and even more from the large plot-structures that build mirages on classical foundations we draw an entire intuitive experience of lost worlds.

Contrary to romanticist notions of the splendid isolation of writers, verbal art involves implicit dialogue, which Plato and Aristotle considered to be the very form of thought itself. "Dialogism and Poetic Discourse" argues for the cognitive necessity of at least a virtual addressee, revising Bakhtin's belief that the lyric genre transcends the inherently dialogic nature of the verbal sign and tracing the dialogic imperative in forms from book inscriptions to magical spells to Dante's *Comedy*.

Formal analysis of verbal art works can be a valuable interpretative proving ground or filter of biographically (or autobiographically) derived information, bringing to light previously unattested phases of the creative process—and new and valid meanings. Chapter 8 encompasses two aspects of "Pushkin's Mentors" which show two quite different sets of results. Each part of the chapter focuses on the assimilation of an entire mentality, showing how the seemingly "external" means afforded by stylistic criteria enable us to see within. The discussion of Pushkin's debt to Lomonosov, perhaps an example of dialogism at the most clearly evident level of poetic practice, goes beyond the "footnote" material of thematic suggestions and scattered stylistic imitations to show how Pushkin's critiques and qualified tributes to his predecessor iconize Lomonosov's own poetic persona, uncovering a strong Lomonosovian aspect of the Russian national poet's own work. Exploring Pushkin's assimilation of Petrarch through his reading of a Russian contemporary, Batiushkov, who championed Petrarch in Russia, the second part deals in greater detail with Pushkin's total psychological experience of the Petrarchan world—from the benefit accorded him by Petrarch's limpid, semiprecious lexical selectivity to the spontaneous reinterpretation of Petrarchan ambiguity. In this section the reader will also find the investigation of comparative sonority between representative works of the two poets which gave rise to the Shakespeare chapter and which is included here with a view to illustrating its usefulness in revealing profound—sometimes otherwise unsuspected—poetic affinities or discontinuities.

"The Meaning of Meter" plunges us into the problematics of a matter as old as Aristotle's *Poetics*, whether different meters have what contemporary Russian verse theorists call a "semantic aureole." The answer to this question is pursued along a path that has existed since the heyday of European structuralism but has remained hidden in plain sight, namely in the concept of markedness, which is the form of meaning, otherwise the evaluative third member—what Peirce termed the interpretant—that gives sense to fundamentally triune relations between the other two members of the semiotic situation, sign and object. An analysis in markedness-theoretic terms of formal properties of the classical Russian syllabotonic meters and their historical development yields a new and far-reaching conception of the coherence of metrical form.

An appraisal of form in ordinary language occupies the last two chapters. "Wimp English" is a kind of trial balloon, an invitation to further exploration of how apparently trivial details of contemporary speech can enlighten us as to the cognitive states and worldviews of speakers. Wimphood includes—among many other traits—preference for passive and conditional grammatical structures, fear of figurative language (balanced by the overuse of tired, lexicalized "metaphors"), and the effete substitution of "authenticity" for truth.

"Boundaries," the concluding chapter, is an inquiry into the ways in which the purely mental nature of bounded entities and the imputation of their purposiveness affect language and culture. We apply the superficially opposed functions of binding and separating within any unified structure to questions of linguistic usage—such as why many speakers have come to treat the coordinate *you and I* as a phrasal compound insulated from individuation at its internal boundaries, or why one increasingly hears locutions like *the problem is is that...*, or the pleonastic *continue on.* The argument expands to include problems of figurative language and then the effects of the negativity, rehierarchization, and instability fundamental to the establishment of cultural norms and, indeed, of any continuum.

1

SOUND AND MEANING
IN SHAKESPEARE'S SONNETS

More has been written about the Sonnets than any of Shake-speare's works except *Hamlet*. Surprisingly, however, practically nothing in this vast secondary literature offers a comprehensive answer to one of the basic questions of poetics: whether the sounds of the Sonnets are an echo of their sense. George T. Wright's bibliographical overview (1985: 371–72) singles out two studies—by David I. Masson (1954) and Stephen Booth (1969: 66–79 et passim)—that investigate the Sonnets' phonetic structure in some detail, but neither of these authors has much of systematic purport to say beyond Shakespeare's obvious utilization of alliteration, assonance, and consonance in the service of syntactic and semantic parallelism.[1] Indeed, with respect to alliteration, the following might well function as an indirect characterization of the status of research on this problem:

> If Roman Jakobson had analyzed [Sonnet] 55, one of the things he would have noticed in its first strophe is the high incidence of alliteration on "m," "p," and "s,"

which is repeated in the third strophe. That Shakespeare "affects the letter" in these strophes, and that
they are thereby linked at the phonetic level is not in
question. Our question is what performative relation
this purely formal linkage at the level of the signifier
might bear to the sonnet's signification, its "contents"
as Shakespeare equivocally puts it. Here Jakobson can
be of little help, taking as he notoriously does, meaning or content for granted or reducing it to the received
ideas of other commentators. In terms of his analysis,
the most the empirical fact of alliteration can be is an
earnest of poetic power, alerting us that some extra-
communicative intention may be at work; in itself it
cannot be a source or explanation of that power. Occurring as it does within a semantic field that the alliteration does not itself generate, the function of
alliteration cannot be causal or integral to signified
meaning. Rather, it operates here as what Puttenham
would call a figure of "ornament" of the kind Shakespeare designates and illustrates as such in the previous sonnet ("O how much more doth beauty
beauteous seem / By that sweet ornament..."). As ornament or decoration, alliteration bears the same superficially attractive but functionally inessential
relation to the poem as "gilt" does to the "monuments
/ O princes" mentioned at the outset. Gilding is to
monumental sculpture as alliteration is to the sonnet.
(Felperin 1985: 176–77)

If alliteration is largely irrelevant to understanding the significance of the sound pattern, what else, then, could there be of
phonetic relevance in Sonnet 55? That a systematic answer to
this question might exist has been obscured, first and foremost,
by the lack of an appropriate methodology. We need to pose

questions regarding the data that presuppose abandoning the fruitless atomism of previous approaches while addressing the phonetic structure in terms of *groups* of sounds and their possible alignment with meanings. More positively, we need to face squarely the problem that sound-meaning correspondences, where they can be shown to exist, always involve the crossing of ontological domains—there being no "natural" connection between any sound and any meaning in isolation. Sets of sounds have *relational values* vis-à-vis each other, in the same sense as when we say that sets of meanings are structured relationally. The correspondences between sounds and meanings in poems are grounded in the relational values of these units in the structure of the language that serves as the raw material for the poetry.

In this light, a natural beginning to a methodological answer lies by way of an appeal to some general principles of linguistic structure. The sound patterns of all languages past and present are characterized by one fundamental division, that between sonorants and obstruents.[2] The class of sonorants includes all vowels and vowel-like sounds, i.e. nasals, liquids, and glides (sometimes called "semi-vowels"); the class of obstruents includes all other sounds, i.e., the "true" consonants (cf. Hymes 1960: 116).[3] In contemporary English, as in Early Modern English, the sonorants are (using orthography instead of phonetic transcription) the nasals *m, n, ng;* the liquids *l, r;* and the glides *h, y, w.*

Sonority is typically defined as the relative loudness of a given sound vis-à-vis other sounds with the same length, stress, and pitch; alternately, it is defined as the position of a sound on a scale that reflects the degree of openness or unobstructedness of the vocal apparatus. Sonorants are more "singable" than nonsonorants and may thus contribute to the perception of mellifluousness when found in non-discursive implementations of speech (cf. n. 10). A synoptic view of both aspects—loudness and unobstructedness—is encompassed by the concept of the relative amount of acoustic energy produced by a sound. A sonority hierarchy based on these phonetic characteristics can consequently be established, going from most sonorous to least sonorous sounds: vowels are ranked as most sonorous, followed in diminishing order of sonority by glides, liquids, nasals, and obstruents.

For our purposes, which have to do with the contexture of verse, it is enough to distinguish sonorants from obstruents. Only one further point needs to be taken into account: since the smallest phonetic domain of verse structure is that of the sylla-ble,[4] our analysis will concern sounds at the syllabic margins (on-sets and codas) of words. With respect to sonorants, any sequence of two or more of these sounds—whether or not it is separated by a vowel—counts as what will henceforth be called a sonorant unit (SU); a sequence of *n sonorants* is equal to *n – 1* SUs. Correspondingly, any cluster of two or more obstruents—whether it occurs within a word or at word boundaries without an intervening pause—counts as what will be called an obstru-ent unit (OU).[5]

Returning to Sonnet 55, here is a demonstration of the method of reckoning sonorant and obstruent units (single and double underscores mark SUs, dotted underscores mark OUs):

> Not marble nor the gilded monuments
> Of princes shall outlive this powerful rhyme,
> But you shall shine more bright in these contents[6]
> Than unswept stone, besmeared with sluttish time.
> When wasteful war shall statues overturn,
> And broils root out the work of masonry,
> Nor Mars his sword nor war's quick fire shall burn
> The living record of your memory.
> 'Gainst death and all oblivious enmity
> Shall you pace forth; your praise shall still find room

Even in the eyes of all posterity
That wear this world out to the ending doom.
So, till the judgement that yourself arise,
You live in this, and dwell in lovers' eyes.[7]

A count of the number of SUs yields 47. There are 140 syllables (14 per line times 10 lines) in the sonnet.[8] Dividing the number of SUs by the number of syllables, we get .336: this is the sonority quotient (SQ) of the poem. A perusal of the values of all 155 sonnets (appendix 1) reveals the fact that Sonnet 55 is one among only six whose SQs are above .300, making them the most sonorous in the entire sequence. The other five—all more sonorous than 55—are 13, 33, 71, 72, and 81 (see appendix 2).

A corresponding count of the OUs in Sonnet 55 yields the number 28, which when divided by 140 results in an OQ of .200. The range of OQs goes from .357—the least sonorous (in Sonnet 73)—to the most sonorous .100 (in Sonnet 72). This means that .357 is relatively neutral with regard to obstruency. In the relation between SQs and OQs, the SQ is normally more significant as a measure of a given sonnet's sonority than is its OQ.[9] In the case of Sonnet 55, then, whatever its OQ, an SQ of .336 is unattenuated as an indicator of high sonority.

The question arising at this point, of course, is the relevance of the sonnet's high sonority to its meaning. Sonnet 55 in its barest outlines is an assertion of the liberating power, via their incorporeality, of words ("rhyme," i.e., verse), as contrasted with the limitations inherent in monuments and other static objects. The renewed life the subject will gain is construed not only as a value in itself but as a dynamic liberation from oblivion in the course of time (" 'Gainst death and all oblivious enmity / Shall you *pace forth...*" [emphasis added]). This idea—whose compass in the Sonnets includes even Cupid, "a boy who is warned that he must in due course succumb to Time's inexorable law of death" (Pooler 1918: xxx)—is punctuated in the first line of the couplet, where "judgement" refers to the Day of Judgement: the addressee of the sonnet, will "arise" from the dead, but more importantly for the semantic dominant, will thereby achieve eternal freedom.

The sound pattern of 55 can thus be accounted for in terms of its isomorphism with the poem's meaning, where meaning in Shakespeare's sonnets is uniformly understood—for the purposes of evaluating the sound-meaning nexus—as being subtended in its most abstractly fundamental sense by the *opposition between freedom and constraint*. There is a particular appropriateness to this isomorphism that bears emphasis. Let us recall the nature of sonority in phonetic terms: sonorants are the freest sounds, those produced with the least amount of obstructedness in the vocal tract. With this in mind, we can see the relationship between sound and meaning in the sonnet to be natural and iconic, not arbitrary and emblematic.

Further to this point, it is instructive to take two sonnets that are immediately contiguous (but not linked in the sense to be developed later). Sonnets 33 and 34 contrast markedly in their SQs, which are respectively .371 and .179. In 33 the metaphor of the sun being obscured by clouds leads to the assertion of the sun's primacy as it emerges from the base obscurity which represents the beloved's dissipations. Smith (1981: 19, citing Puttenham for his definition) points out that the sonnet exemplifies a rhetorical figure ("paradiastole") which moderates and abates the force of a bad thing "by craft and for a pleasing purpose." Sonnet 34 has a more "severe" message, addressed straightforwardly to the beloved, with a possible "link between the raindrops on the poet's face and the tears on the Friend's" (Smith, 1981: 20), and the image of a wound that might be cured by a salve but leaves a disgrace behind. This sonnet in turn has a relatively high OQ: .264.

This leaves moot, for the time being, whether or not a sonnet with low sonority can implement the meaning of freedom; and conversely, whether high sonority can co-occur with the meaning of constraint. As a matter of actual fact there are no such cases of mismatches between sound and sense in the Sonnets. At the extreme ends of the spectrum, the match is complete: high sonority is isomorphous with the meaning of freedom, low sonority with that of constraint. At intermediate points, not unexpectedly given the aesthetic nature of the object of study, what we observe is either a loose correlation between sonority and freedom or no conclusive linking one way or the other.

This might be the moment to distinguish between musicality and sonority. Any poetic text labeled "song" might be expected to be full of sonorants and relatively unencumbered by obstruent clusters, which factors, separately and together, would seem to render the poetry "musical." But this intuitive guess turns out to be wrong, at least as far as Shakespeare is concerned. For instance, the Clown Feste's song in *Twelfth Night* ("O mistress mine, where are you roaming?"), which spans 95 syllables, has SQ and OQ values of .210 and .189, respectively—not especially sonorous by the standards of the Sonnets. Or take Thomas Gray's *Elegy Written in a Country Churchyard* ("The curfew tolls the knell of parting day"), which consists of 40-syllable stanzas (except for "The Epitaph" at the end, whose three stanzas are each 120 syllables). Its four-stanza spans of 160 syllables have SQ values in the .231 to .300 range, except for the opening quartet, whose SQ is .375. Coleridge's *Kubla Khan*, often held up as a model of musicality,[10] has an SQ of .264 and an OQ of .161 over its span of 485 syllables—neither of which is notable in terms of sonority.

Taking the other end of the range from Sonnet 55, we examine Sonnet 4, whose SQ of .086 (only 12 SUs!) renders it the least sonorous in the entire corpus:

> Unthrifty loveliness, why dost thou spend
> Upon thy self thy beauty's legacy?
> Nature's bequest gives nothing, but doth lend,

And being frank she lends to those are free.
Then, beauteous niggard, why dost thou abuse
The bounteous largess given thee to give?
Profitless usurer, why dost thou use
So great a sum of sums yet canst not live?
For having traffic with thyself alone
Thou of thyself thy sweet self dost deceive;
Then how when Nature calls thee to be gone,
What acceptable audit canst thou leave?
  Thy unused beauty must be tombed with thee,
  Which, usèd, lives th'executor to be.

We have here a poem which bristles with the imagery of
money, money lending, and inheritance, already familiar as constituent strands of a main theme in some of Shakespeare's most
prominent nonhistorical dramas (e.g., *Love's Labour's Lost, The
Merchant of Venice*)—economic limitations on freedom. The
sonnet is "built almost entirely upon the idea of spending, saving, hoarding, lending, giving, bequeathing, and the like" (Smith,
1981: 95). Smith points out (ibid.) that "live" in line 8 suggests
both "gain a livelihood" and "survive after death," heightening
the connotations of constraint imposed by usury. The fourth and
fifth lines convey this semantic dominant while playing on the
meaning of "lend": "Nature's bequest gives nothing, but doth
lend, / And being frank she lends to those are free."

After Sonnet 4 the least sonorous, based on its SQ of .100
(OQ = .221), is 67:

Ah, wherefore with infection should he live
And with his presence grace impiety,
That sin by him advantage should achieve
And lace itself with his society?
Why should false painting imitate his cheek
And steal dead seeming of his living hue?

Why should poor beauty indirectly seek
Roses of shadow, since his rose is true?
Why should he live, now Nature bankrupt is,
Beggared of blood to blush through lively veins,
For she hath no exchequer now but his,
And, 'prived of many lives upon his gains?
  O, him she stores, to show what wealth she had
  In days long since, before these last so bad.

This sonnet accuses the beloved of artificiality and reflects the "bias against cosmetics and extravagant dress which seems almost a personal trait of Shakespeare" (Smith, 1981: 21). In the terms of the conflict of freedom and constraint, elaboration and ornament impede the emergence of the beloved's true beauty. According to John Kerrigan's commentary,[11] "this poem—especially in the wake of 66, with its self-pitying lament—marks a crucial stage in the poet's account of the youth" (Shakespeare 1986: 257). The linkage of 66 and 67 is reinforced by their unusually low SQs—.136 and .100, respectively. If one acknowledges, with Kerrigan, that Sonnet 68 continues the argument of 67, and that 69 anticipates 70 within a group extending from 66 through 70, then the unique clustering of low SQs becomes a motivated fact of poetic design. At no other point in the whole sonnet sequence do we encounter a set of five poems with three SQs below .200, as we do in table 1.

TABLE 1. SEQUENCE OF FIVE SONNETS WITH SQs BELOW .200

Sonnet	SQ	OQ
66	**.136**	.207
67	**.100**	.221
68	.186	.150
69	**.143**	**.293**
70	.164	**.314**

The average SQ in this quintuplet is .146—unmatched for any set of five contiguous sonnets. Note also the high obstruency of 69 and 70.

This group also "uniquely anticipates (if 5, resolved by 6, is excepted) the issues of 94" (Shakespeare 1986: 257), an "elusive poem...perhaps the most discussed in the collection" (Shakespeare 1986: 290).[12] It is situated in a group of six contiguous sonnets, 91–96, that share thematic issues or emphases (see appendix 4)[13] and constitute—like 66–70—what might be thought of as a *poetic macrocontext*, defined as three or more linked poems. From the standpoint of sonority, this set is held together by the functionally equivalent factors of low sonority and high obstruency, alternating between subsets of two and three contiguous poems, respectively (see table 2).

TABLE 2. POETIC MACROCONTEXT (= SET OF LINKED SONNETS)

Sonnet	SQ	OQ
91	.300	.200
92	.129	.207
93	.114	.193
94	.186	.314
95	.157	.286
96	.207	.300

While 91 is somewhat neutral with respect to sonority, an SQ of .300 not being significant by itself,[14] the SQs and the OQs of the remaining five—as an ensemble–both signify low sonority. It would be tempting to stop at the notion of a binding function for low sonority in this quintuplet, similar topics being echoed by similar sound patterns *tout court*. But on closer analysis, sonnets 92–96 reveal a sound-meaning nexus that conforms to the iconic function of low sonority, namely a diagrammatic representation of constraint.

Sonnet 92 opens with the statement that the beloved is perpetually constrained to belong to the lover despite any attempt at escape (1–2) and goes on to draw an apparent equivalence: his life in turn relies for its continuance on this love. The two are thus inextricably intertwined (5–6). Freedom lies only in death, the escape from vexation (7–9). The legal right of ownership, or "title" (Shakespeare 1986: 278), signifies a strict bond. However, the equivalence is spurious, a fact which further increases constraint: "happy to have thy love" (12) is unambiguous but ambiguated at the end (14: "and yet I know it not"). "Happy to die" (12) would ensue only from loss and misery. The uncertainty here is also a bind in itself.

Sonnet 93 continues the theme of knowledge and ignorance or truth and falsehood in love. The lover compares himself potentially to a deceived husband (2) constrained to ignorance of his wife's duplicity between "looks" and "heart" (4). The negative is entirely excluded from his lover's face, just as—conversely—"moods and frowns and wrinkles" are ineradicable from the faces of others (6–8). The beloved is forced by the "decree" of "heaven" (9) always to seem affectionate; the same decree constrains his "thoughts" and "heart's workings." The lover, in turn, might be like Adam, possibly about to be "betrayed"—again, like the deceived husband of line 2, who remains in the same bind as in Sonnet 92. Masks such as this constrain the truth, but the lover makes no move to uncover false temptation.

In 94 the unmoved move others (4), like godly powers. Their concealed hypocrisy involves constraint. Although the beloved is detached, he might not be free. At lines 5–7 comparisons based on finance, property, and contract law recur. Line 6 can be paraphrased: "protect the riches of nature (here mainly beauty and charm) from wasteful expenditure by means of prudent management" (Shakespeare 1986: 291). The beloved has "complete control" over his features (Shakespeare 1986: 292), gaining his freedom only through constraint, for self-possession involves great effort and loneliness; one is forced into one's own sole company. The flower (11) benefits others, not itself, by its beauty and its fragrance (9–10); and if its nature becomes corrupted, is necessarily reduced to greater baseness than any lowly weed in the eyes of others.

In Sonnet 95 even bad rumor (which is typically very free; cf. *Aeneid* 4, "fama volat"), is constrained to turn positive when it concerns the beloved (1-8), again because of its beauty. The "tongue that tells the story" (5) has its criticism converted to praise; the beloved's "name" (8) determines every outcome. "Vices" (8) may live under a "veil" (11) in this "mansion" (9) or "habitation" (10), which makes seeing believing (12). Good judgment is constrained—more than encouraged—by the evidence of one's eyes. But the lover warns the beloved to rein in deceptive behavior or scheming at the risk of losing his "edge" (14)—the power to constrain others.

Finally, 96 asserts that the lover "owns" everything essential of the beloved (14), including a part of his reputation ("mine is thy good report"). The main preoccupation is again the contrast between an unknown truth about the beloved and a superordinate rule of representation: appearances constrain opinion ("Thou mak'st faults graces..." [4]; also, "So are those errors... / To truths translated..." [7–8]). Context or contiguity work in supplementary ways to help determine judgment; thus a "base" jewel (6) looks precious because it is contiguous to a queen's hand. "Translated" (8) and "translate" (10) mean forced movement and extreme distortion from error to truth and from wolf to lamb, which is in the power of physical beauty.

The dyad of freedom and constraint may eclipse even that of unity and duality in the broad literary context known to Shakespeare. It pervades contemporary instances of the nature versus culture debate (translatable into the terms of Fate and Ability, "fortuna" and "virtu," submission and release). A few outstanding examples have to suffice here. The vigorous Hoby translation of Castiglione's *Book of the Courtier*, which proved a basic text for Elizabethan "self-fashioning," exemplified both thematically and in its conversational form the constraint/freedom dyad. Throughout the four volumes, speaking characters with finely nuanced opinions strive to define a just midpoint between nonchalance (*sprezzatura*) and decorum in manners, language, and art, which they characterize as grace. It is the movement away from constraint toward freedom that motivates the famous section concerning the "best" Italian language. They agree that it is to be based on a literary precedent derived from history but receptive to input from all parts of the country (in contradistinction to persistent latinizing and to the dominance of Tuscany), to foreign language terms, even neologisms.

In keeping with the search for emotional and aesthetic equilibrium, the characters in the *Courtier* agree or are explicitly instructed to avoid extremist arguments or privative oppositions—a state of intersubjective and mutual constraint. Poetic diction of the time, however, is quite another matter. In Castiglione, Thomas More, Montaigne, and Rabelais "the vertical flexibility of man becomes virtually a structural principle" (Greene 1968: 255).

The conventions of pastoral lyric—with its dyad of nature versus culture, paradisiacal freedom versus earthly servitude—make it an obvious instance of the freedom–constraint dyad throughout the sixteenth century and into the next. The stringent demands of courtiership inform much production in this genre. But in lyric poetry a strong revision of Petrarchan conventions and their subtending humanist anthropology, at the same time, created a poet such as Michelangelo, who instantiates the drive for self-creation over and above all determinism, be it transcendental idealism or the obdurate indifference of a lover. Like Shakespeare, Michelangelo was considered an "anti-Petrarchan": an Italian tercet (by Francesco Berni) celebrates Michelangelo's directness and lack of artifice in this vein. Berni's view, of course, depends on a prior link with Petrarch, their common features being taken generally for granted. The series of existential crises that infuse many of Michelangelo's poems depict attempts to "break free of emotional weight or even from an overweight content that strains the limitations of poetic form" (Marianne Shapiro 1980a: 214). He refers variously to heroic Christianity in Dante, or to the divided will of the speaker in Petrarch's Italian lyrics, now analogized to the contest between "virtue" and "fortune." The poems often take their departure from a problem of act or form expressed as the striving of individual human action against the priority of rule-governed motion.

Shakespeare is "not so much concerned to reforge and refashion himself as to escape [existence], transcend it, leave it behind" (Leishman 1966: 132). The perennial themes of the constraints of time, the unwanted dominance of the calendar and the seasons, the desire to experience nature as the affirmation of one's "innate" character rather than as fate and destiny infuse the lyric of as conventional a poet as Torquato Tasso and betray themselves as diversionary preoccupations in his epic. Like the Spanish Golden Age, Tasso's work is shot through with liberating dreams of the New World. He praises exploration for its very transgression of ancient boundaries. Worn-out rhetorical topics such as lists of desired things are transformed by strong negatives.[15] An outstanding example of such revision in Shakespearean lyric is Sonnet 130 ("My mistress' eyes are nothing like the sun"), which arrogates to itself complete freedom from Petrarchan conventions of praise. The SQ here is actually on the high side (.264), meaning that the sonority correlates well with the content, freedom from the pressures of tradition.

Sonnets 91–96 seem to constitute the largest commonly acknowledged macrocontext but not the only one. Using the Kerrigan commentary as a convenient guide, and adhering to the definition of a macrocontext stipulated earlier (three or more linked poems), we can discern four other such loci (in addition to 66–70): (I) 100–03, (II) 106–09, (III) 144–46, and (IV) 147–49:

TABLE 3. FOUR FURTHER SETS OF LINKED SONNETS

Sonnet		SQ	OQ
I	100	.136 ⎫	.350
	101	.136 ⎭	.243
	102	.279 ⎫	.207
	103	.286 ⎭	.157
II	106	.157	.257
	107	.236	.350
	108	.164 ⎫	.243
	109	.164 ⎭	.193
III	144	.214 ⎫	.200
	145	.214 ⎭	.196 ⎫
	146	.174 ⎫	.210 ⎭
IV	147	.171 ⎭	.236
	148	.179	.221 ⎫
	149	.157	.229 ⎭

The values linked by paired braces lend support to the unity of these macrocontexts. But the matter of linked poems might need to be reexamined entirely in the light of the data in appendix 1, where one finds 33 clusters of poems—some of which overlap—for which the SQs or the OQs are in the same numerical range (defined as beginning with an identical digit):[16] Sonnets 4–6, 7–9, 10–12,15–18, 18–20, 19–21, 22–24, 23–26, 32–37, 38–40, 42–44, 48–52, 56–59, 57–59, 63–67, 66–70, 78–80, 79–81, 82–86, 88–90, 89–92, 92–95, 102–104, 108–10, 109–12, 115–17, 121–27, 127–29, 132–34, 137–42, 139–41, 146–51, and 146–54. It remains for further research to determine whether these sets also form macrocontexts, but the overlap in sound patterns is suggestive.

So far we have concentrated on the SQ of a poem as the significant measure of the alignment of sound and meaning. This emphasis conforms to the idea that SQs are more important than OQs as an indicator of sonority. But the OQs also play a role, albeit a subsidiary one. This can be seen from two contiguous poems, Sonnets 71 and 72, that are highly sonorous and, notably, continuous (share a theme) with each other:

71

No longer mourn for me when I am dead
Than you shall hear the surly sullen bell
Give warning to the world that I am fled
From this vile world with vilest worms to dwell.
Nay, if you read this line, remember not
The hand that writ it, for I love you so
That I in your sweet thoughts would be forgot
If thinking on me then should make you woe.
O, if, I say, you look upon this verse,
When I, perhaps, compounded am with clay,
Do not so much as my poor name rehearse,
But let your love even with my life decay;
    Lest the wise world should look into your moan,
    And mock you with me after I am gone.

72

O, lest the world should task you to recite
What merit lived in me that you should love
After my death, dear love, forget me quite;
For you in me can nothing worthy prove,
Unless you would devise some virtuous lie
To do more for me than mine own desert,
And hang more praise upon deceasèd I
Than niggard truth would willingly impart.
O, lest your true love may seem false in this,
That you for love speak well of me untrue,
My name be buried where my body is
And live no more to shame nor me nor you;

For I am shamed by that which I bring forth,
And so should you, to love things nothing worth.

These two sonnets have the lowest degree of obstruency in
the entire sequence, with OQs of .136 and .100, respectively.[17]
Correspondingly, Sonnet 71 has the highest sonority of all the
poems—.393; this makes it the single most sonorous sonnet in
the whole group, when both the sonority and the obstruency
quotients are considered in tandem. Here, again, the iconic function of the sounds mentioned earlier is confirmed. The poet is allowing his addressee complete freedom to forget him after he is
dead. Nothing will constrain the beloved: no requirement of
mourning, no need of remembrance. According to Smith (1981:
17), the beloved is also being liberated from potential "social em-
barrassment or disgrace," for "the 'wise world' [might] mock him
for caring about one so lowly." Sonnet 72 continues in the same
vein: the SQ is .307, reinforcing the maximally low OQ of .100.

TABLE 4. INVERSE CORRELATION OF SQS AND OQS

SQ Range	Average OQ
.086–.099	.279
.100–.199	.241
.200–.299	.223
.300–.393	.172

OQ Range	Average SQ
.100–.199	.222
.200–.299	.197
.300–.357	.189

Sound–meaning coherences of this kind lend credence to
the reality of the iconic function of sonority in Shakespeare's

Sonnets. Reinforcing this is the negative relationship between sonorant and obstruent quotients over all the sonnets in the sequence. When the sonnets are grouped by the numerical ranges of SQs and OQs respectively that span one digit, there is a patterned relation between the averages such that higher sonority is always associated with lower obstruency and vice versa. The complete set of relevant data covering the entire sequence is to be found in appendices 2 and 3. Table 4 is an abbreviated version that places the relationship in relief.[18]

As the sonority increases, the average obstruency decreases, and vice versa—from a low average obstruency of .172 characterizing sonnets in the high sonority range of .300–.393, to a high average obstruency of .279 characterizing those in the low sonority range of .086–.099.[19] The intermediate averages are progressively more obstruent: .241 > .223. Data derived from the converse of the above comparison bear out the overall validity of the pattern. When OQ ranges differing by one digit are used to group poems, the SQ averages also array themselves by progressive sonority (full data in appendix 3). Again, as the obstruency rises, the sonority falls, and vice versa.

Shakespeare's use of these correspondences stands out in a comparison with other contemporary authors. Shakespeare's evidently deliberate placement of a sonnet sequence in a collection with a long poem, *A Lover's Complaint*, appears to have been part of a literary vogue in the 1590s which received its main impetus from Samuel Daniel's *Delia* (1592).[20] It was immediately followed by five similar collections: Thomas Lodge's *Phillis* (1593), Giles Fletcher's *Licia* (1593), Edmund Spenser's *Amoretti* (1595), Richard Barnfield's *Cynthia* (1595), and Richard Linche's *Diella* (1596).

Ten sets of sonnets chosen at random from modern editions of these collections were subjected to the same analysis as Shakespeare's sonnets. For further comparison, twenty stretches of 141-230 syllables[21] selected at random from Book One of Francis Bacon's *Advancement of Learning* (1605) were included as well (see appendix 5).

FIGURE 1. SONORITY VS OBSTRUENCY: SHAKESPEARE'S SONNETS

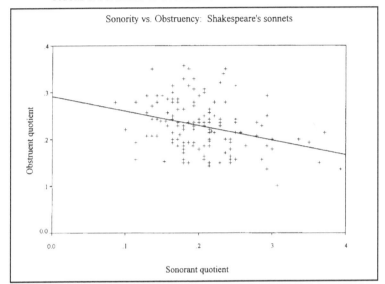

FIGURE 2. SONORITY VS OBSTRUENCY: OTHER TEXTS

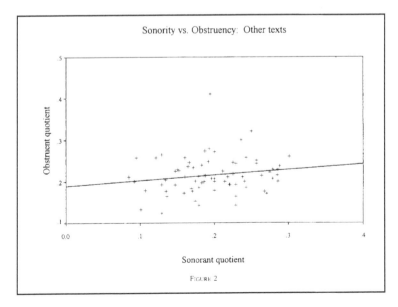

Among these authors, Shakespeare falls clearly in the middle of the range in the matter of sound–meaning correspondences: SQ .16–.24 vs. Shakespeare's .20; OQ .19–.25 vs. Shakespeare's .23 (tables 5 and 6). Statistical analysis (analysis of variance) sets Shakespeare's SQs apart from a high-sonority group composed of Linche, Spencer, and Lodge and a low-sonority group composed of Bacon, Barnfield, Daniel, and Fletcher; the same analysis fails to distinguish any difference among the authors in their average OQs. However, the negative relationship of SQ and OQ within Shakespeare is notably absent in the other authors (figures 1 and 2 on page 25; see table 6 and appendix 1).

TABLE 5. MEAN SQ	
Bacon	.161
Barnfield	.170
Fletcher	.181
Daniel	.197
Shakespeare	**.203**
Spenser	.238
Linche	.236
Lodge	.243

TABLE 6. MEAN OQ	
Fletcher	.195
Bacon	.203
Spenser	.204
Barnfield	.220
Daniel	.221
Shakespeare	**.228**
Linche	.231
Lodge	.245

Statistical testing confirms this relationship: SQ and OQ are negatively correlated within the corpus of Shakespeare's Sonnets (correlation—.312; probability of similar or stronger result by chance—less than .001), and are not correlated within the corpus of the other authors (correlation—.16; probability of similar or stronger result by chance—.17, failing usual statistical criteria for significance).

In addition to underscoring the uniqueness of Shakespeare's poetic technique as regards sonority in the Sonnets, the difference seen between Shakespeare and the other authors demonstrates that the negative relationship between SQ and OQ in Shakespeare is not, as might be guessed, a structural feature of text (SQs and OQs are negatively correlated because textual places occupied by sonorant units are thereby made unavailable for obstruent units). In fact, although obstruents and sonorants are mutually exclusive and jointly exhaustive, OUs and SUs are not jointly exhaustive and, therefore, SQ does not in principle vary inversely with OQ.[22]

Shakespeare's achievement, against this background, is to be located in his unwaveringly motivated implementation of sonority. The judiciousness of his poetic technique in this respect merits special attention. Just as there are Shakespeare Sonnets that eschew alliteration or other forms of paronomasia, so sonority or obstruency quotients can be neutral vis-à-vis the poem's semantics, neither confirming nor disconfirming the meaning. However, when these quotients are significantly high or low, within the statistical parameters of the entire sonnet sequence, we find a uniquely Shakespearean sonority that is never deployed indiscriminately: without fail the poet's ear gives warrant to a sound pattern that is an icon of the sense.

APPENDIX 1. PROFILE OF SQS AND OQS IN SHAKESPEARE'S SONNETS

Sonnet	Total Syllables	Sonorant Quotient	Obstruent Quotient
1	140*	.221	.279
2		.192	.186
3	142	.148	.239
4		.086	.279
5		.214	.236
6		.143	.207
7		.207	.157
8		.229	.321
9		.229	.229
10		.114	.279
11		.179	.329
12		.186	.350
13		.350	.193
14		150	.293
15		.186	.193
16		.293	.136
17		.179	.150
18		.207	.186
19		.293	.293
20		.293	.250
21		.171	.200
22		.243	.164
23		.200	.243
24		.214	.243
25		.193	.221
26		.171	.229
27		.214	.150
28		.193	.228
29		.214	.257
30		.171	.186
31		.193	.193

*In these appendices, whenever a sonnet has the standard of 140 syllables, this datum will be omitted and is to be assumed.

Sonnet	Total Syllables	Sonorant Quotient	Obstruent Quotient
32		.171	.264
33		.371	.214
34		.179	.264
35		.143	.279
36		.250	.243
37		.136	.271
38		.207	.186
39		.207	.157
40		.221	.250
41		.179	.193
42		.236	.200
43		.179	.229
44		.193	.271
45		.164	.193
46		.214	.264
47		.207	.307
48		.157	.257
49		.164	.286
50		.214	.214
51		.279	.236
52		.171	.229
53		.250	.157
54		.164	.300
55		.336	.200
56		.179	.179
57		.243	.150
58		.250	.157
59		.236	.171
60		.193	.329
61		.193	.221

Sonnet	Total Syllables	Sonorant Quotient	Obstruent Quotient
62	.214	0.143
63	.236	0.200
64	.193	0.236
65	.250	0.236
66	.136	0.207
67	.100	0.221
68	.186	0.150
69	.143	0.293
70	.164	0.314
71	.393	0.136
72	.307	0.100
73	.179	0.357
74	.143	0.243
75	.214	0.221
76	.179	0.157
77	.207	0.229
78	.171	0.286
79	.114	0.157
80	.179	0.171
81	.364	0.150
82	.207	0.236
83	.229	0.150
84	.200	0.179
85	.250	0.314
86	.214	0.200
87	.171	0.186
88	.207	0.164
89	.243	0.200
90	.250	0.214
91	.300	0.200
92	.129	0.207
93	.114	0.193
94	.186	0.314
95	.157	0.286

Sonnet	Total Syllables	Sonorant Quotient	Obstruent Quotient
96		.207	.300
97		.171	.200
98		.257	.214
99	150	.233	.340
100		.136	.350
101		.136	.243
102		.279	.207
103		.286	.157
104		.229	.243
105		.179	.186
106		.157	.257
107		.236	.350
108		.164	.243
109		.164	.193
110		.186	.193
111		.243	.193
112		.214	.186
113		.164	.279
114		.164	.314
115		.200	.293
116		.164	.214
117		.229	.236
118	144	.153	.153
119		.171	.279
120		.293	.186
121	142	.155	.239
122		.221	.214
123		.164	.200
124		.186	.236
125		.236	.200
126	120	.217	.217
127		.193	.221
128		.164	.300
129		.164	.250

Sonnet	Total Syllables	Sonorant Quotient	Obstruent Quotient
130		.264	.186
131		.164	.279
132		.243	.179
133		.236	.279
134		.207	.250
135		.300	.179
136		.243	.157
137		.207	.229
138		.171	.264
139		.286	.229
140		.200	.236
141		.200	.236
142		.129	.293
143		.193	.307
144		.214	.200
145	112	.214	.196
146	138	.174	.210
147		.171	.236
148		.179	.221
149		.157	.229
150		.193	.279
151		.136	.207
152		.221	.279
153		.129	.257
154		.279	.236

APPENDIX 2. PROFILE OF SONNETS BY SQ RANGES
AND OQ AVERAGES

A. SQ = .300 – .393 (8 sonnets = 5%)

Sonnet	SQ	OQ
13	.350	.193
33	.371	.214
55	.336	.200
71	.393	.136
72	.307	.100
81	.364	.150
91	.300	.200
135	.300	.179
	AVERAGE OQ = .172	

B. SQ = .200 – .299 (68 sonnets = 44%)

Sonnet	SQ	OQ
1	.221	.279
5	.214	.236
7	.207	.157
8	.229	.321
9	.229	.229
16	.293	.136
18	.207	.186
19	.293	.293
20	.293	.250
22	.243	.164
23	.200	.243
24	.214	.243
27	.214	.150
29	.214	.257
36	.250	.243
38	.207	.186
39	.207	.157
40	.221	.250
42	.236	.200
46	.214	.264
47	.207	.307

B. SQ = .200 – .299 (68 sonnets = 44%)

50	.214	.214
51	.279	.236
53	.250	.157
57	.243	.150
58	.250	.157
59	.236	.171
62	.214	.143
63	.236	.200
65	.250	.236
75	.214	.221
77	.207	.229
82	.207	.236
83	.229	.150
84	.200	.179
85	.250	.314
86	.214	.200
88	.207	.164
89	.243	.200
90	.250	.214
96	.207	.300
98	.257	.214
99	.233	.340
102	.279	.207
103	.286	.157
104	.229	.243
107	.236	.350
111	.243	.193
112	.214	.186
115	.200	.293
117	.229	.236
120	.293	.186
122	.221	.214
125	.236	.200
126	.217	.217
130	.264	.186
132	.243	.179

B. SQ = .200 – .299 (68 sonnets = 44%)

133	.236	.279
134	.207	.250
136	.243	.157
137	.207	.229
139	.286	.229
140	.200	.236
141	.200	.236
144	.214	.200
145	.214	.196
152	.221	.279
154	.279	.236
	Average OQ =	.233

C. SQ = .100 – .199 (77 sonnets = 50%)

2	.192	.186
3	.148	.239
6	.143	.207
10	.114	.279
11	.179	.329
12	.186	.350
14	.150	.293
15	.186	.193
17	.179	.150
21	.171	.200
25	.193	.221
26	.171	.229
28	.193	.228
30	.171	.186
31	.193	.193
32	.171	.264
34	.179	.264
35	.143	.279
37	.136	.271
41	.179	.193

C. SQ = .100 – .199 (77 sonnets = 50%)

43	.179	.229
44	.193	.271
45	.164	.193
48	.157	.257
49	.164	.286
52	.171	.229
54	.164	.300
56	.179	.179
60	.193	.329
61	.193	.221
64	.193	.236
66	.136	.207
67	.100	.221
68	.186	.150
69	.143	.293
70	.164	.314
73	.179	.357
74	.143	.243
76	.179	.157
78	.171	.286
79	.114	.157
80	.179	.171
87	.171	.186
92	.129	.207
93	.114	.193
94	.186	.314
95	.157	.286
97	.171	.200
100	.136	.350
101	.136	.243
105	.179	.186
106	.157	.257
108	.164	.243
109	.164	.193
110	.186	.193
113	.164	.279
114	.164	.314
116	.164	.214

C. SQ = .100 – .199 (77 sonnets = 50%)

118	.153	.153
119	.171	.279
121	.155	.239
123	.164	.200
124	.186	.236
127	.193	.221
128	.164	.300
129	.164	.250
131	.164	.279
138	.171	.264
142	.129	.293
143	.193	.307
146	.174	.210
147	.171	.236
148	.179	.221
149	.157	.229
150	.193	.279
151	.136	.207
153	.129	.257

Average OQ = .241

D. SQ = .086 – .199 (1 sonnet = 1%)

4	.086	.279

APPENDIX 3. PROFILE OF SONNETS BY OQ RANGES AND SQ AVERAGES

A. OQ = .100 – .199 (46 sonnets = 30%)

2	.192	.186
7	.207	.157
13	.350	.193
15	.186	.193
16	.293	.136
17	.179	.150
18	.207	.186
22	.243	.164
27	.214	.150

APPENDIX 3. PROFILE OF SONNETS BY OQ RANGES AND SQ AVERAGES

30	.171	.186
31	.193	.193
38	.207	.186
39	.207	.157
41	.179	.193
45	.164	.193
53	.250	.157
56	.179	.179
57	.243	.150
58	.250	.157
59	.236	.171
62	.214	.143
68	.186	.150
71	.393	.136
72	.307	.100
76	.179	.157
79	.114	.157
80	.179	.171
81	.364	.150
83	.229	.150
84	.200	.179
87	.171	.186
88	.207	.164
93	.114	.193
103	.286	.157
105	.179	.186
109	.164	.193
110	.186	.193
111	.243	.193
112	.214	.186

APPENDIX 3. PROFILE OF SONNETS BY OQ RANGES AND SQ AVERAGES

118	.153	.153
120	.293	.186
130	.264	.186
132	.243	.179
135	.300	.179
136	.243	.157
145	0.214	.196

Average SQ = .222

B. OQ = .200 – .299 (91 sonnets = 59%)

1	.221	.279
3	.148	.239
4	.086	.279
5	.214	.236
6	.143	.207
9	.229	.229
10	.114	.279
14	.150	.293
19	.293	.293
20	.293	.250
21	.171	.200
23	.200	.243
24	.214	.243
25	.193	.221
26	.171	.229
28	.193	.228
29	.214	.257
32	.171	.264
33	.371	.214
34	.179	.264
35	.143	.279

B. OQ = .200 − .299 (91 sonnets = 59%)

36	.250	.243
37	.136	.271
40	.221	.250
42	.236	.200
43	.179	.229
44	.193	.271
46	.214	.264
48	.157	.257
49	.164	.286
50	.214	.214
51	.279	.236
52	.171	.229
55	.336	.200
61	.193	.221
63	.236	.200
64	.293	.236
65	.250	.236
66	.136	.207
67	.100	.221
69	.143	.227
74	.143	.243
75	.214	.221
77	.207	.229
78	.171	.286
82	.207	.236
86	.214	.200
89	.214	.200
90	.250	.214
91	.300	.200
92	.129	.207
95	.157	.286
97	.171	.200
98	.257	.214
101	.136	.243
102	.279	.207
104	0.229	0.243

B. OQ = .200 − .299 (91 sonnets = 59%)

106	.157	.257
108	.164	.243
113	.164	.279
115	.200	.293
116	.164	.214
117	.229	.236
119	.171	.279
121	.155	.239
122	.221	.214
123	.164	.200
124	.186	.236
125	.236	.200
126	.217	.217
127	.193	.221
129	.164	.250
131	.164	.279
133	.236	.279
134	.207	.250
137	.207	.229
138	.171	.264
139	.286	.229
140	.200	.236
141	.200	.236
142	.129	.293
144	.214	.200
146	.174	.210
147	.171	.236
148	.179	.221
149	.157	.229
150	.193	.279
151	.136	.207
152	.221	.279
153	.129	.257
154	.279	.236

Average SQ = .197

C. OQ = .300 – .357 (17 sonnets = 11%)		
8	.229	.321
11	.179	.329
12	.186	.350
47	.207	.307
54	.164	.300
60	.193	.329
70	.164	.314
73	.179	.357
85	.250	.314
94	.186	.314
96	.207	.300
99	.233	.340
100	.136	.350
107	.236	.350
114	.164	.314
128	.164	.300
143	.193	.307
	Average SQ =	.189

APPENDIX 4. POETIC MACROCONTEXT

91
Some glory in their birth, some in their skill,
Some in their wealth, some in their body's force,
Some in their garments, though new-fangled ill,
Some in their hawks and hounds, some in their horse;
And every rumour hath his adjunct pleasure,
Wherein it finds a joy above the rest.
But these particulars are not my measure;
All these I better in one general best.
Thy love is better than high birth to me,
Richer than wealth, prouder than garments' cost,
Of more delight than hawks or horses be;
And, having thee, of all men's pride I boast—

Wretched in this alone, that thou mayst take
All this away, and me most wretched make.

92

But do thy worst to steal thyself away,
For term of life thou art assurèd mine;
And life no longer than thy love will stay,
For it depends upon that love of thine.
Then need I not to fear the worst of wrongs,
When in the least of them my life hath end.
I see a better state to me belongs
Than that which on thy humour doth depend.
Thou canst not vex me with inconstant mind,
Since that my life on thy revolt doth lie.
O, what a happy title do I find,
Happy to have thy love, happy to die!
　But what's so blessèd-fair that fears no blot?
　Thou mayst be false, and yet I know it not.

93

So shall I live, supposing thou art true,
Like a deceived husband; so love's face
May still seem love to me, though altered new,
Thy looks with me, thy heart in other place.
For there can live no hatred in thine eye;
Therefore in that I cannot know thy change.
In many's looks, the false heart's history
Is writ in moods and frowns and wrinkles strange,
But heaven in thy creation did decree
That in thy face sweet love should ever dwell;
Whate'er thy thoughts or thy heart's workings be,
Thy looks should nothing thence but sweetness tell.
　How like Eve's apple doth thy beauty grow,
　If thy sweet virtue answer not thy show.

94

They that have power to hurt and will do none,
That do not do the thing they most do show,
Who, moving others, are themselves as stone,
Unmovèd, cold, and to temptation slow;
They rightly do inherit heaven's graces
And husband nature's riches from expense;
They are the lords and owners of their faces,
Others but stewards of their excellence.
The summer's flower is to the summer sweet,
Though to itself it only live and die;
But if that flower with base infection meet,
The basest weed outbraves his dignity:
    For sweetest things turn sourest by their deeds;
    Lilies that fester smell far worse than weeds.

95

How sweet and lovely dost thou make the shame
Which, like a canker in the fragrant rose,
Doth spot the beauty of thy budding name!
O, in what sweets dost thou thy sins enclose!
That tongue that tells the story of thy days,
Making lascivious comments on thy sport,
Cannot dispraise but in a kind of praise;
Naming thy name blesses an ill report.
O, what a mansion have those vices got
Which for their habitation chose out thee,
Where beauty's veil doth cover every blot,
And all things turn to fair that eyes can see!
    Take heed, dear heart, of this large privilege;
    The hardest knife ill-used doth lose his edge.

96

Some say thy fault is youth, some wantonness,
Some say thy grace is youth and gentle sport;
Both grace and faults are loved of more and less;
Thou mak'st faults graces that to thee resort.
As on the finger of a thronèd queen
The basest jewel will be well esteemed,
So are those errors that in thee are seen
To truths translated and for true things deemed.
How many lambs might the stern wolf betray,
If like a lamb he could his looks translate;
How many grazers might'st thou lead away,
If thou wouldst use the strength of all thy state!
    But do not so; I love thee in such sort
    As, thou being mine, mine is thy good report.

APPENDIX 5. PROFILE OF SQS AND OQS IN SONNETS
BY SHAKESPEARE'S CONTEMPORARIES

Bacon

Passage	Total Syllables	Sonorant Quotient	Obstruent Quotient
1	144	.174	.153
2	194	.160	.211
3	170	.241	.200
4	147	.218	.211
5	177	.147	.192
6	157	.134	.204
7	141	.170	.177
8	156	.179	.186
9	150	.187	.273
10	141	.135	.177

APPENDIX 5. PROFILE OF SQS AND OQS IN SONNETS
BY SHAKESPEARE'S CONTEMPORARIES

Bacon

11	146	0.178	0.212
12	230	.152	.226
13	179	.196	.207
14	170	.129	.124
15	151	.166	.245
16	148	.095	.257
17	191	.147	.225
18	185	.092	.200
19	151	.225	.245
20	158	.101	.133

Barnfield

Passage	Total Syllables	Sonorant Quotient	Obstruent Quotient
1	144	.188	.214
2	140	.129	.264
12	140	.150	.229
13	146	.192	.247
14	140	.200	.271
15	142	.225	.218
16	142	.169	.183
17	142	.183	.197
19	142	.085	.211
20	142	.183	.239

Daniel			
Passage	Total Syllables	Sonorant Quotient	Obstruent Quotient
1	144	.174	.201
2	145	.159	.172
3	140	.229	.243
4	142	.268	.176
8	144	.160	.257
9	140	.193	.279
57	140	.271	.264
58	140	.271	.143
59	140	.207	.279
60	140	.150	.250

Fletcher			
Passage	Total Syllables	Sonorant Quotient	Obstruent Quotient
1		.200	.207
5		.229	.193
6		.271	.171
11		.214	.200
12		.200	.207
15		.136	.164
16		.107	.179
31		.200	.179
32		.129	.193
38		.121	.257

Linche			
Passage	Total Syllables	Sonorant Quotient	Obstruent Quotient
1		.236	.300
2		.264	.214
3		.250	.321
8		.200	.200
9		.286	.229
15		.186	.214
16		.257	.250
35		.229	.164
36		.186	.200
38		.264	.214

Lodge			
Passage	Total Syllables	Sonorant Quotient	Obstruent Quotient
1	150	.220	.193
2	146	.301	.260
3	144	.285	.215
12	144	.194	.410
13	147	.238	.211
17	153	.275	.222
18	146	.171	.233
19	142	.211	.225
20	146	.288	.237
40	140	.186	.293

	Spenser		
Passage	Total Syllables	Sonorant Quotient	Obstruent Quotient
1		.279	.229
2		.164	.236
3		.286	.200
4		.279	.207
5		.221	.193
15		.257	.243
16		.179	.143
20		.243	.186
21		.243	.257
30		.229	.143

2

REREADING DOSTOEVSKY'S *THE DOUBLE*

Dostoevsky's unique status as commentator on Russia and the Russian soul over more than 150 years has resulted in the concentration of critical attention on his novels of ideas, to the sorry detriment of his experimental short fiction—most of all his second short novel from 1846, *Dvojnik* (*The Double*). Dostoevsky himself contended (and not only at the time of writing) that *The Double* had given voice to one of his most important conceptions. *The Double* is in Dostoevsky's words "a dissection of all Russian attitudes toward authority,"[1] and to be justly viewed as "a cosmic allegory in which the author analyzes multifarious relationships to all authority, ranging from the medical to the divine" (Rice 1985: 59). To date, critical readers of *The Double* have unwittingly attested to the power of this work by confusing its inner and outer reality—namely, fantasy versus actuality, inner versus outer life, the "social" versus the "psychological" perspective—whereas each is part and parcel of the other, each the other's concomitant. In confusing these levels, the critics have made themselves willing participants in one of the most adventurous and experimentally fascinating works in Dostoevsky's oeuvre.

A momentous wrong turn caused the author himself to impute the critical failure of the story to his inexperience or ineptness. Dostoevsky worked on the story in the summer of 1845 and finished it in the following year. A letter to his brother Mikhail dated February 1, 1846 informs him that the work has just been finished *(PSS* 28/1: 117).[2] The critical reaction was overwhelmingly negative and generally remains so to this day.[3] Belinskii's well-known opinion allowed for praise of the social criticism implicit in the Goliadkin ambiance but otherwise reflected to perfection the judgment of his times, finding *The Double* "long-winded, lacking in measure, unclear in point of view, and, most important, 'fantastic.'"[4] Often Dostoevsky was berated for his implementation of Gogolian themes, though, surprisingly, not his techniques. Mochulski considers Dostoevsky's early work a "rethinking" of several Gogolian themes.[5] Vinogradov, on the other hand (1979: 220), ingeniously notices that Dostoevsky's is "one of the principles...of literary reformation" whereby "a sort of 'metaphorization' of an integral verbal composition or of its parts" can occur in which "the thematics of the plot are perceived in a double literary entity."[6] In the same review, Belinskii adds, "There should be nothing dark and unclear in art" (in Wasiolek, 189). The behavior of the protagonist Goliadkin proved so mysterious to those critics entrapped by Goliadkin's numbing facelessness that their views tend to read like Goliadkin's own reactions to the appearance of his double, witness Belinskii's:

> It is all the more amusing that neither by fortune [nor] rank...can he [Goliadkin] in any way awaken envy in anyone....He could very well live in the world comfortably, but a pathological suspiciousness and sensitivity to insult are the dark demons of his character. ...[7]

Again, Mikhailovskii (much later, in 1882) on the advent of the second Goliadkin: "Why did [he] appear? There are no satisfactory reasons for his appearance in that corner of life which *The Double* represents. Goliadkin Jr. is dragged in by force and against living truth."[8] The mental construct of a double, then, seems causeless.

One of the obstacles between *The Double* and the paean it deserves is the blurring—indeed, Dostoevsky's erasure—of the boundaries between literal and figural meanings, between the senses of doubling that Dostoevsky plumbs by a rich variety of means, among them a free use of repetition, irony, intersecting self-deceptions—all forms of doubling. There follows no reunification, no explication in a nutshell of the wellsprings of action and feeling, no reintegration of personality. This is a tragedy without anagnorisis. Even the conclusion, Goliadkin's transport to an insane asylum, is engineered to be merely the last thing of its kind—the last of many Goliadkin deaths—that happens, a conventional endstoppage to the narrative offering no resolution. Shklovskii has justly termed the novel "a travesty of the Romantic *Doppelgänger* theme."[9] Finally, while looking back 30 years later, in an 1877 entry of *A Writer's Diary* (= *PSS* 26: 65), and thinking that he had failed to give the novel's form its due, on the way to that opinion Dostoevsky also saw his Goliadkin as the rendering of "a very great type in its social significance."[10] In keeping with the latter judgment we will argue that the work is a masterpiece of tragicomic mimesis instancing a foresighted, inspirational literary logic; that the social corollaries to Goliadkin and *The Double* are replete with significance; and that the psychological rendering of the Goliadkinist pathology is equal if not superior to that of the books known as Dostoevsky's great novels.

The action takes place over four days. Mr. Goliadkin is a bureaucrat who serves in an office copying documents—like many an exemplar of his kind—thus one is on the lookout at the outset for a cog in the wheel, a duplicator of others' thoughts. A toady, coward, and petty deceiver of women, he is sketched almost all at once as a "social type" in flat perspective. From the first morning of our acquaintance with him, he has presentiments of an imminent psychic collapse. Awakening from a dream, he checks to see if he has changed, and seeing nothing, is nonetheless overcome by the desire to conceal himself from others: acquaintances, bosses, the very doctor with whom he pleads for help. G[oliadkin] S[enior]'s reputation precedes him, but he foists unwanted confessions on the same office wags who generally ridicule him; gate-crashes a ball where his behavior sets off a chain of havoc; pleads, threatens, and flees. Ejection from the party finds him at least ready to live through what has been indistinctly hovering in shadow: in the first chapter Goliadkin wonders: "Прикинуться, что не я, а что кто–то другой, разительно схожий со мною? (113)" ("Shall I pretend it's not me, but someone extraordinarily like me?" [8]).[11] Shame brings on the appearance of his double, surfacing in the street.

First experienced as a shock, the double reveals itself also as a figure of mysterious allure. At this stage he follows GS home and, once admitted, tells GS a tale of woe that is bound to charm him, since it is in part GS's own early life in an expurgated version.

At first the double, "Goliadkin Junior" (GJ), models himself on the host figure; soon he has worked himself free, caught up, and has revealed his worldly, conniving traits. GJ—dancing, strutting, frolicking, adept at flattery and good-fellowship—sets about frustrating all of GS's efforts to cling to dignity and realize his little hopes; no impulse is free of GJ's jeers and manic parodies; no intention remains unmasked. A morbid oppression overtakes GS, so that everything, once simply charged with menaces or riddles, becomes an occasion for radical terror. While GS bangs his head against failure, GJ triumphs in the world. GS, profoundly chagrined, dogged by ineptness and confusion, exists in trembling fear of the consequences and engineered by terror of discovery. GS is sporadically gifted with just enough foresight to know he will fail; his timing and judgment suffer an extra increment due to foresight, much in the way of the falling sickness. The end of the story is a climax of hindsight: "Герой наш вскрикнул и схватил себя за голову. Увы! он это давно уже предчувствовал!" (229) ("Our hero gave a scream and clutched his head. Alas! He had felt this coming for a long time!" [144]).

Let us suppose the entire novella takes place "inside GS's head." Then why is the social conflict so believable? (It doesn't matter.)

The most troubling aspect of the double (GJ) is his double visibility, to GS and to the rest of society, where he is immediately accepted without surprise or outrage by anyone except Goliadkin Senior. Their first conversation at GS's house, where the "inner" aspect predominates for lack of other viewers, is shortly counteracted by a sequence of appearances at the office. These manifestations of otherness, however, retain their "inner" side as GJ launches grotesque hostilities on GS—pinches, kicks, withdrawals of a handshake; mocking repetitions of GS's precise words; actions that hurl GS's desire to merge with his double into his own face. The author sustains a doubling scheme that encompasses intimate formulations of GS's wishes as well as burlesque, reiterated pursuits along the same track. GJ's hypocritical jeers, such as "Жизнь не игрушка, сами вы знаете"(203) ("Life isn't a game—you know yourself") [114]), join with GS's self-deception as further forms of doubling, often structurally paired.

GS's longstanding tendency to blame others for his own actions becomes justified when it is no longer clear who or what they are. It is as if the author himself were groping for secure ethical terrain: are not others, in some measure, "already" to blame? GS has an overwhelming need to be a Goliadkin who is admired, respected, and envied, an aim easily confused with wanting to be a "good" Goliadkin. Psychic damage serves eventually to crowd GS out of every arena but the "inner" one in which secret dialogue, maturing plans, digressions, and longings hold sway. At the final stage, St. Petersburg decides to tolerate him no further, and the psychic, paranoid-schizophrenic aspect of the double *récit* comes to the fore. As he is dragged off to the madhouse, GJ's taunts and smirks escort him out of life in society. But this conclusion was always foreseeable!

Yet, although he is programmed not to see what is before his eyes, GS's maladies are an aggravated and "officially" certifiable form of a ubiquitous set of ambient ills. Once this is accepted it inoculates Goliadkin against irrelevance, and it becomes clear why he could not have been a member of the Poor Folk, an Akakii Akakievich, or anyone whose victim status depends on socio-economic want; why it is that Dostoevsky's opening scene instantly locates GS amid imitation/bogus mahogany, surly servants, and comical chirruping samovars rather than anything that would express the pathos of genuine poverty. The gimcrack comforts GS enjoys at home are tainted by the aprioristic fakery and tawdry third-rateness that the narrator lavishes with contempt, mocking the set for its very obliqueness and insincerity, as part of a giant false front.

Would GS see them for what they are in his discourse? GS has to exist in oblique, slanted, uneasy accord with the social lessons that belong to Dostoevsky's parody of the office, the ballroom, the doctor's surgery, sharing with those who surround and challenge him the same obfuscating love of etiquette and the proprieties, obedience to regulations, and indifference to compassion. Goliadkin has to lack full outsider credentials in order to need a double and yet be unable to coexist easily with him—for the pieces *not* to fit. His ambitions have to be small scale: compliments paid by peers, the upward crawl rung by rung, an ever-so-slightly higher-paying job, the merest chance at a pretty woman's favor (rather than "favors"!), not only so that the author can establish GS and GJ as belonging to a social type but, more forcefully, to reveal GS's very roots as enmeshed and inveigled within his context rather than ever running counter to it. Several weaker, feuilletonistic subplots involving letters both signed and anonymous, intrigues concerning the German woman with whom GS had been involved, and a coming and going of letters to false friends and servants function to advance the social aspect.

GS's search for guarantors to clear his good name moves these plots into conformity with GS's search for safe havens and good fathers. The story remains in one sense at the crossroads between Gogol's "Nose" and the reforming project Belinskii (who did approve of the first two chapters, locating Goliadkin in his setting of petty social life) would wish to see the author engaged in.

That GS's motives suit his petty status in life successfully inserts him into the prevailing cycle of insult and injury, stimulus and response. It has indeed become axiomatic to classify *The Double* as a Gogolian derivative, and not entirely without cause. Gogol's "Diary of a Madman" tempts obvious comparison (although "The Nose" is so much more apt!), but its protagonist, formed in opposition to the hospital personnel who are his only interlocutors, lives in complete isolation from public satire. It is essential for Goliadkin to have "external" as well as "internal" tormentors, and for the reader to remain unable to distinguish between them finally. It is indeed essential that GJ's existence as much as GS's (though for opposite tropological purposes) be confirmed in the eyes of "others." Again, the poet of *Dead Souls* is most freely recalled in passages that dwell on social satire, such as the extensive description of Klara Olsuf'evna's first ball, all self-deflating hyperbole and literary parody:

День, … ознаменовавшийся блистательным, великолепным званым обедом, таким обедом, какого давно не видали в стенах чиновничьих квартир у Измайловского моста и около. (128)

(The day [...] was marked by a dinner, splendid, magnificent, and such as has not been witnessed within the walls of any civil servant's apartment in or about the neighbourhood of the Izmajlovsky Bridge for many a day. [26])

"О! для чего я не обладаю тайною слога высокого, сильного" (129) (Oh, why do I not possess the secret of elevated, forceful style [28])—all this a loving imitation culminating in an explosion of modesty-topics: "О, если бы я был поэт!—разумеется, по крайней мере такой, как Гомер или Пушкин; с меньшим талантом соваться нельзя." (128) (Would I were a poet! A Homer or a Pushkin, of course, for with a lesser talent one would not attempt it. [27])—and Gogolian preterition: "Я ничего не скажу." (129) (I will say nothing. [28])—only to gas on about the party at considerable length.

By subtitling his novella *A Poem of St. Petersburg* Dostoevsky immediately engages with Gogol's *poèma*, the better to foreground his divergence from it. Another undisguised homage to Gogol, indeed, constitutes the very opening of the narrative. It is as if Dostoevsky were at first bowing in half-mockery to the source of a "social type," such as Khlestakov or Chichikov—down to the servant Petrushka, the expressive samovar, and even (in more strained fashion) by the encounter of GS's carriage with that of two gibing colleagues on the road. The Gogolian antecedents of GS's tiny character have been noted, but scarcely the fact that the preambular resemblance only throws Dostoevsky's astonishing originality into better relief: this new story is to be an internal description of what in Gogol remains purposively flattened. Everything onstage is laid out in *Dead Souls* style, until GS enters Dr. Rutenspitz' office for the first time, and their interview marks the turning point from the "source." Further Gogolisms have the mnemonic function of cluing readers in to the radical differences in aim between the two authors. The moment is both a tribute to Gogol and a valediction to Gogol's resolute externalism.

The free passage between public and private realms that powers *The Double* is recognizably akin to Gogol's "Nose." On one side, the major Kovalev loses his nose; on the other side, people routinely see either Kovalev or his detached appendage without evincing any surprise. The author takes their stultification for granted, while keeping his eye resolutely on the interaction between them and the self-propelling nose. The situation satirizes social clichés, stale pieties, bureauspeak, and hypocrisy, while demurely ignoring the private side. It would be fair to say that "The Nose" stimulates a dialectic that culminates in Dostoevsky's decision to plumb the workings of *The Double*, GS/GJ, while holding fast to his typicality. The utter capriciousness of the Gogolian world is now revealed in its tragic character: everything from unbending social hierarchy, with its minute, petty divisions and discrepancy between talent and reward, to the submersion of individual human identity. From the social perspective *The Double* is indeed a tragedy of individualism.[12]

Among critics, Bem and Vinogradov recognize *The Double* as an anti-Gogolian production, "a unique artistic protest against Gogol's 'The Nose'";[13] and again, a unique "literary refutation" of the earlier work, in the service of which the blatant imitations of Gogol appear.[14] Bem (240) also pays just attention to the "idea of *authority*" as a tragic motive playing "an essential role for Dostoevsky," with reference to Dostoevsky's notebooks. An example:

Г—н Голядкин—младший растолковывает старшему: что так, значит, принимаю благодетельное началь-ство за отца и что тут рыцарское …Тут анатомия всех русских отношений к начальству. (*PSS* 1: 432)

(Mr. Goliadkin Jr. explains to Sr.: that I, you see, regard

the benevolent authorities as a father and there's something chivalric in this...Here is the anatomy of all Russian relationships to authority.)

Again: "Юридически начальство только по законам поступает, это только грубая подчиненность и послушание начальству." (*PSS* 1: 432) (From a legal standpoint the authorities only act on the basis of laws, and this results only in gross subservience and obedience to authority.) It is surprising that this emphatically social aspect is so often neglected in criticism.[15]

What Dostoevsky accomplishes is nothing less than a total reconsideration and overhaul of Gogolian thought and technique, beginning with what may be provisionally identified as GS's discourse mannerisms: the obsessive and thought-deflecting use of clichés; nonsequiturs; vagueness and sidestepping; filler such as umming (followed as in Gogol by three dots); hypercorrectness and excessive decorum; exempla from legends of or random reference to great men; references to well-worn literary works.[16] The epistolary moments are no less emptily rhetorical than GS's speech and protests of sincerity. All of the above are recognizably parceled out among various minor Gogolian characters (such as, say, Ivan Shpon'ka or Podkolësin in *The Marriage)*, but most significantly among the landowners in *Dead Souls* and the local officials in *The Inspector General* and distilled via the behavior of their heroes, Chichikov and Khlestakov. *The Double*, like the Gogolian works, uses these discourse features to underscore social satire; but whereas Gogol distributes them widely and generously among groups, Dostoevsky unveils their full pathological import by making them emanate almost entirely from the two Goliadkins.

Bakhtin (1984: 211–27) devoted more space to his classic analysis of Goliadkin's language and its bearing on the psychic aspect in *Problems of Dostoevsky's Poetics* than to any other sin-

gle work. He characterizes GS's discourse as "first and foremost
…the collision and interruption of various accents within the
bounds of a single syntactic whole… ." (224). Although his account appears to take the social and environmental aspect for
granted, Bakhtin's analysis does take its departure from GS's
emotional dependence on the discourse of others, since he lives
by interpreting his reflection in others' eyes. Accordingly,
Bakhtin isolates three interrelated reactions in GS to the discourse of others: (1) "self-reassurance and comfort" (2) "the desire to hide from the other's discourse, avoid attracting attention
to himself" (3) "concession or subordination," a submissive assimilation of that external discourse. I recur to these useful categories, with two caveats. Firstly, unlike (1) and (3), reaction (2)
is concerned entirely with empirical, practical being. Secondly,
unlike the other two, it does not generate further speech in GS.
It takes the form of a sudden clash, an alarm that brings on silence; it characterizes the moments when GS desires nothing
more than a respite from discourse or the advent of clarity ('Ах
ты, господи бог мой! Господи бог мой! да о чем же это я
теперь говорю?'[220]) ('Oh God! What on earth have I just been
talking about?' [134]). It is the collusion of (1) and (3) that
furnishes the typical raw materials of Goliadkinist speech, determines GS's physical movements, and occludes his hopes. Reaction (1) takes logical precedence because it is most of all the
inchoate drive of his ego to withstand the blows dealt it by
shame. "Goliadkin's desire to do without an actual other's consciousness, to avoid the other and assert his own self, to find for
himself a substitute for the other" (215) belong to an alliance of
(1) and (2).

Dostoevsky's letter to his brother (October 8, 1845; *PSS*
28/1: 113) about the progress of *The Double* enfolds GS's motto:
'Он покамест сам по себе; … он ничего' ('He's on his own;…
he's all right'). Since GS "lives by his reflection in others"
(Bakhtin 1984, 232), the simulation of independence directs it-

self not toward another but toward GS's own self: he persuades himself, reassures and comforts himself, plays the role of another person vis-à-vis himself. Blustering, the umbrella Goliadkinist tactic, responds to alarms from the weakest, least defended "I."[17] The kinship of (1) and (3) comes to the fore when GS's "concessive" overtures to others, whether in thought or speech, are rendered as bluster: let it all happen, since I am ready to surrender! Or in full tilt against himself about whether to "accept" and learn to like his double:

> "Я смирением возьму. Да и где же опасность? ну какая опасность? Желал бы я, чтоб кто–нибудь указал бы мне в этом деле опасность?" (170)

> ("I'll triumph through meekness. Where's the danger in that? What danger is there? I'd just like someone to show me." [76])

Here GS peters out dialogically:

> В глубине души своей сложил он одно решение и в глубине сердца своего поклялся исполнить его. По правде–то, он еще не совсем хорошо знал; но все равно, ничего! (167)

> (In his heart of hearts he had formed a resolution which in his heart of hearts he had sworn to carry out. To be truthful, he still did not quite know or rather, he had no idea what steps to take. But it didn't matter! [73])

A more typical example:

> "А что до того, так пусть его служит, пусть его слу-

жит себе на здоровье, лишь бы никому не мешал и
никого не затрогивал; пусть его служит, — согла-
сен и аппробую!" (151)

("And as far as this other fellow is concerned, let him
work here. Let him, and good luck to him, provided he
doesn't hinder or interfere with anyone. Let him—he's
got my consent and approval!" [54])

The centrally situated and lengthy rationalization of GS's replacement by GJ faithfully annotates some main themes:

"Так из чего же по–настоящему здесь хлопотать?"
(171: bluster)

("What actually is the point of fussing about here?"
[78])

"Из чего же мне хлопотать?" (171: identification with
power)

("...why should *I* have all the bother?" [78])

"Рассудим так: является человек ... с достаточной
рекомендацией ... способный чиновник, хорошего
поведения, только беден ... ну, да ведь бедность не
порок; ...так уж его за это не принимать в департамент?!" (171–72: same identification, with sidestepping)

("We'll argue it this way: along comes a man with adequate references, a capable clerk, well-behaved, but
badly off [...] Well, poverty's no crime [...] Can you
refuse to employ him because of that?" [78]).

"Коли уж судьба, коли одна судьба, коли одна сле-
пая фортуна тут виновата ... тут сердце болит ...
хороши бы были начальники, если б так рассуж-
дали, как я, забубенная голова! ... Эка ведь башка у
меня! На десятерых подчас глупости хватит!" (172:
self in full tilt against self; contiguity disorder)

("If it's fate—if it's only fate or blind fortune that's to
blame [...] Your heart aches for him [...] Fine people
departmental heads would be if they argued the same
way as a ruffian like me! What a brain I've got! Sometimes I'm as stupid as a dozen fools put together!" [78])

Thus the overconfident and the slavishly concessive regis-
ters, (1) and (3), wage joint warfare against the struggling and
rather prudently timid (2). In fact, if GS were capable of tailor-
ing his actions according to (2), he could smuggle himself into
the blessed realm of social acceptance "like everyone else." It is
the second voice that occasionally confronts terror verbally and
directly, or at least permits it to appear in blurred focus, or
masked lightly: "Уж лучше мы с тобой потерпим, Яков Петрович, подождем да потерпим!" (151) ("We'd better have patience, Yakov Petrovich. We'll have patience and wait!" [54]). But
from a slightly different angle, (2) and (3) share the objective of
reducing GS to perennial emotional stasis and terror.

All three voices anticipate and fill in the responses of another, making for relentless inner dialogue in which GS speaks
for everyone. Reaction (1) is most evidently keyed to grandiose
bluster, in which the aggressive impulse turns on an imagined
"outward." Reaction (3) decrees, subsequently, that GS's actual
confrontations with authority will unleash a superabundance of
slavish verbiage at the interlocutor. Reaction (2), we believe, is
the bridge between them and generates the voice most likely to
rehash successful clichés, spells, and formulas, in which GS hides

from "readings" by others, avoiding attention, trying to bury himself in a crowd of similar-looking people. Because cliché—after all, little more than an exaggeration of social acquiescence—is ubiquitous and general, it has some capacity to repulse consciousness (as of mortal slights). Prepacked in modules, GS's prefabricated dialogue already strives to assure another of his good fellowship or fealty. That may further understanding of why cliché and bureauspeak actually occur more frequently in the "inner" dialogues than in GS's addresses to employers, clerks, or party guests. The narrative subordinates plot events (such as the courting of Klara Olsuf'evna, the crossings of defamatory letters) to the inner voices they stimulate. But the *superiors*, the *socialites*, etc. actually "sound" sensible most of the time, albeit harsh or impatient. They are not windbags, for example. Except for the two Goliadkins no characters inhabit any large or dominant role but provide raw material for the work of consciousness. It is the second reaction or voice that formally substitutes for the inadequate recognition GS receives from empirical others. This voice, therefore, has to pretend most urgently that it belongs to another empirical person, has to appear, unventriloquized, as if expressed from the presumed viewpoint of that person. When GS visits the mesmerizing Dr. Rutenspitz, he refers to himself at first as a "close friend," using a standard gambit of self-concealment. A hiatus ensues as GS awaits the reply, for waiting for the doctor's formulation is his only hope of coherence—despite (or indeed, because of) his immediately preceding outbursts of independence. Actual collision with someone else, then, happens in contrast to the unctuous interaction between "you and [me], my friend Goliadkin," where GS's inner dialogue proves the most fertile ground for exfoliating clichés, as would be the case with someone practicing to learn a bewildering new language.

Although it serves the coward and the bluffer equally well, most of all cliché satisfies GS's generic desire to yield to authority. Obeisance to elegant form is an attitude he freely admits, as in the use of French expressions. When the desire to yield overwhelms him, cliché may emerge in a quasi-religious register, as if addressing the deity. Here the referent is the boss of bosses: "'Принимаю ... благодетельное начальство за отца и слепо вверяю судьбу свою'" (196) ("'I look upon our benevolent superior as a father, and blindly trust him with my fate'" [106]). Again, where worship is qualified by a stealthier, affiliative yearning, GS's thoughts proliferate with specifically social and quasi-professional mottos, old saws, and proverbs; and the voice speaking out of his body is more obviously appropriated from the very powers whose attention the subordinate craves. The progress of GS's struggle to persuade, unite with, or triumph over authority is determined by an uneven flow of permissible linguistic matter, while the substantially same raw material in the hands of GJ is controlled by a phalanx of mental agents and subagents who have fully mastered their job descriptions. The wild swings from impervious bluster to abject surrender, the narrower oscillation between aggression and placation, may be performed alone or in the formal company of "others."

GJ is a wish-fulfillment figure begotten by rage upon shame, a retaliatory Goliadkin whom GS hopes he may incorporate in order to outfox the world. This genesis of the "internal" aspect by the narcissistic personality's utter dependence on affirmation from without runs parallel to the "external" society's glad reception of the new clerk. Why not have a miracle? Exemplifying the fulfillment of Goliadkin's wishes (for fame, fortune, a somewhat higher-paying job) means satisfying all the others, too, according to the miracle worked by Dostoevsky, that fleshes GJ out as a charter member of the club—and, of course, GS's most dangerous superior.

Yet the fantasy of a benevolent superior never quite vanishes. To the last, GS desires union with his double; at the last, he accepts GJ's outstretched hand (so often previously snatched away). "Это мирить нас хотят" (227) ("They want to reconcile us" [142]), he muses—a notion still appealing despite many series of (paired) rebuffs, despite the double's treacherous smile accompanied by a wink at the crowd.

The tactic of recourse to cliché finds a corollary in GS's aspiration to decorum and propriety. He is prey to an extreme degree of a common failing: keeping score, with high marks for flowery phrases or fawning gestures, demerits for errors or defections:

"Поклониться иль нет? Отозваться иль нет? Признаться иль нет? … или прикинуться, что не я (113)

("Shall I bow? Shall I make some response? Shall I admit it's me, or shan't I?" [7])

The department head, Andrei Filippovich, is passing in a droshky. So far this could be anyone trapped in a chance encounter with the boss; but the pivotal word "admit" (*Признаться*) gives the pathology of this instance away.

Then:

"Или прикинуться, что не я, а что кто-то другой, разительно схожий со мной, и смотреть как ни в чем не бывало? Именно не я, не я, да и только!" (113)

("Or shall I pretend it's not me, but someone extraordinarily like me, and just look as if nothing had happened? It really isn't me, it *isn't* me, and that's all there is to it!" [8])

What began as a contretemps ends in frantic burrowing for self-concealment from the "магнетизм начальничьеских взоров" (113) ("the magnetic influence exerted by the gaze of the departmental head" [8]).

This scene leads to another in which, arrived at Dr. Ruten-spitz' office, GS sits down, then recalls that he has not yet been invited to sit:

> [Он] поспешил поправить ошибку свою в незнании света и хорошего тона, немедленно встав с занятого им без приглашения места.(114)

> ([He] made haste to rectify this breach of social etiquette and *bon ton* by rising from the seat he had so unceremoniously taken. [10])

and this gestural series is followed by muttered apologies, lapses into muteness, and especially, defiant facemaking, which comes from the internalized source of the dialogue:

> этот взгляд вполне выражал независимость господина Голядкина, то есть говорил ясно, что господин Голядкин совсем ничего, что он сам по себе, как и все, и что его изба во всяком случае с краю.(114)

> (a look that gave full expression to Mr. Goliadkin's independence, making it clear that he had nothing to worry about, that he went his own way like anyone else, and had in any case nothing to do with what concerned other people. [10])

Goliadkin's fixed stares also signify by seeing nothing, as if blindly, inwardly directed. The graded sequence tipped by non sequitur, hyperbolizing the spectrum of slavishness/defiance, is generated by what GS at first perceives as his own lapse of propriety.

The narratorial voice stays loyal to GS's obsession with

decorum, deploring a toast drunk at Klara's name-day party "таким приличным забвением приличия" (130) ("by this decorous breach of decorum" [28]); praising "весьма приличные и любезные откровенности" (130) ("eminently decorous and amiable confidences" [29]) overheard on that occasion. The word *propriety* appears no fewer than eight times in this single scene (Danow 1997: 28). This party scene is closely correlated with the splendid satirical digression in which the narrator laments his own failure of high style ("o! для чего я не обладаю тайною ..." [129]; "Oh, why do I not possess the secret..." [28]), but finds a "grand" word—*гомеопатически[е]* (130) 'homoeopathic' (29)—to describe the feet of the ladies present. The narratorial voice, capable of minute oscillations between sympathy and contempt, proves too nimble, however, to settle for satirizing misguided notions of literary elegance or misprision of literary precedent.

At what might seem the gravest junctures, Mr. Goliadkin makes appeal to petty infractions of rule. In contemplation of begging the chief clerk to fire GJ: "'Ваше превосходительство ... перемените ... велите ... безбожный, самовольный подмен уничтожить ... не в пример другим'" (213) ("'Replace him, Your Excellency [...] put an end to an ungodly and unwarranted impersonation, that it may not serve as a precedent for others'" [126]). This utterance must not be taken as plain nonsense. Its Goliadkinistic semantics do at least two enlightening things. First, by urging a "replacement," the speaker contradicts his main plea that the imposture be destroyed. Second, by yoking together the portentous "ungodly" and trivial "unwarranted," he betrays his inability to distinguish between uncanny horrors and infractions of rule. However, GS never questions his own propriety and etiquette when he crashes Klara Olsuf'evna's parties, for he is nursing an outlaw mentality that effectively does away with ethical self-searching.

When he spots the two colleagues in their droshky, one

possibly pointing at him, the narrator chides them for behavior "весьма неприлично на улице" (112) ("very unbecoming in the street" [7]), then yields to GS himself, who reacts by attributing the colleagues' ridicule and offhand manners to arrogance at being in a carriage: "'Ну, что же такого тут странного? ... человеку нужно быть в экипаже, вот он и взял экипаж.'" (112) ("'What's so unusual about being in a carriage? If you need a carriage, you take one.'" [7]). To his two office colleagues:

> "Говорят еще, господа, что птица сама летит на охотника. Правда, и готов согласиться: но кто здесь охотник, кто птица? Это еще вопрос, господа!(125)"

> ("'The bird flies to the huntsman,' they say, gentlemen. That's true, I'm ready to admit. But who's the huntsman here, and who the bird? That's another question, gentlemen.'" [22])

Here, against the noise of the clerks' laughter, the presence of the uncanny is discernible: GS is being spoken through.[18]

Most of GS's non sequiturs, however, belong to irrelevant officialese, for example: "'Кто разрешил такого чиновника, кто дал право на это?'" (147) ("'Who admitted this clerk? "Who authorized it?'" [48–49]). Or, secreting himself on Klara's stairs: "'Эх ты, фигурант ты этакой!'' (132) ("'A walking-on part—that's all you've got!'" [31]).[19] Confronting his office superior:

> "Я говорю ... что это моя частная жизнь и что здесь, сколько мне кажется, ничего нельзя найти предосудительного касательно официальных отношений моих." (127)

> ("I say that this is my private life, and that regarding my official relationships, nothing reprehensible is, so

far as I can see, to be found in my presence here." [24])[20]

Many non sequiturs obviously spring from GS's urge to expel the truth of his being in the face of authority. Despite its prevailing inconsequentiality, GS's harangue to an absent Klara Olsuf'evna retains the same link to Goliadkinism: "Без благонравия в наш промышленный век, сударыня вы моя, не возьмешь" (221) ("...in our industrial age, young lady, you won't get anywhere without good behaviour" [134]). The irrelevance here is invariably based on cliché.

Suppressed resentment contending with a passionate submissiveness has another Goliadkinistic outlet: invoking the names of great men and celebrated examples of virtue. Dragging in important names also reassures Goliadkin that he belongs in their company and occasionally contributes to his store of portentous or sentimental rhetoric. The associated language of praise conflates (great men's) motives and their destinies:

"Ведь и великие люди подчас чудаками смотрели. Даже из истории известно, что знаменитый Суворов пел петухом ... Ну, да он там это все из политики." (152)

("[...] even great men have looked silly at times. History even tells us the great Suvorov used to crow like a cock...Still, all that was for political reasons." [55])

The "still" is an extra fillip betraying GS's predilection for "political" tactics. Or:

Вот он ... и выжидает ... тихомолочки, и выжидает ... ровно два часа с половиною. Отчего же и не выжидать? И сам Виллель выжидал. (132)
(And there he was, staying quiet just as he had been

for the past two and a half hours. But why shouldn't he? Villèle waited. [31])

The name of the monk-impostor Grishka Otrep'ev, who impersonated the tsar-apparent before the ascension of Boris Godunov and is known as the False Demetrius, is farcically connected to Goliadkin Junior ("Гришка Отрепьев только один, сударь, взял самозванством, обманув слепой народ, да и то ненадолго." (168–69). [" 'The False Demetrius was the only one to gain by imposture, sir —after deceiving a blind people—but not for long.' " (73)].

In diametric opposition to the moments of "death" and stasis where the naked truth takes over, bluster has an almost superhuman psychic power capable of moving GS at breakneck speed and in contradictory directions, just as its cessation freezes him in his tracks. Dostoevsky transposes GS's moves to an otherworldly cinematic realm *avant la lettre*—such as running, jumping, falling, fainting—all a form of expressive "speech." Of the multifarious means employed to ward off introspection, the Chaplinesque mode,[21] fast-forwarded motion, is one of the most strikingly modern, foresighted inventions. Everything we "see," too, has in a sense "always already" happened.[22]

A breakthrough strategy of Dostoevsky's is to make sure GS remains paradoxically a prisoner of centrifugal motion possessed by irrepressible kinetic energy that moves him cinematically, running, jumping, skidding, shooting off in directions opposed to his "spoken" intentions. The psychic force of automated movement of course derives from GS's need to blow smoke over the mental residue of semantically charged failure, shame, mortification. Anything mechanical is to be preferred, so that the more irrelevant a move looks the more significance it has for the maintenance of GS's delusions.

An important subsection of Goliadkin's bluster comprises declarations of sincerity and plain dealing. Most of the time these belong to the realm of unwanted confessions, functioning also in desperate contrast to GS's visceral need of self-concealment with moments of breakdown in his defenses. With the doctor: "Я … не мастер красно говорить … я не так как другие … придавать слогу красоту не учился." (116) ("'I'm no great talker…I am not as other people. I haven't learnt to embellish what I say.'" [11]).[23] One is reminded that this is all too true, though neither the intention nor the result will benefit the speaker. "Зато я действую … зато я действую, Крестьян Иванович." (116) ("'But to make up for it, I'm a man of action, a man of action, Doctor.'" [11]). This gambit does double duty as a social cliché reactivated by the weak. The scene culminates in GS's weeping, which is sincere. His company face returns to the fore at the office:

> "Есть люди, господа, которые не любят окольных путей и маскируются только для маскарада. Есть люди, которые не видят прямого человеческого назначения в ловком уменье лощить паркет сапогами." (124)

> ("There are people, gentlemen, who don't like beating about the bush, and mask themselves only to go to a masquerade. There are people who don't see that man's one purpose in life is to be adept at bowing and scraping." ([22])

To a bunch of clerks assembled around their laughing stock, he proclaims (in Gogolian form): "'Вы, господа, все меня знаете, но до сих пор знали только с одной стороны.'" (124) ("'You all know me, gentlemen, but up to now you have only known one side of me.'" ([21]); and this debouches into several standard sincerity topoi: he doesn't beat about the bush; he is innocent of intrigue; a challenge only brings him courage. "'В дипломаты бы я не годился." (125). ("'Asa diplomat I'd be no good at all." [22]). Proclaiming his forthrightness to the doctor, the employer, the colleague, even the double, he ironizes on the smokescreen that perennially enfolds him; but it is also the parody of the time-worn social discourse of sincerity and honesty in which Goliadkin's superiors are also likely to indulge. His bravado takes it to extremes because his illusions call for the further one, that he can express himself directly and unashamedly. Of course Goliadkin meanwhile holds fast to the notional god of his own cunning.

From his earliest encounters with colleagues and with Dr. Rutenspitz, readers are given to understand that in the Goliadkin system no one questions a winner's ethics, nor does GS try to conceal the wrongness of his own past wrongful actions (seduction of the German cook; the imbroglio with false letters) from himself any more than he does those committed against him. The profoundly chagrined GS is in one aspect only one among all the moral relativists populating *The Double* who would reproach themselves only for ineptness, bad luck, or bad timing, and there is a carefully observed sportsmanship in the way even his severely neurotic mind withholds moral blame while condemning the appearance of impropriety.

GS's pathology is front and center from the outset; everything pertaining to his "character" is fully formed as soon as the story opens, thus protecting the whole text from incremental development and Bildung, and later from novelistic models that call for anything more than minimal change. The result for the plotting is infernal repetition, a Dostoevskian decision that hurls readers into the no-exit position that is GS's very plight. Disparagers of the story's reduplications fail to understand the potential value of their own exasperated response. The beauty is precisely that the absence of climax and release dramatically inveigles readers into a situation with no exit, rather than a plot offering facile relief.

Although GS owes something to other models of automata

(as in Poe and E. T. A. Hoffmann), he differs from them capitally—as a specifically human byproduct. The narrative voice impels him onward almost into freewheeling expressive realms as yet unrealizable in visual terms but beyond the possibilities of speech. Playing out the contrast of high-speed centrifugal motion within a torturously repetitive scenario, GS chases his own tail, frantic, exasperated, casting about for alternatives, while the narrative collaborates in the suppression of any "rational" alibi. Interference, hiatus, ruptures of dialogue that would otherwise lead to false continuities occur via physical motion that betrays deeper structural incongruities, a noise within the consciousness, an exchange of sense for nonsense. Most obviously self-negating are the moments when GS proclaims himself free and clear (of obligation to or mockery by others), only to lurch yet again into his infernal pursuit; ejected from Klara Olsuf'evna's ball, GS runs off to "freedom," but "wherever his legs may carry him" proves no place to find it. For GS, the succession of automated moves simulates having somewhere to go; readers, on the other hand, are made painfully aware that this is false. Stasis, for GS, means having to take in the truth, and signals a paralysis of his will, a repudiation of self. The sacrifice of the self is its own pleasure. This is not the same as seeking to identify the self with some other, through efforts to resemble them. Rather, self-torment is at a given moment a sort of deep pleasure for Mr. Goliadkin, amounting almost to voluptuousness.

Usually GS will shoot off in some evidently unintended direction, or in the one perfectly opposed to his declared intention. Saying to himself "I must go home" practically mandates a rush to the office. Accordingly, his fears assuaged for not showing up at the office the day after he first sights the double,

Взялся он за трубку, набил ее и, только что начал порядочно раскуривать,—быстро вскочил с дивана, трубку отбросил, живо умылся, обрился, пригладился, натянул на себя вицмундир и всё прочее, захватил кое-какие бумаги и полетел в департамент. (145)

([...] he picked up his pipe, filled it, and had no sooner got it drawing nicely, than he sprang up from the sofa, tossed it away, quickly washed, shaved and combed his hair, dragged on his uniform jacket and other things, and grabbing some papers, shot off to the office. [46])

A brilliant authorial strategy is to deploy GS's moves at a speed nearly impossible to track. Dostoevsky comes close to overcoming this narratorial handicap—as Goliadkin says the same thing over and over with glances, movements, sprints, all registered with tedious precision—so that the tightness of continuity defies efforts to linearize GS's actions as discrete and thus subject to judgment. The fast-forwarding produces a sense of overlapping and a ceaseless din at the level of "plot." But the perpetual-motion mode has further import: it helps to impose the idea of continuity in general, making it obvious that no action here can be definitively isolated from its context.

Like speech-based filler, the succession of motor activities provides GS with relief via busy-ness, assuaging his desperate need for change. But just as filler has no semantic value as language, the kinetic fireworks have no semantic value as point-to-point communication. Gestures function as correlates of the verbal cliché and vice versa. Goliadkin's speaking—or rather, telltale hand and foot movements—begin well in advance of the double's advent, with simultaneous reference to Goliadkin's own social life and to their meanings in society generally. Early on, the narrator observes coldly that Goliadkin "изредка подмигивая своей думке выразительною гримаскою" (112) ("making an expressive grimace as a thought occurred to him" ([6]) is at the same time oblivious to the "grins and grimaces" ("не заметил улыбочек и гримас") the servant Petrushka directs at him while assisting in his toilet. There is also the early fake-chivalrous or rakish man-about-town, jauntily greeting a strange female:

> Заметив одну женскую фигуру ... господин Голядкин послал ей рукой поцелуй. Впрочем, он не знал сам, что делает, потому что решительно был ни жив ни мертв в эту минуту. (125)

> (Noticing the figure of a woman [...] Mr. Goliadkin blew her a kiss. But he had no idea what he was doing, for at that moment he was neither dead nor alive [23])

Whereas, at first, mechanizing GS's grotesque moves appears mostly to underscore his soul-deadness, as in the case of other automated characters, the process comes to reveal the completeness of the alienation between "inside" and "outside." Both sound and movement are driven by external compulsion, displaced from volition.

The clash between frantic physical movement and the quagmired spirit is offset by the claustrophobic environment. The hero runs in circles, at times amid crowds of people and all in the same few settings: the office, the repeated soiree where others participate in the automated action. In chapter 4, Klara Olsuf'evna mechanically extends her hand to Mr. Goliadkin so that they may execute a clipped little dance, a meaningless social gesture that typifies the party. But Goliadkin's clumsiness brings on the downfall of the little social machine and undoes the automatic convention in slapstick mode. Chaos ensues on the dance floor. In the course of this scene it transpires that psychic damage has already crowded GS out of the social sphere, or "process." Goliadkin's non sequitur on this occasion hews close to the form of form: shamed again, he mutters a formula preceded by a distancing qualifier: "Полька, сколько ему по крайней мере кажется, танец новый и весьма интересный, созданный для утешения дам …" (137) ("The polka was, as far as he could see, a novel and extremely interesting dance, contrived to delight the ladies" [37]); a beginning that shapes up into a blustering show of concession: "но что если так дело пошло, то он, пожалуй, готов согласиться" (137) ("But if this was how it had turned out, he was prepared to acquiesce" [37]).

The alienation that propels GS's stiff little body and superintends its grotesque twitches and governs his lightning changes of mind overdetermines his (and our??) disconnection between subject and object, inside and outside. Only the double, GJ, retains his analytical ability, keeps his counsel, and therefore restricts his behavior to well-judged observance of the forms. This is no philosophical panic, but a psychic clash, the immediate panic of being-in-life, far more profoundly rooted than a fully nihilistic Gogolianism. Speech filler (which is like movement)—the repetitious don't-you-thinks, here's whats, umms—in short the "spam" and residue deposited by rational dialogue—is a close relation of cliché and repetition but more specifically associated with hesitation and uncertainty. It is also more intimately bound up with the fear of silence—anything to keep communication open, or at least closed for renovations. In GS's case, of course, it helps stymie the flow of consequential thinking and is a purer form of self-concealment than hoping to sound like everyone else while trying to mean what they mean. By fully abstracting from meaning, unlike bluster (which remains in an intelligible dialogic relationship to the speech of others), filler raises the stakes of self-delusion, as an acoustic portrait of the noise in GS's head against the background of the nonsense buzzing around him.

Dostoevsky expends filler in the service of fully representing the inanition of the speaker. The well-known Gogolian rhetorical move of interlarding speech with false starts, pauses, harrumphs, and other filler easily usurps the place of normal subject matter to a degree unexplored even by Gogol, especially when GS strains most ardently to match his consciousness to that of his interlocutor(s). For example, in the throes of realizing that he has been replaced at the office by his double, GS undergoes several phases of alternating panic and blustering. It occurs to him then to enlist the support of the other clerks, "забежать вперед зайцем ... подойдя как будто бы за делами, между разговором, и намекнуть, что вот, дескать, господа, так и так" (151) ("of somehow stealing a march on them, and, approaching them ostensibly on business [...] of making in the course of conversation some reference to the subject such as 'Such and such, and such and such, gentlemen' [53]). Giving full display to GS's misprision of social exchange and of what have been called the "prescribed informalities," Dostoevsky lampoons those very things. Of course it is in the expectation of social exchange that GS's solipsistic side reveals itself most tragicomically. What normally signals indecision, offers a gain of time, or the need to break bad news lightly, and therefore can be a useful weapon, turns against the speaker vis-à-vis society just as it mercifully screens GS from himself in interior dialogue. When his internal rhetorical temperature rises and he needs to summon up a high tone, the entanglement in retarding formulas impedes or staves off the unwelcome message he has for himself.

Among the most striking of the verbal pyrotechnics deployed in the service of pathology is a propensity for stringing together a progression of attributes or adjectives whose meanings would be contextually interpreted in descending order of importance, but hyperbolizing the least important ones. In other words, the series begins forte and concludes pianissimo, with the least powerful adjective in final position:

Господин Голядкин почувствовал, ... что сбывается с ним небывалое и доселе невиданное и, по тому

самому, *к довершению несчастия*, неприличное
(147; emphasis added)

(What was happening to him was, he sensed, unprecedented, unheard-of, and therefore, *to crown his
misfortunes*, unseemly [49])[24]

Goliadkin's verbal syntheses generally fall prey to contiguity disorder, in harmony with his unconscious parodies of normative ethics. He specializes in sidestepping the intolerable clash
with the enemy by a foggy understanding of menacing events.
When he has undertaken a preemptive march (on the party, the
chief clerk), the retreat is likely to express itself in the same
peremptory terms. Of Anton Antonovich's refusal to hear out
his plea: "'что означает этот новый крючок?'" (163) ("'What
does it mean, this new piece of pettifoggery?'" [68]). When the
full force of GJ's desertion occurs to him: "'Не отступиться ли
запросто?'" (170) ("'Why not just break with him without any
formality?'" [76]). At the first horrified sighting of the double,
GS's brainwork bypasses the onset of "fear and anguish" "'Ну,
ничего … ну, ничего; может быть, это и совсем ничего и
чести ничьей не марает'" (140) ("'Well, it doesn't matter [...]
Perhaps it's nothing, and not a disgrace to anyone's honour'"
[40]). The peculiar aptness of this is reflected by the use of officialese, but more potently relies on that sadly foresighted "anyone," which even in eliding the presence of the real subject
foretells his own loss of "honor."

GS's fears are deeply rooted and (via the conspiracy between his infirmities and the social environment) well justified
by the time we meet him, and his anticipation of disaster
grounded in probability. To allege simply that he creates his own
enemies is to abolish the social significance of the double, his
public self. That operation can lead only to the conclusion that
Goliadkin has created the whole society around him, and that

we are reading the narratorial reproduction, down to the last diacritic, of Goliadkin's dictation.[25] Failing this, one is left to accept that Goliadkin's preemptive strikes and his hindsight of foreknowledge are necessary to each other, in a psychological process that runs on a double track (at the behest of a cruel fate which has also generated the society around him).

However, Dostoevsky does not turn anyone explicitly against Goliadkin from the outset (with the exception of Rutenspitz or a few gibing younger colleagues). His acquaintances are simply indifferent, his servant annoyed, his colleagues mildly derisive. No one on the stage or in the office hierarchy is plotting his downfall or his dismissal from work; his failure in "love" is not a dire experience if only because love is not even under contemplation. The "psychological" critic could allege that in Goliadkin we have nothing but a triumph of solipsism. Yet society's indifference to suffering is under authorial indictment. That it is reflected in a protagonist already inoculated with it makes this indifference no less a social illness, nor does its deployment in a situation where the protagonist is certainly a cause. The office staff and party guests show themselves willing to meet one of their own halfway, but never to go the extra distance: it is made patently no one's business to forgive and cure. No one would doubt that Goliadkin would see matters in the same way, given another scapegoat.

Cyclical recurrence is a structural and mimetic support, which at the level of prosody already affords us the very experience of an infernal machine. GS is quagmired in a no-exit situation rather than a plot. It is surprising to find nonetheless that the author has structured events firmly around the core of chapter 7, which includes the midpoint. Most important events are doubled.[26] The trick of self-deception, whereby GS mistakes a door for a mirror occurs twice,[27] for the first time in chapter 9:

В дверях в соседнюю комнату, почти прямо за спиною конторщика и лицом к господину Голядкину, в дверях, которые, между прочим, герой наш принимал доселе за зеркало, стоял один человек. (174)

(Standing in the doorway of the next room, almost directly behind the waiter and facing Mr. Goliadkin—standing in the doorway, which till then he had taken to be a mirror—[stood a certain] man [80])

And again, in chapter 12:

В дверях, которые герой наш доселе принимал за зеркало, как некогда тоже случилось с ним, появился *он*,—известно кто. (216)

(In a doorway, which till then our hero had as on a previous occasion taken for a mirror, *he* appeared, the *he* who is already familiar to the reader. [129])

The essential doubleness of the text is completed by the absence of a summation: GS is escorted to the insane asylum by a cohort including Dr. Rutenspitz with the double cavorting alongside his coach. But this feuilletonistic ending (chapter 13) does little more than top off Goliadkin's first visit to the doctor (chapter 2), and underscores its repetitiousness with verbal echoes of its predecessor:

"Я надеюсь, что здесь нет ничего … ничего предосудительного … или могущего возбудить строгость … и внимание всех касательно официальных отношений моих?"

("I trust there is nothing reprehensible...concerning my official relationships...that could provoke any severe measure...and excite public attention?" [143])

GS's fatal defects are sketched in from the opening scene, and thus recall the arbitrariness of Greek tragedy (insofar as they have to bring him down inexorably). Another tragic feature is that most of the "action" has taken place already by the time the story opens, "and the narrative deals only with the final dissolution" (Ayers 1988). Goliadkin Senior falls from the pinnacle of his possibilities through individual failings which may be part of a predetermined fate. And the novel also represents a wider conflict within the surrounding ethical sphere (cf. the hierarchy of bosses at the office). The author alternates Goliadkin's actions as contingent or necessary. At the same time he demonstrates the real existence of suffering outside of Goliadkin's delusions; this world is tragic and in need of transformation.

The criticism of *The Double* over time tends to replicate the conflict within the story. Pity and fear, copresent, occur in readers as the byproducts of a complex interplay between identification with GS (pity) and the fearful recognition of and fascinated revulsion from the realia of GS's behavior (fear). Yet compassion for GS would not require simple cognitive identity with him but would call on readers to "love" the sufferer as one might "love" someone being subjected to scapegoating by others. As a scapegoat GS has the function of reaffirming the horrid orthodoxy around him. Self-deception is already a form of doubling, so that GS contains his double a priori, but as a scapegoat he fills another doubling role, encounters with which trigger a recognition (or should) that the social order needs to be transformed. The slippage between the realm of social order and that of psychological disease raises a challenge to traditional notions of tragedy, which do not gladly accommodate GS's shabby fantasies. Much as people prefer being accused of bad judgment to being taxed with bad taste, the subject is distasteful, a negative image of the beliefs that form ordinary social life and as such would rather be kept secret. But the conception of human subjectivity, by laying bare the sheer paltriness of human subjectivity, translates into modern terms the central experiences of tragedy—except that of self-knowledge and resulting transformation.

Does Dostoevsky make suffering pleasurable to consume in literary form? If so, the aesthetic pleasure derived from watching someone suffer in a successful representation scapegoats the protagonist, Goliadkin. Much of the criticism, especially that of the last twenty years in the English-speaking world, evinces a contempt for Goliadkin that masks the fear-content. If one supposes that readers experience pity and fear of his scapegoat, Dostoevsky complicates these responses by inducing such fascinated revulsion. He does not allow compassion to require a cognitive identity with the protagonist, yet holds the internal and external—that is, psychological and social—forces in balance so as to trigger a recognition that the world that produced such a Goliadkin needs to be transformed. One is invited to identify with the scapegoat and so to feel not horror of it but of the social order whose failure it signifies. It may frustrate readers working their way through Dostoevsky's oeuvre in reverse that no mechanism exists whereby identification with Goliadkin can lead to change in his world. The interplay between an appalled, shaming partial identification with Goliadkin and a general horror at the world that has drawn the full measure of suffering from him is at work. But aside from the hyperkinetic mimesis of the story lies only a deictic thrust: our encounter with the fearful figure of this scapegoat continues to offer the escape valve of ridicule and thereby leaves untouched the world—ours—which the scapegoat inhabits.

If readers retain pity for Goliadkin, do the emotions he elicits stop with their object? Here are striking differences from traditional views of tragedy, as if crafted for postmodern times. For one thing, suffering here has no cognitive value for any character. Never does GS's occasional burst of self-assessment result in a stable self-understanding. He is the ultimate recidivist. More significantly, Goliadkin's errors derive from flaws not of character but of "personality." Does GS make ill-judged moves, or have the gods turned their faces away? or is it all the same? Is GS really his "own executioner," as he complains more than once? He seems to be the slave of a pathological design whose patterns are currency to everyone except him. It is more than usually ironic that GS most volubly protests his clear-sightedness. Behind every mask he fits himself with is yet another mask, until even what seems an ultimate motive is masked (Coetzee 1985). Goliadkin, whose name includes the meaning *naked*, is in fact one of the Dostoevskian characters who cannot tell himself the truth without the copresence of self-deception.

A high-speed, very short route shuttles GS back and forth, between errors and punishments, with a mystical directness that eludes rational dissection and cancels out the possibility of change. The character GS and indeed every character in the story has only to play itself out, the more so since no rescue can be wrested from the stagnant and hypocritical society in which they are rooted. The narrative voice conspires in everything on every side and changes sides flexibly (as via *style indirecte libre*), but never sheds light on causes. Any inquiry into causes will yield the simple conclusion that the gods have chosen GS as the butt of a strange experiment in which inside and outside are no longer distinguishable from one another. GS conflates ends and means like a child concealing himself in a game of hide and seek by covering his own eyes:

"Подменил, подлец! ... не постыдился публичности! Видят ли его? Кажется, не замечает никто ..."
(174)

("He's passed himself off as me, the blackguard [...] He's got no qualms about other people being present! Can they see him? I don't think so." [81])

The interplay of resentment and shame displaces his grasp of the double's motive, for it is the latter's obvious, brazen purpose to garner maximum attention.

That readers are forced to swallow at least the suspicion of supernatural intervention underscores the cruelty. Any individual subject to the social order as Dostoevsky delineates it could have been chosen. For the great divide between GS and his double is that everything GS says and does in public and with respect to social advancement has to fail, while everything GJ does has to succeed in its aims. Not even a tactical reversal is made possible.

It is difficult to understand how, then, critics could have considered GJ as a figure of GS's guilt. The following is a representative statement: "Goliadkin's double represents the suppressed aspects of his personality that he is unwilling to face; and this internal split between self-image and truth [...] is Dostoevsky's first grasp of a character-type that became his hallmark as a writer" (Frank 1976: 311). The urge to slot *The Double* into a dynamic of relentless development toward the Big Books severely mars the analysis, which is wrongheaded first of all because GS wants nothing more than to merge with GJ, thereby transforming himself into a raging success at the office and with his sniggering coterie, even potentially the winner of Klara Olsuf'evna's hand. Here is how Dostoevsky calibrates the events in chapter 8. GJ at first seeks out his "original," almost immediately to supersede him malevolently. Appearing with a sheaf of papers for GS and aping a concerned look, soon GJ will trot, smiling, behind the chief clerk Andrei Filippovich, becoming more contiguous to this personage in the course of the office narrative. And already, GS pursues GJ at the first of the many key moments of "death" or loss of consciousness:

Наконец он опомнился. Сознав в один миг, что погиб, уничтожился в некотором смысле, что замарал себя и запачкал свою репутацию, что осмеян и оплеван в присутствии посторонних лиц, что предательски поруган тем, кто еще вчера считал первейшим и надежнейшим другом своим, что срезался, наконец, на чем свет стоит,—господин Голядкин бросился в погоню за своим неприятелем. В настоящее мгновение он уже и думать не хотел о свидетелях своего поругания."(167)

(At last [GS] recovered. Realising in a flash that he was done for, that he had in a manner of speaking destroyed himself, that he had been disgraced, that his reputation was ruined, and that he had been scorned and ridiculed in front of others—realising that he had been perfidiously abused by him he had considered his greatest and most trusty friend, and finally, realising that he had been utterly shamed, Mr. Goliadkin charged in pursuit of his enemy. He tried not to think of those who had witnessed the outrage. [72-73])

This pursuit parodies the notion of a split personality seeking its other half, but, more importantly, leads naturally to the second reason why GJ should not be thought of as a projection of conscience or consciousness: he is steadfastly the object of pursuit.[28] GS experiences all attacks by self and others as coming from others; he also joins in the creation of an entire, split-off self.

In spirit GJ inhabits, together with GS, a guilt-free realm. Both are firmly ensconced in a shame culture where guilt is simply irrelevant. Dostoevsky lets us know this by providing, almost contemptuously, the convoluted capillary plot having to do with accusations by the German woman and a nest of denunciatory letters. It is the accumulation and fear of shame that brings on the numerous "deaths."[29] Goliadkin is the child of the society for whose protection he longs, as any child would turn repeatedly to a powerful father who has after all bequeathed him his share of genes.

The search for acceptance by a powerful father and concomitant resentment of the available ones emerge in the visit to the doctor, well before the double appears. "Но ведь доктор, как говорят, что духовник,—скрываться было бы глупо, а знать пациента—его же обязанность (113) ("But after all, [Goliadkin thought,] a doctor was supposed to be like a [father] confessor, and to hide away from him would be foolish, since it was his job to know his patient." [8]). But Rutenspitz's indifference and misconstruals goad the patient to tears. The unprincipled or cruel fathers multiply: Anton Antonovich, Andrei Filippovich, the unnamable His Excellency—Dostoevsky's pyramidal indictment of the functionary class extends as far as the divinity, and its sphere of influence attains the supernatural. In GS's very words:

> "промысл божий создал двух совершенно подобных, а начальство благодетельное, видя промысл божий, приютило двух близнецов. Оно, конечно... лучше бы было, кабы не было ничего этого, умилительного." (172)

> ("divine Providence creates two identical beings, the beneficent authorities behold the divine handiwork, and here they are giving them a place of refuge. It would of course have been better [...] if there'd been nothing of this touching business." [79])

On one side the wish to assert himself contends with the perfectly opposed wish not to exist at all: "Goliadkin Jr. is the embodiment of Goliadkin Sr.'s wish simultaneously to be active and effective in the world and to be annihilated" (Sherry 1975, 263). If GS cannot be effective, then he wants to die.

Mr. Goliadkin "dies" many times in the course of the narrative. Ejection from Klara Olsuf'evna's early on causes a deathlike trauma: "Господин Голядкин был убит,—убит вполне, в полном смысле слова" (138) ("He had no more life in him. He was finished in the full sense of the word" [38]). It becomes plain almost instantly that the narrator, following the precise event of the moment, will resurrect Goliadkin at any moment. What moves the narrator to exaggeration is the flood of feeling, or numbness, that is Goliadkin's experience of the instant. Shortly afterward, Goliadkin keeps on running "по какому–то чуду" (138) ("by some incredible miracle" [38]). Goliadkin's deaths are habitual, but no less painful for it:

> он … проникнутый вполне идеей своего недавнего падения, останавливался неподвижно, как столб, посреди тротуара; в это мгновение он умирал, исчезал; потом вдруг срывался как бешеный с места и бежал, бежал без оглядки, как будто спасаясь от чьей–то погони. (139)

> (he would stop short and stand stock-still in the middle of the pavement, completely absorbed by the awfulness of his downfall. At such moments he would depart this life and cease to exist. Then suddenly, off he would go like a madman, and run and run without looking back, as though being pursued. [39])

Spotting the double at the office:

> Он даже стал, наконец, сомневаться в собственном существовании своем … Порой он совершенно лишался и смысла и памяти. Очнувшись после такого мгновения, он замечал, что машинально и бессознательно водит пером по бумаге. (147)

(He began finally even to doubt his own existence [...].
Now and then he would lose all power of reasoning
and lapse into unconsciousness. After one such moment he recovered to find himself automatically and
unconsciously guiding his pen over the paper. [49])

At the end of *The Double*, against a background of crescendoing
catcalls, cries, and gibes, he falls unconscious and recovers to realize that he is being driven to somewhere unfamiliar for the last
time.

The reiterated deaths are real in terms of feeling but also
mock the tragic mode whereby dying can function as belated
and permanent revelation with its complement of decisive
change. These swoons are full stops, indeed, but rather than
transformation, they signal how nothing can be climactic or even
incremental here except to readers stubbornly impatient for
development and resolution. The deaths mark stasis pure and
simple, occasionally providing GS with the narcoleptic self-for-
getfulness that might accompany a spasm or epileptic attack. He
sometimes seems to long for these deaths but equally fears them.
Yet GS is wired to react perpetually to external, contiguous stimuli, including those generated by his alienated self, which produce the same fits and starts of activity. And here Dostoevsky's
sardonic narratorial decisions, which depend on repetition and
on the short-circuiting of consciousness, consistently outclass
the "tragic" bauplan whereby the formal rites of belated self-
knowledge would show us the way out by a well-worn road. Dostoevskian genius thus certifies that the most "final" expression of
dying finds its contrary almost immediately But this putative an-
nihilation is little more than a beaten child's cry for justice, and
the trace of attendant psychic damage. There is no tragic escape
route for author, narrator, GS, or any of the dramatis personae—
except for the double himself. The double's mental constitution,
it may be inferred, is in diametric contrast, analytical. From the

first meeting, he can guess what GS is thinking—get inside him, so to speak.

Merezhkovsky thought of GS and his double as "two halves of a third, cloven entity, who mutually seek and pursue each other" (Rank 1971: 47). This view, reminiscent of Plato's hemispheres seeking completion in the *Symposium*, neglects two capital differences. GS pursues GJ in a rage against his treason and usurpation, but burdened equally with a craven longing to participate in his triumphs, to blend with him, at least to find favor with him, which would meet not with forgiveness but outright gratitude. To the last, GS desires to unite with GJ. As swiftly sketched, the narration nearly achieves the speed of thought:

"Ишь его разбирает!—подумал герой наш,—фаворитом смотрит, мошенник! Желал бы я знать, чем он именно берет в обществе высокого тона? Ни ума, ни характера, ни образования ... ведь как это скоро может пойти человек, как подумаешь, и 'найти' во всех людях! ... Господи боже! Как бы мне это так, того ... и с ними бы тоже немножко ... дескать, так и так, попросить его разве ... дескать, так и так, а я больше не буду; дескать, я виноват" (200)

(" 'He's quite giddy with it!' thought our hero. 'He looks the favorite, the scoundrel! I'd like to know just how he manages to succeed in good society—no brains, no character, no refinement, no feeling! [...] When you think of it, how quickly one can get on, and make friends with everybody [...] Oh God! How could I just ...How could I get in with them as well? "Such and such," I'd say—perhaps I should ask him..."Such and such," I'd tell him, "and I won't do it again. It was all my fault." ' " [110])

Vinogradov notes (219) that Gogol's madman Poprishchin becomes transformed into the object of his fixation, the king of Spain. The transfer suggests the action of Goliadkin Senior in "transforming" himself into Junior.

In fact GS is as much taken in at first as a new lover. Together with a generous amount of drink, the very presence of his new guest engenders "an extraordinary feeling of happiness" (62; "необыкновенно счастлив" [158]). The use of formal address speedily cedes to "tell you what, Yasha" (61; "Ты знаешь ли, Яша" [157]) in a flood of exaltation. To the last GS remains charmed by GJ's ingratiating manners. He likes him, just as all the others do. GJ's ingratiating and unctuous manners exert a quasi-erotic appeal. GS attempts to hide for the last time at Klara's, but GJ reports the guests' demand that GS show himself—"'Осчастливьте, дескать, и приведите сюда Якова Петровича'" (224) ("'Do us the pleasure of bringing in Yakov Petrovich'" [138]—and GJ later assumes "an extraordinarily decorous and well-intentioned air—which was a source of [extreme] gratification to our hero" [139]) ("принявший на себя вид чрезвычайно благопристойный и благонамеренный, чему наш герой донельзя обрадовался" [225]). Respect for the forms equals displaced desire for acceptance and love—so much so that GJ's display of egregious, ersatz politesse can substitute for a social dialogue in which GS might participate.

On GJ's side, at bottom we find only a parasitical and temporary need for a host figure. GJ's immediate purposes in taunting GS do not have to be explicated in the narrative: gratuitous pleasure suffices. While GS is driven to ceaseless pursuit, it is enough for GJ to drop by every so often. Although GJ, of course, needs the presence of GS in order to achieve his destruction, he has no intention of uniting with him.

The second point that forever separates them from being "halves" is that GS was there first, that GJ is parasitical on his victim. One of Dostoevsky's most sardonic and deeply rooted jokes is to show that doubleness is very different from "split personality," that what looks like replication is actually differentiation along crucial lines.

That the double, GJ, is a wish-fulfillment figure, a desired point of arrival and not at all a creature born of guilt[30] is probably clearer to those who accord a just measure of importance to his "public" side, the aspect that gets more frequent and thorough exposure. Since GJ is received everywhere in society, including people who know and could locate the old GS, it is obvious that society prefers the new one. And social approval is GS's sole criterion of enduring value. Junior has everything Senior wants: his deviousness, undetected by everyone except Mr. Goliadkin (who falls victim to his blandishments as well), charms everyone; his gossip and first-naming hit the spot; he conquers the admiring glances of women at parties (without having to prove himself later); his flattery works; his approaches are everywhere welcome; his slimiest speeches are perceived as sincere and heartfelt.[31]

Repetition is of course the elementary form of doubling, and the author deploys its possibilities fully. It is the double's "conscious" speech, conversely taken by others to be sincere and benign, that carries the full weight of irony (one signifier, two signifeds—like allegory, but not it), whereas GS is "spoken through," "unconsciously." GJ of course speaks in GS's own words, different mainly in their tonal variety—moans, wheedles, gibes, and echoes, with a specialty in reversing GS's primary meanings. At first, pretending to be an even more cringing version of GS, the double acts like a double, looking, acting, and miming the third, uncertain, cringing voice in GS's internal dialogue. As he settled in:

Гость был в крайнем, по-видимому, замешательстве, очень робел, покорно следил за всеми движениями своего хозяина, ловил его взгляды и по ним, казалось, старался угадать его мысли. (153)

(The guest showed every sign of being acutely embarrassed and overcome with shyness, dutifully watched his host's every move and caught his every glance, striving, it seemed, to divine what he was thinking. [56–57])

This behavior reproduces GS's usual efforts vis-à-vis superiors, but the prose anticipates success. For the moment, the double

довольно походил в эту минуту на того человека, который, за неимением своего платья, оделся в чужое: рукава лезут наверх, талия почти на затылке, а он … то … сторонится, то норовит куда–нибудь спрятаться. (153)

(was […] rather like a man who, having no clothes of his own, has donned someone else's, and can feel the sleeves riding up and the waist nearly round the back of his neck […] he edges away, tries hard to hide. ([57])

Dostoevsky has opened with a recap of the time-honored comparison between rhetoric and clothing, thrusting GJ into the shrinking second voice and GS into stridency and confidence. As the roles reverse themselves, and the treacherous double takes over the "first" voice, of affectionate, exaggerating familiarity, one linguistic signifier—such as "'мы, дружище, будем хитрить, заодно хитрить будем'" (157); "хитрить мы будем с тобой, Яков Петрович, хитрить" (167) ("We'll fox 'em, my dear fellow. We'll fox 'em together." [61]; "We'll fox 'em, you and I [72])—emerges with GS and GJ as two signifieds in a linguistic reproduction of pure irony. Some of the GS phrases GJ loves to mimic thematize deception: for example, there is the *переулочек* 'little side street' by which GS first takes GJ home, which resurfaces in one of GJ's grotesque farewells; along with the play on *хитрить* '[out]fox.'

Early on in the relationship the pieces of GS and GJ appear suitably fitted; each seems to have found its mate. At first, GS thinks that united, they will "outfox" everyone. The term "outfox" already switches sides by its second occurrence in chapter 8, as GJ turns against GS with a pinch on the cheek. If GJ seeks him out (parodying, again, the shopworn model of two aspects of one personality), it is only to taunt GS with his own faults and gaffes. Some of the latter are deliberately induced as entrapment by GJ, such as the episode where GS is stuck with an inflated payment for eleven meat pies consumed by GJ at a restaurant. Whereas GS at first fed his double gladly and with patronizing benevolence, now he has been forced into it, in a full turn from patronage to submission.[32]

GJ lies to GS routinely, steals the credit for his work, gossips about him with the other clerks, all in speech styles that sedulously refract GS's style, albeit with a supplement of parodic exaggeration (Bakhtin, 232). GJ's hypocritical behavior is perfectly suited to the social context, and impossible to face down. He can even reproach GS for his peccadillo with the German woman. If GS were able, he would turn into his double at once and reap his rewards. GS is simply—terrifyingly simply—incapable of refracting the GJ image toward "the anticipated responses of others" (Bakhtin, 214).

GS does not experience pangs of conscience or remorse except insofar as he can cognize that he has hurt himself. At such moments he is cut to the heart by the perception of his failed tactics, with the result that he is further alienated from himself, as an outsider. GS is a textbook example of subject-object confusion. The same reversal of inside and outside—understood even only in their most mimetic or physical being—that hurls and thrusts his mechanical, misdirected body and tweaks his lightning changes of mind overdetermines the disconnection between what he perceives as coming at him from outside and what is generated within.[33] His own psychic boundaries, where he ends and another begins, remain uncertain to him. His extreme degree of projection, whereby, puppetlike, GS attributes "aspects of [his] self to others" and embarks upon a prolonged relationship of persecution by, opposition to, or identification with those others, is counterbalanced by his double's "ability to 'overstep all the boundaries'" between himself and actual others (Rosenthal 1982, 81–83).

This inside-outside confusion also rules over the schism between "social" and "psychological" readers, harmonizes perfectly in purpose and effect with the GS persona. It would be a simple-minded disservice to the genius of Dostoevsky's scrambling of the conventional "internal" and "external" to label anything about GS as one or the other; the author is quite likely to exchange them at any time.

One of the most touching cases occurs where Mr. Goliadkin wants the meaning of his (already uttered) words reversed: apologizing for a combative, resentful letter to GJ, he begs him to replace his words with the opposite:

"умоляю вас читать его наоборот,—совсем наоборот, то есть нарочно с намерением дружеским, давая обратный смысл всем словам." (204)

("[...] I beseech you, read it the other way round in a deliberately friendly way, giving each word its reverse meaning." [115]).

This moment deserves reflection, not for the simplistic reason that it is cowardly or mendacious, but for revealing a new layer of "virtual" falsehood that exists in and of itself, suggesting that opposites also signify "the other way round" (which cannot justly be laid at the feet of linguistic failure). This is not about language's ontological instability (except insofar as one's words may be "turned against" the speaker), but about the menacing possibilities of "a word with a sideward glance" (Bakhtin, 232 et passim). Bakhtin's formulation strikes to the core of *The Double*: not only verbal sarcasm but facial expression, gesture, and motion become the vectors of a potentially unchecked irony, as signified by the double's parodies of affectionate familiarity, crowned (in chapter 8) by his "smile full of the most venomous and far-reaching implications."[34]

The flexibility of the narratorial voice functions as a powerful destroyer of stability. Confounding and conflating, the narrator demands that readers experience the panic of alienation in their own lives, and does so without invoking them directly. The storyteller "is literally fettered to his hero; he cannot back off from him sufficiently to give a summarizing and integrated image of his deeds and actions" (Bakhtin, 225). But the aim of the text is to provide us with an illusion of synchrony—wanted or not. No distance perspective on the outside, no stable emotional position on the inside; the narrator merely "loves" his object with a passion, and makes sure we are there too.

Like an accomplice, or a cameraman working only at eye level, the narrator is welded to GS, but cannot be trusted to defend his charge. Scarcely a word exceeds the possible boundaries of GS's own self-consciousness. The blur of the subplots looks like what Goliadkin Senior himself would see in a vain attempt to taxonomize the events of his days. But to anyone trying to interpret the whole as a product of Goliadkin Senior's own self-consciousness, the narrator—by his ubiquity and his doubling voice—functions paradoxically as an effective impediment. Even if the other characters were no more than isolated elements of that self-consciousness, even if the convoluted and weak subplots were analogously part of GS's dreams, even if the intrigue concerning the double could be read as the dramatized crisis of one fevered mind, the fastidious formality and unlimited flexibility of the narratorial voice convert the first person into a relentless third.

The narrator sees nothing that Goliadkin does not see. In fact, as Bakhtin notes, the narrator often picks up GS's words and thoughts, intensifies the mockery assigned mostly to GJ, engages in his own nonsense and filler, parodies GS's acts, gestures, movements. There are in fact three interdependent personae at front and center of this claustrophobic stage: GS, GJ, and the narrator, who shows himself as dramatically enmeshed in GS's being as a perfervid reporter or cameraman who knows nonetheless when to pull out and coolly retail the moves of GJ.

The setting becomes more and more like a stage and less like the extensive map of a city. Bad actors vie exclusively with other, sometimes better actors. And yet Petersburg presents an ominous face to Goliadkin's fruitless pursuit, as he executes a "closed loop" through the city, "a 'city-enemy'" (Shklovskii 1957, cit. Gasperetti 1989: 219). Is this "poem of St. Petersburg" composed in Goliadkin's head out of myths of the city and badly assimilated novels?[35] Perspective is abandoned: the narrator never pans above his characters. The text problematizes the actor or role as a standard or model of human behavior, attacks the idea that man is ontologically an actor who has to strut his stuff on the stage of life. GS the puppet moved to do the things he wants least to intend, or that will produce the direst outcome, perfectly complements GJ, whose decisions are deliberate and (on the terms shared by both Goliadkins) productive. None of GJ's thinking is articulated; his motives are plain and his success assured.[36]

Quotation marks could be inserted into the narrative without changing the tone, or the construction, of any énoncé. Bakhtin (drawing on Vinogradov) points out various means whereby the voice of the narrator merges on occasion with that of GS so as to complete one of his thoughts. An unsegmented continuum unfolds so that the field of action shrinks to the dimensions of one hijacked consciousness. The first line GS speaks, as Bakhtin (225) points out, can be "an obvious response to the sentence preceding it in the narration:"

> Не то чтоб он боялся недоброго человека, а так, может быть ... "Да и кто его знает, этого запозда-лого,—промелькнуло в голове господина Голяд-кина,—может быть, и он то же самое, может быть, он-то тут и самое главное дело, и недаром идет, а с целью идет, дорогу мою переходит и меня заде-вает." (140)

> (Not that he was afraid of it being anyone unpleasant, but..."Who knows who this belated fellow may be?"'flashed through Mr. Goliadkin's mind. "Perhaps he's the same as the rest ... Perhaps *he's* the most important part of it, and isn't just out for his health but with the express purpose of crossing my path and provoking me." [41])

The consummate brilliance of this inveigling strategy brings into being a wryly experiential, practical relation to an enduring Dostoevskian Great Idea that we are all one, that no man is an island. But this ethical principle is often rehearsed and recapitulated with little regard for its practical implications. It is all very well to be told by the Greater Dostoevsky that we (humanity, society, all Russia, all Christians) are all implicated: this dictum belongs to things that student papers are expected to summarize and is obligingly repeatable. It is quite another thing—and even in expert literary hands, very difficult to repeat—to be inveigled by the Lesser Dostoevsky into just that position. The former tells us; the latter shows us, and forces the experience on us.

That is a significant function of GS's few but well-scattered lucid intervals, which brilliantly prove that the Goliadkins are acting out their being, as it were, under a new dispensation: understanding comes to readers only via experience. The snapshots of a stalled Mr. Goliadkin, reeling between "life" and "death," find him, for mere seconds, sufficiently possessed by fear to cast aside all efforts at disguise. There is also a moment with the cabman who has brought him to Klara Olsuf'evna's for the last time (chapter 13) in which Mr. Goliadkin temporizes against his fear in a new way: by engaging the other man in talk of matters that concern cabmen/serfs (what village does he hail from? has he a good master? even rich men sometimes weep, etc.). Why rehearse so many of these little deaths, and why recount in detail a banal dialogue with a coachman? In order to follow Mr. Goliadkin meticulously, almost everywhere, and to punctuate by contrast (via lucid intervals) the otherwise relentless possession of his very soul.

GS's initial reactions to injury and insult (however variously motivated) succeed in foreshadowing a more upstanding image. Inveigling readers into yet another dialectic, a passage begins:

> Не спорим, впрочем, не спорим. Может быть, если б кто захотел, если б уж кому, например, вот так непременно захотелось обратить в ветошку господина Голядкина, то и обратил бы, обратил бы без сопротивления и безнаказанно (господин Голядкин сам в иной раз это чувствовал), и вышла бы ветошка, но ветошка—то эта была бы не простая, ветошка эта была бы с амбицией, ветошка—то эта была бы с одушевлением и чувствами, хотя бы и с безответной амбицией и с безответными чувствами и далеко в грязных складках этой ветошки скрытыми, но все—таки чувствами (168–169)

(But let there be no argument about it. Perhaps if anyone had wanted—had suddenly felt a desire to turn Mr. Goliadkin into a boot-rag, they could have done so with impunity, encountering no resistance—Mr. Goliadkin had occasionally sensed that himself—and a boot-rag there would have been, and not a Goliadkin; a nasty, dirty boot-rag, it's true, but still no ordinary one; this boot-rag would have had pride, would have been alive and had feelings; pride and feelings might have remained concealed deep in its filthy folds and been unable to speak for themselves, but all the same they would have been there. [74–75])

Can anyone pronounce GS's and the narrator's collaborative statement decisively false? No more suspect of simple falsehood is GS's affirmation of his uniqueness (in chapter 9), which feeds ironically on the concept of doubleness and emerges in diction that is full of Goliadkinistic bluster, nonetheless moving the speaker to the periphery of psychological disorder because the instant transports GS without his double to a world of principle and compassion, a beyond where every living being would be unique in the mind of every other, representing a valid self-worth.

When this text relies on a presumption of readers' benign ethical norms as a control, the very implication of high-minded axioms drowns in the experiential issues of reading. The noise intensifies and the prospect of canned unilateral conclusions fades out. Thinking about a "unique" Goliadkin could easily narrow one's sights only to the "social" aspect (of collective injustice against a solitary being) and reduce him to yet another (though somewhat more complex) Akakii Akakievich turning on his tormentors. But Akakii, besides his conspicuous humbleness, has an integrated character whose thoughts never resort to canned verbiage or nonsense bureaucratese, much as he loves copying. The practical result of any summarizing or integrative perspective would be to elide the specific predicament of Mr. Goliadkin or smudge it into either the diagnosis of a malady or the indictment of "society." One side would have to win, and the "social" or the "pathological" aspect carry the day. It is intrinsic to the experiential impact of GS's torments that the creature seemingly brought into being by his own dementia achieves public kudos. The semantic supercharge not only threatens boundaries between public and private, outside and inside, psychological and social categories. *The Double* extends to those in search of nostrums a cordial invitation to make a variety of category mistakes, and persuasively—deceptively—solicits facile mockery, especially from anyone seeking the sheltering, protective father under the mask of the tyrant.

Dostoevsky was no exception, in a way. A progress report to his brother (October 8, 1845) adopts basic style features shared by Goliadkin and his narrator:[37]

Яков Петрович Голядкин выдерживает свой характер вполне. Подлец страшный, приступу нет к нему; никак не хочет вперед идти, претендуя, что еще ведь он не готов, а что он теперь покамест сам по себе, что он ничего, ни в одном глазу, а что, пожалуй, если уж на то пошло, то и он тоже может, почему же и нет, отчего же и нет? Он ведь такой, как и все, он только так себе, а то такой, как и все. Что ему! Подлец, страшный подлец! Раньше половины ноября никак не соглашается окончить карьеру. Он уже теперь объяснился с его превосходительством и, пожалуй, (отчего же и нет) готов подать в отставку.

(Yakov Petrovich Goliadkin holds his own completely. He's a terrible scoundrel and there's no approaching him; he refuses to move forward, pretending that he's not ready yet, that for the present he's on his own, he's all right, nothing is the matter, but if it comes to that, then he can do that too, why not, what's to prevent it? He's just like everyone else, he's nothing special, just like everyone else. What's it to him! A scoundrel, a terrible scoundrel! He'll never agree to end his career before the middle of November. He's just now spoken with His Excellency and he just may (and why shouldn't he) be ready to announce his retirement.)

A harmless bit of mockery, or evasion, or both? Dostoevsky was convinced after the puzzlement that greeted *The Double* that its central idea should be made more effective by revision. Goliadkin was to become a socialist, with dreams of fomenting an uprising in Russia. Goliadkin Junior was going to work for the police. Stylistic changes appear in a further version; some parts are abbreviated; he ended up believing that he had not mastered the material. The layered Goliadkinisms in this (October 8, 1845) letter seem to prophesy the obstacles *The Double* would encounter in polite society. Since there was nothing to compare it to, the conviction that "I never brought to literature a more important idea" was answered for practical purposes by "Will it be all right? Is it a proper thing to do?"

At this stage of his creative life Dostoevsky's work harbors no conception of spiritual resurrection. *The Double* transports carnival lunacy to a vision of revenge, yet it shows Dostoevsky (already!) at the height of his empathetic powers, succeeding triumphantly in the task of rendering an aberration typical of something wider and more diffuse. In its "semantics of a social type," *The Double* shrinks from nothing and bounces the great ideas back into the thinker's court. It is still capable of arousing overt hostility because its frame of reference is overtly personal: Goliadkin is not only a type as viewed through a telescope, but a pitiable weak person such as one is afraid or ashamed to know.

As Gogol claimed to hold up his world as a mirror to the audience whose reflection is simply ridiculous, Dostoevsky finishes the job, plumbing the nether reaches of falsehood, solemnity, and false sentimentality in search of visceral response to a text that implicates readers in the very misprision they are quick to detect in others. Whether or not *The Double* "exists" only in Goliadkin's mind, he represents the juncture between an individual consciousness and collective ideology. A paranoid schizophrenia based on narcissism attacked by shame reveals itself as a sign not only of a rupture between interior and external worlds but also of their prolonged and cyclically formed collusion. GS's psychological destruction is unleashed by the desire to be a successful someone else, which he expresses by forcing social barriers, to the certain enhancement of his humiliation.

In narrative method as well as in the social types depicted and because of its weblike construction, allowing of no relief for anyone who would seek finally to separate Goliadkin's projections from an objective rendering of events, the story is modern. True, we still experience a romantic-parody ending, with fiery eyes burning into Goliadkin's, brilliantly and with sinister, infernal joy. This scene corroborates interpretations of GS's thwarted narcissism, his fear of entrapment and unmasking by another's glance, but it is also a sop to an outdated Romantic tropology. The eyes might well be those of E. T. A. Hoffmann or of his Doctor Coppelius, or someone out of Lautréamont, and the image bespeaks Dostoevsky's wavering confidence in the audacity of revealing the lurking, contaminating omnipresence of evil in everyday life.

Nor does the story require a recognizably pathetic "social alibi" such as Dostoevsky was wont to give himself in the early works.[38] Here there would be nothing—neither mannerisms nor grand designs born of excess feeling—for Nabokov to despise, and not a little to emulate.

Nabokov remarked in his *Lectures on Russian Literature*

that *The Double* is the very best thing Dostoevsky ever wrote.[39] For all Nabokov's avowed contempt for Dostoevsky and accusations of false sentimentality against the Great Novels, *The Double* is an inspiration to the complex organization of *Pnin*. At the simplest level of plot, Pnin himself parallels Goliadkin Senior in his ineptness and failure to make a professorial career. The glib and deceptive narrator does double duty as storyteller and also occupying the place of Goliadkin Junior. His account often objectivizes Goliadkin Senior, and ironizes copiously on events: the two have similar backgrounds, though the narrator's is more advantaged. He alleges intimacy with Pnin as a subject although he cannot follow him everywhere; he intersects mysteriously with Pnin at life crises. This amounts to a claim of identity. Eventually the narrator usurps Pnin's job at Waindell College, with the extra fillip of tenure. Pnin's departure from the book is a gradual, miraculous fadeout in his jalopy that represents in outline Goliadkin's coach escort to the madhouse. Though in a different spirit, this ending brings to a climax the magical-realistic aspect of Nabokov's novel, also moved by the uncanny in Dostoevsky's *The Double*.

3

DOSTOEVSKY'S MODES OF SIGNIFYING

We use the phrase "modes of signifying" as applied to Dostoevsky in order to explore the immanent semiotician within Dostoevsky's fiction—not the writer and his views on what we now call the artistic sign (these topics have been dealt with, for instance, by Linnér 1962 and Jackson 1966), but the way in which Dostoevsky actually poses and works through problems of signification, alias representation.[1]

To begin with, the simplest instance of representation by structural analogy already appears in Dostoevsky's texts preceding the major fiction. At an immediately perceptible level of sign function, the topography of setting in *Notes from Underground* functions by analogy to the U[nderground] M[an's] entire persona. When Liza unexpectedly pays him a visit, we get from him the following reaction: "A dismal thought was conceived in my brain and spread throughout my whole body like a nasty sensation, such as one feels upon entering a damp, moldy underground cellar." (60; *PSS* V: 152, 27–9).[2] The UM's moral landscape is a case of what can be called mimetic iconicity. In this form of semiosis, elements of the text which are icons (images, diagrams, or metaphors) contribute to the text's representation of the world of reference it depicts by establishing figurative equivalences which are also concrete.

A little later in the same section, the UM stops his dialogue with Liza to ruminate over his condition before resuming (61; *PSS* V: 153, 27–39):

> Images of the previous day began to come to mind all on their own, without my willing it, in a disordered way. I suddenly recalled a scene that I'd witnessed on the street that morning as I was anxiously hurrying to work. "Today some people were carrying a coffin and nearly dropped it," I suddenly said aloud, having no desire whatever to begin a conversation, but just so, almost accidentally.
>
> "A coffin?"
>
> "Yes, in the Haymarket; they were carrying it up from an underground cellar."
>
> "From a cellar?"
>
> "Not a cellar, but from a basement...well, you know...from downstairs...from a house of ill repute. ... There was such filth all around. ...Eggshells, garbage ...it smelled foul...it was disgusting."

The contiguity of the prostitute's coffin and the underground cellar is an iconic index that further reinforces topographically the UM's moral landscape. Its occurrence here can be compared to the topography of the Karamazovs' house and garden in *The Brothers Karamazov:* those saved are outside its pale; those who perish, inside.

As is known, *Notes* (while denouncing all forms of totalitarian determinism) is also an exercise in understanding pathosemiosis, the inner logic of the mentally diseased, the psychological self-revelation of a pathological personality. It is moreover a theological cry of despair over the evils of "human nature," and yet also a defiant assertion of human personality against *all* attempts to limit its potentialities. This latter point is the one André Gide appropriates from Dostoevsky (Todorov 1990: 76).

In one of his lectures on Dostoevsky, Gide denounces what he deems to be the French attitude to "ce qui reste en nous de refoulé [repressed], d'inconscient" (Gide 1923: 165), in the effort to maintain the unity and continuity of personality. By contrast, Gide observes, Dostoevsky's characters "cede complaisantly to all the contradictions, all the negations of which their real nature is capable" (Gide 1923: 255; cit. Cadot 1993: 204). If this is true, the UM's defense of his right to act on impulse and his repudiation of absolute determinism would derive coherence from the breadth of their common context, despite the implicit contradiction between the UM's spurning of his own nature and his insistence on acting out its demands.

Pathosemiosis, however, dominates the text. One fertile source of this is to be found in the use of literary citation and allusion in the *Notes*. The incorporation of aspects of one's predecessors' texts is always manifestly semiotic, and Dostoevsky's fictions are full of intertexts—particularly, *The Brothers Karamazov* (cf. Perlina 1985, Belknap 1990). In *Notes*, the UM is also dominated by bookishness, "speaking like a book" even to Liza— that is, as if from a book, not from the spontaneous workings of an existential consciousness. And at the end of *Notes* there is a final reference to books and how they can corrupt spontaneous feeling. Earlier, the UM had inveighed against the fiction-making process; he seems prey to an ascetic neoplatonism that pokes fun at the lies told by writers: "Of course it was I who just invented all these words for you. That, too, comes from the underground. ...It's no wonder that I've learned it all by heart and that it's taken on such a literary form" (26–27; *PSS* V: 122, 8–12).

The UM is himself a lowly but supremely self-conscious

equivalent of the Superfluous Man—a literary artifact in his turn, ostensibly based (already) on the egoism and vanity of the gentry in the 1840s liberal intelligentsia who were allowed to live in a dream-world of universal beneficence while neglecting the simplest and most obvious moral obligations. This background confers additional significance upon the socially centered prostitute of Part II. The latter plot element—and others, such as the officer-in-the-street episode that parodies an incident in Chernyshevsky's *What Is to Be Done;* the moment recalling Gogol's "The Overcoat," in which a parodistic, half-baked version of Akakii Akakievich gets a new coat to impress his old schoolmates and gives the coat a new beaver collar (there is even an Important Personage involved)—function to situate recognizable literary topoi in a context where the literary no longer can justify itself as a matter of overweening concern but must give way to the urgent claims of ethics and history. Thus reference and allusion, the second-order trace of the self-consciously literary, become a means for Dostoevsky of demonstrating the inadequacy of words to the achievement of full humanity. The character yearns for integrity at the same time as he fears what would turn up among the self-discoveries that would force themselves upon him. Literature only functions for him as yet another smoke screen.

Bakhtin's long analysis of the UM in the chapter entitled "Discourse in Dostoevsky" of his *Problems of Dostoevsky's Poetics* concentrates on speech and on the word, and is instructive as far as it goes. Since the *Notes* are presented in a confessional mode, it is indeed understandable that (as Bakhtin has it) the form of the discourse has an overarching effect on the revelatory content—so much so as to determine the UM's personality: to speak means for him to be *tout court.* But his speech, while repeatedly addressed to someone, including himself, is ultimately only self-directed. Whether he "squints his eyes to the side...toward the witness, the listener, the judge," there is still in the UM's world "nothing merely thinglike, no mere matter, no object—there are only subjects" (Bakhtin 1984: 237). He can talk about something only as filtered through his acutely subjective, almost solipsistic, perception of it.

The extent of his subjectivism betokens mental illness in the context of the UM's world—and, generally, our own. Yet it must not be overlooked that his very humanity, and any aspect of him that should be salvaged, also depend upon this subjectivism. Moreover, subjectivism is the common font of the Dostoevskian character. As René Girard observes, "l'univers dostoïevskien est...dépourvu de valeurs objectives" (Girard 1963: 49). The shifting context is part and parcel of the human condition his values embody. Whatever depends upon human subjects is unstable at its roots.

Therefore, Bakhtin's exclusive preoccupation with voice and discourse and addressivity, while making us aware of the power of words as such, misses the main semiotic purport of the discourse (which actually subsumes the mockery of fiction-making outlined earlier): though all thought is in signs, and primarily of the nature of words, in Dostoevsky's world "words might turn round and say, you mean nothing which we have not taught you and then only so far as you address some word as the interpretant of your thought" (Peirce 1982: 496). That element by which thought would be interpreted—in other words, the subject—is necessary to semiosis without being sufficient for it. Without the subject there is no sign interpretation; and without the *possibility* of interpretation, grounded in some relation of sign to object, there is no sign. Without the *possibility* of a subject, then, there is no sign. The paradox thus created is that the subject, though unstable, is necessary. That is also the reason why an oeuvre is always far beyond the author himself, alone.

The divine Word stands above this interpretative turmoil; the human word, never. Deeds count far more than words in the consecutive evaluation of a character. Man is a sign who is subject as such to the interpretations of him by others. The UM enters into the most intense polemic with the anticipated responses of an imaginary interlocutor, but the ellipses, the abrupt changes of tone, the sudden dialogic reversals only punctuate "his own dependence on this other. He fears that the other might think he fears that other's opinion" (Bakhtin 1984: 229). Through this fear, the UM immediately demonstrates his own inability to be at peace with an integrated definition of self. The UM can recover his self-respect only by some victory over his offenders, yet only the same offenders are capable, within his sights, of securing that victory for him. The contempt he means to inspire in them is the very thing that confers upon them an outsized, unsolicited power.

The same vicious circle entraps many a Dostoevskian character—hence, self-interpreter—in a "myopie existentielle" (Girard 1963: 38). The circle, linking dialogue (thought) and self, ultimately defines the UM's impotence. The eternal incompletion toward which his dialogue drifts is signaled by the way in which Dostoevsky concludes *Notes*: "But enough. ...However, the notes of this paradoxicalist don't end here" (89; *PSS* V: 179, 9–13). The ending also demonstrates Dostoevsky's cognizance of having created a multifarious paradox, in which self and other (arbitrarily labeled as such and haplessly interdependent) war endlessly into the future. Dostoevsky seems to be commenting negatively on something like the proposition that "semiosis explains itself by itself" (Eco 1976: 71; cit. Colapietro 1989: 36), for the vicious circularity of object and interpretation, the infinite vacillations of the UM's discourse, end by explaining nothing to him. In his straitjacket of objects taken for signs and his implicit insistence on stonily meditating upon them, he reduces meaning to a hermetic game. He remains an enigma to himself: a mystery infinitely iterated is a mystery still.

In the words of Charles Peirce, sign interpretation "is very inferior to the living definition that grows up in the habit" (Peirce

1976/III: 493)—that is, in a general predisposition to *act*, and in a particular way. Dostoevsky seems to furnish artistic examples or test cases of this very attitude toward the relation between the semiotic value of words and of deeds in his famous silent scenes (particularly pregnant with meaning in *The Idiot*; see Danow 1991a, especially chapter 1), where gestures not only stand for but supersede words.

When Christ kisses the Grand Inquisitor at the end of his long disquisition-cum-interrogation, the power of the mute act emanates not only from its godly origin or from its immediate emotional context but, significantly, from its implicit contrast to the purely verbal semiosis in which it is embedded. That this act has semiotic import pointing beyond itself transpires from Alyosha's immediate imitation of it when he kisses Ivan, who recognizes its true meaning only in part, delightedly calling it an act of "plagiarism." Alyosha's kiss symbolizes both a growth in knowledge of his brother and, more importantly for Dostoevsky's scheme, a growth in self-knowledge. The Devil is to be conquered by an all-encompassing love, but that love must be specific not general, and it must take place in the world and therefore in a replica—hence the imitation of Christ's kiss by Alyosha. Christ's own pragmatistic admonition, "By their fruits shall ye know them," would be in perfect alignment with the symbolism of subjective and wordless giving.

As Bakhtin says, "the '*truth*' at which the hero must and ultimately does arrive through clarifying the event to himself can essentially be for Dostoevsky only *the truth of the hero's own consciousness*. It cannot be neutral toward his self-consciousness. In the mouth of another person, a word or a definition identical in [surface] content would take on another meaning and tone, and would no longer be the truth. Only in the form of a confessional self-utterance, Dostoevsky maintained, could the final word about a person be given, a word truly adequate to him" (Bakhtin 1984: 55–56).

We would add here that for such a confessional dialogue to have the epistemological effect Bakhtin rightly associates with it, the interlocutor—the sounding board—of the hero must be disengaged and have no personal stake in the outcome of the journey to self-knowledge. Zosima, for all his interest in Alyosha's spiritual development, functions precisely in that way, as does Tikhon in *The Devils* when he hears Stavrogin's confession (in the famous chapter "At Tikhon's" that was dropped from the final version). Alyosha will ultimately double Zosima in this function vis-à-vis Lise and Ivan, among others, as we will show.

Another point regarding confession must be made despite its seeming obviousness: it is always provisional and subject to further revision. "Celui qui dit 'je,'" in a sense, can never stop speaking; that condition rests heavy on the epiphanic possibilities of confession. The ontological instability of the UM may be hyperbolized, but it is also to some degree the mode in which every person—however aware—makes his statement of self. Silent, symbolic action, however, cannot be undone, but it has its own way of semiotically determining its interpretation.

Christ's gesture, later imitated by Alyosha, has two highly significant pathological counterparts that are to be found in IV. iii and XI. iii, called, respectively, "A Meeting With the Schoolboys" ("Связался со школьниками") and "A Little Demon" ("Бесенок"). Both are important points on a trajectory defined by a gradual increase in self-knowledge for the character of Alyosha and the unmasking of self-blindness for characters like Lise. The abyss separating good from bad interpreters emerges as part and parcel of the entire structure which may be (at least provisionally) defined as winnowing the saved from the damned. Two episodes need to be considered together; they form the beginning and the end of an important segment, both involving the maiming of a finger, whereby Dostoevsky implicitly couples their meanings. On his way to the Khokhlakov house after leaving his father's, a ruminative Alyosha happens on six boys throwing stones at Ilyusha Snegiryov, whom Alyosha does not yet know. The boys suspend their fracas to talk to Alyosha, but in the ensuing resumption of the fight Alyosha becomes the target of Ilyusha's stones. The painful direct hits he suffers are only a prelude to the climactic act, toward the end of the chapter, when Ilyusha, in answer to Alyosha's confronting him ("Aren't you ashamed? What have I done to you?"), rushes at him and bites the middle finger of his left hand to the bone. After a full, silent minute passes, during which Alyosha bandages his bleeding finger, he addresses Ilyusha again (164; *PSS* XIV: 163–164):

> "Very well," he said, "you see how badly you've bitten me. That's enough, isn't it? Now tell me, what have I done to you?"
>
> The boy stared in amazement.
>
> "Though I don't know you and it's the first time I've seen you," Alyosha went on with the same serenity, "yet I must have done something to you—you wouldn't have hurt me like this for nothing. So what have I done? How have I wronged you, tell me?"
>
> Instead of answering, the boy broke into a loud, tearful wail and ran away. Alyosha walked slowly after him towards Mikhailovsky Street, and for a long time he saw the child running in the distance as fast as ever, not turning his head, and no doubt still keeping up his tearful wail. He made up his mind to find him out as soon as he had time, and to solve this mystery [загадку].

Note the serenity with which Alyosha repeats his previous question, "Aren't you ashamed? What have I done to you?" This calm comes from the force of good habit, as does Alyosha's thinking of the boy probably still wailing as he runs, and his need to solve the "mystery"—which, of course, points beyond itself to analogs both in Alyosha's behavior as a conscious being and in his incremental, less self-conscious imitation of Christ. Indeed, the New Testament would yield numerous glosses to the mysterious action of the boy (e.g., Galatians 5:15: "If you bite and devour one another take heed, or you will be consumed by one another.").

But Ilyusha, by contrast, after biting Alyosha's finger cannot speak. First he "stares in amazement," then he runs off weeping. We are in the presence of another of Dostoevsky's silent scenes. Alyosha's question has performed the service of articulating both for himself and, inchoately, for Ilyusha an interpretation that is tentative now but pinpoints the existence of a "mystery" (human evil) and its solution in the full recognition of human communality.

Here opens a mini-subplot involving cruelty, sadomasochism, and self-interpretation that extends over several chapters to feed once more into the more detailed events that concern the brothers and the parricide. A paradigm of sacrifice and salvation it certainly is; in addition, Dostoevsky characteristically probes from this beginning new themes of sadomasochism and its implicit division of integrity that crucially affect his calculus of good and evil. Is it shame or fear, or first one then the other, that send Ilyusha off howling?

Ivan Karamazov asks the question, "What of the children, Alyosha?," and as is well known, this crux is answerable only by silence and faith. As if in answer to it, the entire novel finds its end in the anticipation of a resurrection and in the form of a love-feast where these very children are gathered around a table recalling their former life and converted to the new one. This passage, as Terras points out (1981: 442), "is one of very few in all of Dostoevsky in which the beneficial effect of institutionalized religion and its ritual on a troubled human soul is shown." This rarity renders the moment all the more crucial to its understanding as the culmination of bread-and-stone symbolism throughout the book. Now at the end, Ilyusha's "stone, under which they wanted to bury him" (733) symbolizes an "edifice of new harmony created by Alyosha and his disciples" (Terras 1981: 442), whereas in the early scene it stood for a hardening of the heart that petrifies even Alyosha, for a minute.

To one attuned to the context of stone-throwing that is appropriate to the intuitive Alyosha, the rocks being hurled first at Ilyusha, who immediately transfers the injury onto Alyosha, initiate a series of sacrifices then and there. Eating, or biting, points to a symbolism of sacrifice and resurrection that culminates in the final scenes of the novel, replete with Eucharistic features. To the manifest Christian symbolism, though, Dostoevsky from the first adds this link that ties evil to individual personality and also makes evil contagious, so that each recipient passes it on. Who cast the first stone? Who remembers? What is important is that Ilyusha, functioning as the present link in the chain, turns against his benefactor, defends his right to be humiliated and humiliate another in turn. The sign function of masochism, expressed in the need to reproduce injury (to oneself, then to another) supersedes that of giver/taker, which would have put an end to the series of insults and injuries, replacing it by a relation of reciprocity.

In the absence of a (Eucharistic or otherwise reconciliatory) covenant, where it is every man for himself, all men are beasts. The trap of subjectivity is as evident as it is in *Notes from Underground:* every subject reifies an object (makes it "thinglike," as Bakhtin has it), as if that object were mere fodder; to assert one's subjectivity is to treat the other as object. But for Dostoevsky the suffering of children in particular is a heightened example of a sacred order, carrying with it a redemptive possibility; to accept such suffering with total selflessness and no thought of passing on vengeance would have been to put an end (however finite) to the otherwise eternal succession of violent acts, making possible a communion that was not there before. But at the moment in question Ilyusha refuses the gift of his freedom from Alyosha, although he does so in a state of evident confusion.

Note that for Peirce the example "gives to" constitutes "a triad," hence a lawlike sign that cannot be reduced to dyadic relations: "Indeed the very idea of a combination involves that of thirdness, for a combination is something which is what it is owing to the parts which it brings into mutual relationship." ("A Guess at the Riddle," in Houser and Kloesel 1992: 251–52). Peirce contrasts this triadic relation with "a dual relative term such as 'lover' or 'servant'...a sort of blank form, where there are two places left blank. ...in building a sentence around lover, as the principal word of the predicate, we are also at liberty to make anything we see fit the subject, and then, besides that, anything we please the object of the action of loving. But a triple relative term such as 'giver' has two correlates, and is thus a blank form with three places left blank" (Houser and Kloesel 1992: 252). The systemic relations described in Peirce's remarks are clearly instantiated in the relations between characters in the chapters of *The Brothers Karamazov* that begin with the stoning and Alyosha's visit to the Khokhlakovs (IV. iv.) and culminate in XI. iii, "A Little Demon."

The second finger-maiming, this time self-inflicted, occurs at the end of "A Little Demon," where Lise deliberately slams the door on her finger, causing it to bleed and turn black. That the two episodes are connected is already evident from the character of the act, but it is also relevant that the temporal span indicated for both is also the same, "about ten seconds" (*PSS* XIV: 163, 37; 15: 25, 42). Both episodes are pivotal to the growth in self-knowledge of Alyosha.

In this scene Lise confesses to Alyosha various impulses and desires for self-destruction and destruction of others, expressing envy of a boy who committed suicide and daydreaming of setting her house on fire. Alyosha understands that provoking him is only part of her purpose, which also includes taking pleasure in evoking pain verbally, thus directing pain inward, back to her self. The two-part dream she recounts to Alyosha has her first crossing herself against devils, then reviling God and succumbing to them. Alyosha confesses to having had the same dream, but there the resemblance which she emphasizes, mistakenly, ends all at once. For she adds another daydream, based on "the trial of a Jew, who took a child of four years old and cut off the fingers from both hands and then crucified him on the wall, hammered nails into him and crucified him" (552; *PSS* XV: 24, 4–7). She goes on to relate her own desire to crucify such a child and take pleasure in his moans, "and I would sit opposite him eating pineapple compote. I am awfully fond of pineapple compote. Do you like it?" Again Alyosha is momentarily silent.

Comparing this episode with that of the earlier finger-biting, we note the substitution of the pineapple compote in the use of eating as a sign of self-hatred. The self-consuming lacerations (надрывы) here bring back the theme of the suffering of children, in a fantasy where Lise damns herself for the same curse of which the child Ilyusha was first an innocent victim, then an agent of evil.

"You take evil for good," Alyosha ventures, near the beginning of the conversation (550; *PSS* XV: 22). By that token the same dream of God and devils will produce different meanings for each of the two, and yet they are nefariously related. The difference is that Alyosha perceives and accepts that relation as larger than himself. He also accepts the similarity Lise reveals between herself and his brother Ivan, "who believes in the pineapple compote himself" (553; *PSS* XV: 24, 39–40).

The dialogue between Alyosha and Lise does produce an increment of understanding for Alyosha (but not Lise): when Lise asks him whether Ivan despises her, or laughed at her fantasies, first he answers no, but very soon his thought evolves so as to yield the opposite result (553; *PSS* XV: 24, 42–46):

"He doesn't despise anyone," Alyosha went on. "Only he does not believe anyone. If he doesn't believe in people, of course, he does despise them."

"Then he despises me?"

"You, too."

But Lise rejects the possibility of self-understanding, as she has from the beginning of the dialogue (549; *PSS* XV: 21, 16–22):

"Alyosha, why is it I don't respect you? I am very fond of you, but I don't respect you. If I respected you, I wouldn't talk to you without shame, would I?"

"No."

"But do you believe that I am not ashamed with you?"

"No, I don't believe it."

Lise laughed nervously again; she spoke rapidly.

The nervous laughter and quick switch to a new subject betray the rejection, within her consciousness, of Alyosha's awareness of her fear and shame. Later she will even reiterate that she feels no shame before Alyosha (552). The possibilities of learning afforded by the dialogue had been successfully blocked by that same dyad of emotions, so that in the last bit of eating symbolism in the scene Lise declares that if Alyosha does not hand the letter to Ivan, she will poison herself (554).

The dream as a sign (note its duality) prefigures death—of body and spirit severally, again in twos. But the symmetrical inversion in the Lise case is characteristic of self-hatred in particular. It foreshadows an infernal cannibalism which perverts the natural desire to eat. Alyosha and Lise find themselves now at nearly opposite poles of a salvation drama in which two separate modes of signification are involved: dyadic and triadic. For Alyosha not only assures Lise that he "loves" her, but that he will give her the gift of his tears (553). When near the end of the scene Lise gives something to him, it is not a gift but a letter for Ivan. It is just afterward that Lise slams the door on her finger. The disengaged love Alyosha freely dispenses is here opposed to inversion and self-mutilation. The significance of these exchanges reverberates throughout the rest of the book and, retroactively, over all of Dostoevsky, in a calculus of ethics that intertwines good and evil; it insists—by allowing a blurring of the boundaries between them—on their reciprocal dependence *in situ*, i.e., in real human characters. This means that even in the most evil and repugnant of Dostoevsky's characters, what brings about their destruction is not their evil thoughts or even their evil deeds: it is rather their inability to grow in self-understanding. The mysteries infinitely repeated do not cease to be such. We might be reminded by Liza and her dreams of the Underground Man:

> But it's precisely in that cold, abominable state of half-despair and half-belief, in that conscious burial of itself alive in the underground...because of its pain, in that powerfully created, yet partly dubious hopelessness of its own predicament, in all that venom of unfulfilled desire turned inward...herein precisely lies the essence of that *strange* enjoyment I was talking about earlier. (9; *PSS* V: 105, 5–12, [emphasis added])

By the criterion of inability to grow in self-understanding through internal dialogue, to converse with one's own soul in an exchange untrammeled by fear and shame, Lise is of a piece with Smerdyakov, Svidrigailov, and Stavrogin (who are also bound by the identical initial letter of their surnames). In certain respects, all three of the latter are more clever—fiendishly clever—than any of the other of the dramatis personae in the three separate great novels they inhabit. But all three share the same fate: death by suicide (which Lise's final utterance adumbrates). It is as if Dostoevsky were declaring that their self-destruction is in each case the inevitable consequence of the character's fundamental failure to heed the injunction "Know thyself," the Socratic position presupposed by the Old Testament's "Love thy neighbor as thyself." For it is only through self-knowledge that one can aspire to know God, and all three are atheists through and through—to the bitter end. Of the two ultimate objects of love— God and the self—they chose the latter, to which, then, everything was permitted. Smerdiakov hangs himself, and like Svidrigailov and Stavrogin he does so only after fulfilling the heuristic function of the disengaged interlocutor in the three meetings with Ivan in Book XI. No matter how devilish Smerdiakov is in relation to Ivan, there is no denying that he has nothing to gain in promoting Ivan's growing insight into himself. Self-knowledge can be helped along by either a good or an evil interlocutor—provided only that the interlocutor has no personal stake in the outcome of the process. This would be a paradox, in the light of the same functions being fulfilled by such as Zosima and Tikhon, were it not for the insight that Dostoevsky gives us into the unity of humanity by distributing good and evil *complementarily* among his characters. It is, in fact, the most salient way Dostoevsky has of structurally validating Zosima's maxim that "everyone is really responsible to all men for all men and for everything" (VI. ii [a], 268; *PSS* XIV: 262, 31).

Invoking complementarity in the analysis of Dostoevsky brings us in a roundabout way to what has been called "the dominant human problem and philosophical theme in Dostoevsky …the double, from which body forth all of the polyphonic ramifications of character and, on the other hand, the ubiquitously fragmenting discontinuities, projections, and disorientations of narrative manner" (Rice 1985: 245). Complementary distribution is a commonplace in the analysis of language, but the process is not merely linguistic: it is a semiotic process par excellence. When two entities or units are distributed complementarily, this is a *sign*: it signifies that the entities or units involved are really *variants of one unit*. Now with reference to Dostoevsky's constant recurrence to the principle of doubling, we would do well to elide the search for its origins in the history of abnormal psychology and to investigate the semiotic implications of doubling with reference to the problem of identity.

Naturally, this inquiry takes us to Dostoevsky's earliest experience as a writer and to his short novel *The Double*. Chizhevsky (1929: 17) has rightly underscored the point that the ontological instability of personality imaged forth by the double is fundamentally independent of a psychological or sociological instability. Chizhevsky also has it right when he notices the sounding of a "new and deeper note" (14) in the second half of *The Double*, when Goliadkin-Jr. begins to supplant Goliadkin-Sr. in all aspects of his life, including substituting for and ultimately displacing him at work, in his private life, in the Olsuf'ev family (that of the woman he hopes to marry), and among his friends and co-workers as expressed by Goliadkin-Sr., his double "forces himself into the circle of my being and all the respects of my practical life." Expressions denoting substitution or taking the place of (R *подменяет, занимает место*) abound in Goliadkin-Sr.'s characterization of his double's behavior. This leitmotif of usurpation is particularly clear in Goliadkin-Sr.'s dream, where Goliadkin-Jr. is said to "take his place at work and in society" ("*занимает место его на службе и в обществе*"). The words самозванство ("usurpation") and самозванец ("usurper"; literally: "self-appointed-ness/-one") and also Grishka Otrep'ev (the False Demetrius) occur repeatedly in the text, where Goliadkin-Sr. condemns his double.

The Double has been taken as Dostoevsky's first depiction of a split personality (R *раздвоение личности*, which is much closer linguistically to the idea of the double: R двойник; cf. R двойничество "doubling"), to be repeated later in a whole gallery of more important characters. We would like to suggest, however, that from the semiotic standpoint Dostoevsky seems fundamentally to be exploring something else, namely the ontology of human identity (cf. chapter 2 above). Specifically, starting with Goliadkin in 1846 and culminating in Ivan Karamazov in 1880, Dostoevsky pursues and develops his grand artistic vision of the warped personality as the history of a failed attempt to unify opposites, a history shared by all the Efimovs, Ordynovs, Valkovskys, and Nastas'ya Fillipovnas that come in between *The Double* and *The Brothers Karamazov*.

In any binary (i.e., minimal) opposition we have two terms, one of which is necessarily *in praesentia* when the other is *in absentia* (and vice versa). The two terms are mutually exclusive. This is not true of mere contrast, which is defined by gradations and not by privative opposites. In logical opposition, the difference translates into contrary and contradictory, respectively. In a unified ego the various hypostases of human personality are distributed complementarily. The particular manifestation at any one time is determined by context, and the congruence of variants with contexts occurs regularly—whence the coherence and integrated nature of the person. When the ego is whole, the persona remains the same under transformation, varying uniformly with varying contexts. The ego is invariant as a unit, and the regularity of its contextual variability is a sign of its unity, of its being one (integrated) thing.

But in Goliadkin's case—which Dostoevsky repeatedly, mainly through the character's self-assessments, depicts as one of usurpation—the ego cannot be unified because it has bifurcated into two opposites: only one of these can be in one place at one time, to the exclusion of the other. Literally, then, as the plot bears out, Goliadkin-Sr. and Goliadkin-Jr. cannot share the same "place" either psychologically or socially. Nowhere is this point better made textually than in the opening sentence of Goliadkin-Sr.'s letter to Goliadkin-Jr. in chapter 10: "It's either you or me, but not both of us together" ("Либо вы, либо я, а вместе нам невозможно!"). The character's verbal ineffectuality is itself a semiotic analogy for his inability to enter into a "self-relating relation" that would allow him to commune with others as well as with himself in the light of something that would encompass them all. Instead, both "personalities" enter into a contiguity relation that is not one of complementarity or mirroring, but rather one that parallels structurally the metonymic chain of insults and injuries with which our analysis of Dostoevsky's crucial stoning scene began.

The subject is ontologically unstable and does indeed risk excesses of many kinds (ethical, moral, stylistic) in creating its objects. That risk carries the results Dostoevsky presents in terms that add up to psychopathology—in self-devouring or self-consuming lacerations. However, without anchoring every utterance in a subject we have no sign function, or a degenerate sign function at best. The subject is the starting point of the utterance, not just as the utterer but as the main criterion by which the coherence of the sign relation will be measured when it comes to human beings. Another way of describing Goliadkin's split is to say that it displays a fundamentally dyadic conception of himself as a sign, which leads to an artificial concentration on the form of expression (i.e., words) to the detriment of the intelligible, or cognitive, part of sign structure and hence, of signification. Goliadkin's style proves to be a fundamentally cognitive category (though not for him, personally).

Dostoevsky's exploration of human identity and of its fission can perhaps further our understanding of just why the Existentialists coopted him. Impelled in the first instance by their spiritual father Kierkegaard, such representative thinkers as Nietzsche and later Sartre saw in Dostoevsky's fictional brief for the supervening moral value of individual personality a powerful, implicit refutation of the Hegelianism against which they had taken up the cudgel. Indeed, Dostoevsky stands today more than ever as a monument to the belief that "the capital error of Hegel which permeates his whole system in every part of it is that he almost altogether ignores the Outward Clash" (Peirce 1993/V: 225). The case for Dostoevsky as an explicator of sign function—a semiotician *in actu*—rests in the final analysis on the ineluctable presence in his fictions of that Outward Clash as an organic component of symbolic meaning, which alone reconciles the human urge for apprehension and structure with the realm of phenomena, or appearances.[3]

4

LITERARY-HISTORICAL CONSEQUENCES OF THE RUSSIAN NON-RENAISSANCE IN A COMPARATIVE CONTEXT

The year 1550 in Western Europe already finds Leonardo da Vinci a historical figure—wistfully recalled by Vasari in his *Lives of the Painters*. Rabelais and Montaigne are in the past. The Western Renaissance had come and indeed almost gone. Already long before, Petrarch (1304–74) had understood the fundamentals of the "middle ages" and revolted against them, had helped usher in an awakening to politics and secular reasoning, to relativism and to an idea of change in the world that could not be governed by the caprices of nature or the weather. The Middle Ages, he had said, were the time between Antiquity and the great renewal of Antiquity. The notion emblematic of the Renaissance, that mankind stands at the very center of a hierarchy running from God at the pinnacle down to the various forms of animal life, was already so well cherished that it stood in virtual danger of being taken for granted and, accordingly, revised.

A second and probably corollary feature of Russian culture

in the year 1550 is the absence of an investigation of the universe based on theology and on Aristotelian methodology. The Aristotelianism which characterized late medieval theology in Western Europe is not to be found in the Russian development. That is to say, no systematic theology or scientific method underlies the Russian expression of Christianity. Throughout the 16th and the 17th centuries there is no movement or document that could be linked to the European ambition to synthesize faith and reason—except for a few Polish and Ukrainian scholars with some Latin learning. There is little if any seepage, not even an importation of foreign techniques or models. This state of things ended very abruptly with the accession of Peter the Great in 1689, which saw the foundation of some sort of verbal art in the literary sense. Foreign models grafted themselves awkwardly onto Russian culture; the secondhand imitation of France, as of this period, becomes something literary history has to contend with. But the "Renaissance" stage had never existed.[1]

The Italian Renaissance was construed in reaction to the Middle Ages, even by persons still living in them (such as Petrarch, who complained about it). In Russia, either the Middle Ages never appeared—or they are still going on. We want to sketch out some of the consequences of this cardinal distinction within the history of Russian literature. We should stress at the outset that these consequences are largely positive for literary production, and it is the positive side we intend to concentrate on here. To analyze the crucial differences in literary production and influence, in the modern period, between countries that underwent a Renaissance and the Russian situation, one need not go to the extreme of dwelling upon Western Europe. René Wellek (1963: 23) discredits the view that the sixteenth century was a Czech Golden Age or "renaissance." Apparently, Bohemia had no renaissance either. Taken together with other factors, Czech literature is all the stronger for that.

By contrast consider Poland, which by 1550 had celebrated

its cultural union with Italy.[2] The marriage of King Sigismund and his second wife, Bona Sforza of Milan, took place in the year 1517—about the same time as Rabelais was composing *Gargantua*, Ariosto the first edition of *Orlando Furioso*, the young Ronsard his lyrics. For the wedding Jan Dantyszek (called Ioannes Dantiscus, 1485–1543) composed a marriage-celebration poem (*Epithalamium Reginae Bonae*), where Venus rewards the widowed Sigismund for his many recent military victories. Mars is accordingly asked to interrupt the ongoing war between the Poles and the Muscovites so that he may convey the will of the gods to Sigismund: that he remarry the Italian duchess. Meanwhile, Venus travels to Italy to collect Bona and her entourage and bring them to Poland. The sea, forests, and mountains join her retinue on the way. Dantyszek uses the occasion to praise the Italians, making a point of how much at home they should feel in Poland: it is, he says, as if all the Italians were moving north. He means that Italian culture was flourishing there, so she would never miss home.

This marriage, in turn, gave decisive impetus to the spread of Italian influence in Poland: the result was a genuine invasion of Italian courtiers, clergymen, architects, and artists. Even vegetables were imported from Bologna and Padua, together with some of their names. The Jesuit order, eventually brought to Poland in 1564, was already active in transplanting Italian styles of church building. Erasmus of Rotterdam was surrounded by veneration in Polish intellectual circles, his works avidly read. Faithful readers would send him golden knives and forks as well as rings and money. One of his pupils, Jan Laski, bought Erasmus' library to help him, then gave him lifetime use of it.

Jan Kochanowski (c.1530–1584), the most eminent Slavic poet until the beginning of the 19th century, was six years younger than Ronsard. The year that Kochanowski left Poland at 22 to continue his studies in Padua, the Italian Torquato Tasso was a child of eight. One of Kochanowski's nephews is known still for his excellent translation of Tasso's *Jerusalem Delivered*. This nephew studied philology at Padua as well, read Homer and Pindar in Greek, and—more importantly—adapted epic tableaux and set pieces to Polish history (Miłosz 1969, 63). His poem "The Banner" represents the ceremony of homage paid by the prince of East Prussia in 1525 to the king of Poland: on one side of a certain banner, held at that ceremony, appears the history of Polish-Lithuanian relations with the Teutonic order, while the reverse side pictures the entire history of the Slavs, beginning with the Amazons, who, rather early on, landed in Scythia and then migrated north over the Don and founded two Sarmatias, Russia and Poland.

These are simply two examples of a widespread phenomenon that is perhaps well known: Italianism, joined by significant Frenchifying and the importation of the Renaissance, spread like wildfire—adaptations of Horace, devotion to antiquity, imitation of Italian lyric, Petrarchism. These did not end with the 17th century and the parallel onset of the baroque in both countries. The poetry of self-conscious craft and recherché conceits drew from the Italian model of Marino and the Italian baroque. The Polish baroque, like the Italian, also shows a macaronic bent. As late as the 1920s the outstanding poet Julian Tuwim (1894–1953) implements this tradition both in his tragedies and in his light verse. Miłosz observes (1969, 387–89) that Tuwim's "Czarnolas Speech"—which refers to Kochanowski's estate—achieves a genuinely "classical conciseness." Indeed, when in the late 17th century the Polish literary language went through a genuine revolution and a clear, precise style became the ideal, this was now modeled on French classicism. The Polish incorporated antiquity and still sought authority in Boileau: having codified the laws of French versification, Miłosz (1969, 162) observes, "Boileau was considered a lawgiver in Poland too." When linguistic purity was stressed, periodicals and leaflets were filled with polemics centering on the rules of good taste. In addition it was backwards, toward the Polish Renaissance poets—models of a limpid and balanced style—that literary attention refocused itself. "Good taste" dictated literary fashion even during the first decades of Polish romanticism: they were the rule in literature, theater, and the fine arts (Miłosz 1969, 163). There was a marked division into highbrow and lowbrow genres—poetry and verse drama, submitted to rigorous rules were "high," sentimental novels and "bourgeois" drama (so-called) were ranged in the lowbrow class.

A Polish classicist, Aloizy Felinski (1771–1820), returned to Renaissance subject matter in somewhat the same way as Stendhal did in his Italian stories—to none other than Bona Sforza and King Sigismund, now seen via their unhappy descendants (Miłosz 1969, 205–6). The subject matter, however, is topical: Bona is now the queen mother. Her son the crown prince of Poland secretly marries Barbara Radziwiłł, the daughter of a Lithuanian lord but not of royal parentage. Upon the death of the king, the Polish Senate therefore voted their opposition to the prince's ascension and made the demand that he divorce or renounce his throne. The leader of the anti-Radziwiłł faction was Bona herself. True, the subject matter, acting as it did on the popular imagination, is not an example of Renaissance or of classicism; but the conflict between love and duty, as it plays out, is formed upon some of the best known classical models—painstakingly read into the Polish national past.

Fast forwarding to the modern novel, we witness a revolt against importation and the search for authenticity. These characterize the work of Witold Gombrowicz (1904–1969), who made of his entire oeuvre a quest for a world where "eternal actors" and forms are no longer imposed from outside (Miłosz 1969, 432–47). "Each book of his," says Miłosz, "is a renewed attempt to smash one more sacrosanct rule of art" (434). His "Transatlantyk," for example, brings into the open the theme of how to transform one's "Polishness"—felt as a kind of wound or affliction or inadequacy—into a source of strength. The looming authority of foreign models is part and parcel of the difficulty. And this impediment does not remain within the precincts of criticism, extending to literary creative production itself.

Moving now to Croatia, it came to be known in the course of the Turkish wars as the farthest outpost of Christianity. Here the influence of the Catholic church helped the Roman script and the Latin language to gain literary sway (Tomasović 1981; cf. Čiževskij 1971). The 15th century already shows us Dubrovnik poets who represent Petrarchistic lyric, with its usual gamut of emotions, courtings, and disappointments. Three outstanding Dalmatian writers best represent the period of literary activity that lasted from the late fifteenth through the entire seventeenth centuries. They were humanists, largely educated in Padua and Bologna (neither of which was famous for home-grown literati!). They composed in Latin and read the works of Ariosto and Bembo. These Latinists were among the most representative of Croatian writers. Jakov Bunić (1469-1534) furnishes a typical example of how classical mythology was incorporated into Christian poetic epic-writing at the same time as Ariosto's first redaction of *Orlando Furioso*. Bunić tells of the conquest of Cerberus by Hercules, who descends to the underworld to lead the dog away, and as in Italian work, is a figure of Christ. Again, a Latin, moralistic work of the moralist Marko Marulić (1450-1524) was the only book St. Francis Xavier took with him when he left Rome in 1540.

In spite of themselves modern writers retained many of these paradigmatic traits: the leading Communist author Miroslav Krleža (1893–1981) did not shake off his attachment to the Catholic liturgy (Wierzbicki 1981). Although he hated the dogma and the hierarchy, it is in a novel about Michelangelo that Krleža's protagonist undergoes an epiphany about the meaning of life that is quite unmarked by communistic ideals.

It would be impossible to explore in any depth every one of

the varied causes that seem to have mandated the subordination of these two literatures, in terms of influence and even the expression of individual geniuses, to that of Russia. Several features call for mention, however: the relative lack of a strongly rationalized theology in Russia—also a phenomenon of the early as well as late Catholic Renaissance. The lack of imitative constraint is another. The two become entwined in literary history: take the "ut pictura poesis" idea, extrapolated from Horace, that a literary work is like a picture (never mind, at least for the moment, what Horace might "actually" have meant). It became a relatively modern instantiation of Aristotle's principle that art imitates life, and that mimetic force is among the most important criteria of art. "Ut pictura poesis"—Horace to Lessing—is imitative in that both poems and pictures are said to imitate nature, and in that literature imitates visual art. (For Western literature, the Catholic Middle Ages already acknowledged the world as book, picture, and mirror.) But, as we believe, Russia created a literary art which did not impose upon itself to imitate "nature" or even ordinary life. Russian literature is a worldmaking literature which puts before us *alternative worlds*, which are different from merely "fictional" worlds. This is simultaneously the source of confusion to critics and to scholars, and of Russian literature's positive uniqueness. A third is the absence of Aristotelianism from the precincts of either theology or verbal art.

One consequence of the lack of a Renaissance in Russian literature is that it pays little obeisance to principles of genre, such as are derived essentially from Aristotle. *Hybrid genres* appear in the service of alternate fictional worlds. Once there are no statutes of propriety concerning, say, unified characterization or the three unities of time, place, and subject matter, a novel can be (as for the author of *Dead Souls*) a "poèma." Pushkin's *Eugene Onegin*, conversely, can be fully appreciated in the designation he gave it of a "novel in verse." These works obviously postdate the European Renaissances; our point, however, is that Russia did not have to go through the long apprentice-ship in which the imitation of models of classical antiquity would have worked to transmit an inflexible idea of generic appropri-ateness. Consider the reaction that was formed by macaronic poetry in Italy and in Poland, and you see this as only the reverse side of the coin: for macaronic poetry to appear comical, one has to have a steadfast notion of the contrasting norm.

We would like to make the point that hybrid genres are a denial of imitation such as that of the Renaissance—even inso-far as the Renaissance itself contained and restrained the hy-bridizing of its own genres by Ariosto and Rabelais, for instance. Imitation and genre go together because the very formation of genres presupposes imitation. Genres create a literary environ-ment. The curious example of the late Italian Renaissance, which entertained polemics about whether the three Aristotelian unities (of time, place, and subject) "had to" be observed, is a classic instance of such containment. The exceptions—always within their bounds of occasional "carnivalism"—are those best loved by Russian criticism. Rabelais, for instance, sends up learned conventions, makes fun of assumptions of the necessity of book learning, and that is an important reason why he repre-sents the carnivalesque for Bakhtin's criticism.

The hybridizing of genres in Russia appeared in a flash of its own genius; we may say so regardless of the educational and literary adventures of authors. The Russia of 1840 as repre-sented by, say, Dostoevsky's reading, has a "confused...roman-tic, baroque, Rousseau-like sensibility, Sturm und Drang, and the romanticism of 1830 in France" (Girard 1991: 99). The young Dostoevsky devoured everything pell-mell: *The Brigands* by Schiller, *Notre Dame de Paris* by Hugo, Byron's mock-epic (note in passing the different development of the Renaissance in Eng-land). It is not far from here to his "Discourse on Pushkin," with its scrambled categories of the pan-European. Again, if one ob-jects that Gogol (however briefly) occupied a chair of European medieval history, we note that his quasi-Hegelian take on medieval Europe is also unilluminated by any ramble through the disciplined gardens of Renaissance learning. These instances cannot simply be attributed to the medievalism of the times: in each case the mind at work has been allowed to leap backwards past the rationalizing stage.

Anyone used to the easy notion that there is no such thing as literary originality is likely to be amazed by the Russian novel. The blend of the social and the psychological that has come to be understood as the matrix of the novel almost invariably gets a twist: yes, the novels deal with character and personality in various ways, but they are *estranged* from the influence of Europe, though not completely severed from it. They do not play by the implicit rules—generic or linguistic. Nabokov makes mincemeat of ideas of common sense that keep the British novel rolling on, and reinvents American English as a hybrid of language-isms. Bely shows how terribly irrelevant European-style political and cultural reforms can be for Russia. Bulgakov gives us a grotesque but profoundly moving form of magical realism that bridges the gap between so-called "real" worlds. Sologub displays a world gone to chaos, frustrating expectations at every turn, even those derived from the recognized features of literary figures such as Pushkin. If one begins with a conception of the novel that emanates from Dickens, Richardson, Balzac, and Stendhal, one soon learns that in order to read Nabokov, Bely, and Sologub, one has to depart from that conception, estrange oneself from it. You have to exile yourself from the certainties that compose their kind of social criticism and of individual portraiture. You come to terms with the crucial importance of *exile* and *displacement*, as even nineteenth-century novelists themselves did. (We think of Gogol's self-estrangement from the surroundings of a Russia he loved with despairing contempt; we think of his life in Rome.) We are talking, after all, about a literary production that shortly before the great novelists consisted of little besides hagiographic records, folk tales, religious tracts, and—yes—great lyrics. Russia caught up to Europe with a dizzying speed, signposted by Pushkin—but hardly at all before him. Hundreds of years of European literary history rush by, hastily assimilated as Russian intellectuals turn toward western Europe for inspiration; yet the uniquely Russian sociopolitical problems never cease to affect their understanding of European culture. The Renaissance was an awakening to politics, but Russian history is a history of tyranny with no political culture to speak of. No idea of an anthropocentric universe ensues from this; rather we have the idea that man is born profoundly flawed and tainted by sin, and that this common plight helps to create an early but enduring sense of the human condition, often just short of despair.

Girard points out in his book on Dostoevsky that the primary model for Myshkin in *The Idiot* is "a Christ more romantic than Christian...a Christ always isolated from human beings and from his Father in a perpetual and somewhat theatrical agony. This Christ, 'sublime' and 'ideal,' is also a Christ impotent to redeem humankind...Myshkin's anxiety before the too realistic 'Descent from the Cross' by Holbein symbolizes the dissociation of flesh and spirit" (Girard, 79). Of course, the passage carries meaning about Girard as well as Dostoevsky. All the more, actually, the passage juxtaposes Dostoevsky's Christ to a Westernized ideal: all influence of a rationalized psychology of the Crucifixion is absent. Beyond this, too, Dostoevsky gives little if any idea of the societal benefits to which God's sacrifice could be turned.

Comparisons between Dostoevsky and the French novel instinctively recur to the lack of a Renaissance as a key difference. It is expressed by André Gide in terms of light and perspective, in the time-honored Renaissance way: Gide observes that "in one of Stendhal's novels, the light is constant, steady and well-diffused. Every object is lit up in the same way, and is visible equally well from all angles. There are no shadow effects. But in Dostoevsky's books, as in a Rembrandt portrait, the shadows are the essential. Dostoevsky groups his characters and happenings, plays a brilliant light on them, illuminating *one aspect only* [emphasis added]" (Gide 1952: 99). From the perspective of perspective—in other words, using the key conception of visual art contributed by the European Renaissance—this is what you get.

To extend the comparison, the way Rembrandt illuminates the inner life of the portrait sitter disturbed the patrons who were paying for the *Night Watch*—the famous group portrait of burghers in Amsterdam. What they were expecting was likely to be a picture of the sociable and mercantile connection between one man and another. What they were given was more like a picture of the relation between each individual and his own self or his God. Turning back to Dostoevsky, it is again the inner life that is far more highly prized than the relation with one's fellow man—paradoxically—although the individual must always appear embedded in a social matrix. Although the novel may strive for the common good, there is sufficient amorphousness about just what the matrix is—*the* aristocracy, *the* peasantry—to turn the focus repeatedly back upon the irrational, irresolute, irresponsible individual face to face with his own conscience. The psychology, again, is not rationalized: no clear conflict between passion and intellect, or between individual and family, as in Stendhal or Balzac. Rather what we have is the brilliant flash that "changes everything."

Speaking of illuminating *one aspect only*, consider Gogol's statement that he was surveying the whole world—but only "from one side."[3] He created a way of satirizing what he perceived to be the corrupt and barren mores of contemporary Russia by means of a language full of wanderings, divagations, fits and starts, shifting frames of reference, intrusions into thoughts by competing thoughts, extended similes that bear you away from the apparent "subject"—a language full of seeming irrelevancies that actually binds together things that look, initially, unrelated. In this case, by contrast with Dostoevsky, the author is exemplary in his *refusal* to go beyond the externalia of the material and the corporeal to the inner sanctum of the psyche. What he did in *Dead Souls* was to transcend this absence of a thematized psyche by endowing purely external forms with so much vitality that, in Rozanov's words, "nobody noticed that there is nothing in essence behind those forms, no soul or person who would bear them" (1970: 16). Theorists struggle between terms like *realism* and *hyperrealism* even when these are sometimes derived from Gogol's own words, can't hit the mark, or settle into agreement, mainly because the part of Gogol on which disagreement centers concerns an alternative world grafted onto enough reality to remain communicative.

Russian impatience with European literary tradition—as exemplified by clarity, rationality, luminosity—is already expressed by Pushkin. Here is part of a draft note of his, written in 1832, which comes out against the erudite post-Renaissance French influence (Wolff 1986: 320):

> Everyone knows that the French are the most anti-poetical of people. Their best writers, the most famous representatives of this *witty and rational nation* [emphasis added], Montaigne, Voltaire, Montesquieu, La Harpe and Rousseau himself, proved how alien and incomprehensible they found a feeling for beauty.
>
> If we look at the critical judgments current among the people and accepted by them as literary axioms, we will be astonished at how insignificant and unjust they are. They hold Corneille and Voltaire, as dramatists, to be the equals of Racine; J. B. Rousseau still retains the title "great".

Nor is this a broadside for a clichéd Romantic taste. In a somewhat earlier note (1825; Wolff 1986: 126), Pushkin argued for a definition of the Romantic that relied upon form and genre, and the later writing does not contradict this. But he himself called *Eugene Onegin* a novel in verse—unlike the recent *Childe Harold's Pilgrimage* of Byron.

It might be alleged that Pushkin's attitude is little different from that of a European writing from the inside, such as Madame de Stael in her admiration of Germany as against France. But more than the manifestations of Romanticism are involved in the Russian case. The *frustration of expectations* did not restrict itself to theorizing but became a Russian literary tradition in itself. There are two countervailing principles or tendencies that coalesce here. The first one is that Russian formalism springs from the character of Russian and the Slavic languages themselves (Russian is very richly morphologized). On the other hand, there is the *alienation* that is built into the culture—alienation of Russia from itself and from Europe. This marginality produces what seems to be paradoxically copresent: a concentration on form and innovation, and an alienation from culture and convention. These seem to be opposed but they rather tensely coexist. This tension comes to a head in the course of the late nineteenth and early twentieth centuries. Gogol is to be taken as the beginning. The Formalists and Symbolists, of whom Bely and Sologub are two, are the ones who start investigating the formal structure of narrative—particularly that of Gogol, their special forbear. Bely's excellent book on Gogol (1934), Bulgakov's theatrical version of *Dead Souls*, and various other things are connected to Gogol directly. And Nabokov, of course, wrote his book on Gogol (1944) that stands out for its intuitive grasp of the Gogolian style.

Dostoevsky and, in fact, Gogol, belong to a feudal society at the point of disintegration—as do characters such as the Karamazovs or Myshkin. This is the source of their differences from the Western tradition and of Russian literature's great strengths.

The freedom from a requirement of coherence and rationalization is the main advantage: as Girard has it, "intelligibility" emerges, not "coherence" (1991: 56). The psychology of the underground, for instance, or the psychology of the sacrifice, never become reified into concepts—try as one might to do so in academic realms. That is one thing students love about the Russian novel, perhaps without acknowledging it: because it creates alternative worlds it cannot and does not rely on formulas, concepts, nostrums.

If we split all of modern Russian literature into two lines, Tolstoy's and Dostoevsky's, Gogol and his followers belong to the latter—as do Bulgakov, Nabokov, and Futurist poets with their displacement and reliance on mere contiguity relations. (Nabokov emerges, after all, in the line of Russian literary development.) The first is a sparser line, from Pushkin to Tolstoy, and it has no authentic latter-day progeny (with Mandelstam, Pasternak, and Brodsky—note: all [ex-]Jews—as possible exceptions): precisely (we believe) because it is oriented to the past. Of course, Pasternak's *Doktor Zhivago* and Solzhenitsyn's *Krasnoe kolso (Red Wheel)* novel cycle could be considered kind of a latter-day continuation of the Tolstoy line with their past-centeredness, but they are also syncretistic in that they are generic hybrids, Pasternak's novel being more of an extended *poèma* and Solzhenitsyn's fictional history. Alternate worlds such as are created by the second line are part of the future. They could not exist without interpretation in the broad sense, whereas the Pushkin-Tolstoy line is fundamentally historical—including even the history of the individual human psyche of a character. The idea of historical accuracy as applied to individual personality joins with the idea of memory and past-orientedness because the smallest historical unit is the memory of one's own history, and everything else works outward from that.

Russian fiction is peculiarly modern in that historical learning does not provide a key to its interpretation. Not that reference to antiquity isn't there in plenty: but it is easy, clichéd, often half-parodic at least. The work accommodates—even encourages—the disintegration of learned elites. The readership therefore expands naturally, cutting into old hierarchies of "understanding" based on literary knowledge. Source studies often reveal themselves in their genuine irrelevance—a notorious instance being Bulgakov and research on his "theology"—because the representation of antiquity, and of old things in general, is so carefully scrambled in *The Master and Margarita* that the only way to see within is actually from the inside. The idea of the alternative world in this case is actually built right into the plot! The book stands in opposition to the dominant idea that a well-ordered universe has to be extrapolated. Readers happily recognize irrationalism and alogism, the scrambling of order, the unfettering of individual speech. While the Pushkin-Tolstoy line—which is substantially classical, Olympian, explanatory, illuminating—has all but died out, *The Master and Margarita* is a prime instance of Russian fiction in its appeal—unique among literatures belonging in part to Europe—of leaping over the affirmations of reason and the models of antiquity that were the sometimes dubious gift of the Renaissance to Western Europe.

THEORETICAL EXCURSUS

The upshot of all this may be a typology of literature by what suggestively may be called kinds of representation embodied in the narrative: *iconic, deictic (= indexical),* and *symbolic* representation. In terms of temporal orientation, these are respectively directed to the past, the present, and the future. Renaissance literature, with its orientation toward the past, tends toward the iconic type of representation, hence its concentration on imitation and fidelity to models—also why it was so heavily pictorial, with ekphrasis as a dominant mode. The Gogolian strain in Russian literature, with its creation of alternate worlds, is oriented—*by virtue of the "as if" character of the al-*

ternate world—toward the indeterminate future, i.e., toward the subjunctive, the "would be," and thereby relies on the symbolic type of representation. In the middle, finally, is the Chekhovian type of literary art, oriented toward the present—the deictic type of representation—in which meaning is conveyed through context-determined cues, signs, and indications. Since Gogol is full of metonymy, which is a kind of pointing or deixis, i.e., based on contiguity, what then differentiates Gogol from Chekhov? Gogol's method is a teasing out of the hidden; what is made manifest is something that is originally concealed (example: Dobchinskii predicting to Mar'ia Antonovna in *The Inspector General* that she will wear a gold dress at her wedding, "sip various soups"; then shading into the darker prediction that she will have a son small enough to hold in her hand who will "cry all the time...wah, wah"—the concealed terrible aspect of motherhood). However, none of Gogol's characters is revealed through the exteriorization of his or her inner life (example: Akakii). In Chekhov, by contrast, no matter how truncated, the *disjecta membra* of dialogue in both the plays and the short stories serve to construct a purely interior context through which the meaning units are cumulatively constructed. Nothing is hidden in principle, and nothing needs to be teased out. Which is what explains the feeling of hopelessness engendered in readers as well as characters. Chekhovian "mood" is just another word for this purely deictic representation.

5

INTERPRETING BULGAKOV'S
THE MASTER AND MARGARITA

In the 40-year history of critical work on Bulgakov's masterpiece, *The Master and Margarita*, a large body of literature has been devoted to a quest for the single answer that would unite its disparate worlds.[1] This chapter will argue not only that it is precisely the absence of such a point of transcendence that is illustrated in all the worlds of the novel, but that this lack is represented specifically by the self-absenting of God the Father, as it would be perceived through his works, from the sublunary world.

We would like to suggest that this self-absenting permeates the principal figurative aspect of the entire book and creates a distance between the material events and the emotional targets toward which readers are almost irresistibly directed to marshal their own longings. Neither the Symbolist's indefiniteness nor simply any kind of semantic cipher (which would be finally guessed) can be at issue here since Bulgakov's allegory adumbrates ideal meaning without elaborating access to it. The figurative aspect simultaneously creates channels for emotional intensity and directs them to endpoints, yet the dynamic power of longing is aided by the absence just the way a vacuum is produced by a draft. It pulls the reader along on a trajectory classifiable as a nexus of sheer longings which are matched by the feelings induced in the characters.

Ideal meaning not only supersedes but may effectively cancel out the objective correlative. For example, Woland's famous line "manuscripts don't burn" ("рукописи не горят" [283]),[2] an apodeictic generality for which Bulgakov has been variously praised and taken to task, displays not mere indifference but actually an eradication of the literal sense of the proposition it makes.[3] In contrast to a Dante, whose poetics would be at pains to justify the statement's literal sense—if necessary, by constructing a possible world in which it would emerge as objectively true—for Bulgakov the "ideal" and metaphysical meaning would be the only one, canceling the requirement of objective or plausible veracity. The rhetorical power of the statement would derive not from its participation in an experienced literal truth but in its expressive articulation of a superseding desire— be it for the eternity of art or the hope of universal love.

REASONED THEOLOGY "IN" *THE MASTER AND MARGARITA*
It has been well established that the theological syncretism of Bulgakov's treatment makes doctrinal certainty generally unavailable and, when occasionally present, unreliable as a key to the one meaning.[4] Bulgakov scholarship has long striven to link the Yershalaim story to antecedents Hebraic, Gnostic, and Manichaean, and to proceed from there to graded interpretations of truth conditions, and from these to a unified reading.[5] But many of these have proven paradoxically to be all plausible, since Bulgakov entwined elements from each conception in ways that encourage multiple interpretations, as numerous scholars have recently demonstrated.[6] We do not know for certain who wrote the Yershalaim narrative;[7] therefore, even the logical pri-

ority of Yeshua's story to the Moscow narrative, which would derive from certainty of authorship, remains in doubt. Is the Yershalaim narrative a fiction whose "author" has guessed what happened in reality? Are the chapters apparently narrated by Woland and by Ivan Bezdomnyi objective reality as they witnessed or intuited it? If so, does the Master then recognize these chapters as being very close, or even identical, to what he imagined in the chapters of his own novel, which we readers never come to know as such? At the same time, Woland, the Satan-figure who dominates 27 out of the 32 chapters and epilogue (which add up to the number of years Jesus lived, 33), cannot claim final authority over the entire work. We suggest that, in parallel formation, the absence of an author "outside" the Yershalaim narrative and the absence of God the Father "within" it are the very factors which will permanently block the search for a unified reading of the whole.

It should be made clear just what is to be gained by resorting to theological argumentation as far as the interpretation of *The Master and Margarita* is concerned. We want to argue that far from constituting "the key" to the novel (as Ericson would have it), theology furnishes a system of meanings and significances that can be drawn on for *key analogies* to the form of Bulgakov's masterpiece, very much in the spirit of Charles Peirce's idea that those who know the structure of the Christian Trinity know his *semeiotic* or theory of signs. In evaluating the validity of our thesis, it is important to bear in mind that patterns of thought are at issue which might be quite independent of any expressed—or even conscious—design of the author, whether we understand this to be Bulgakov himself (with all the paraphernalia of Bulgakov biography) or characters who are commonly taken to be his mouthpieces. In this sense, theological analysis will function as a heuristic through which the specific interpretation being advanced here for the first time will be shown as centrally relevant.

WOLAND'S AUTONOMY

In contradistinction to conclusions drawn from efforts to normalize Bulgakov's theological underpinnings, Woland cannot be proven to act in earthly matters in concert with—much less on the authority of—a higher power. Valuable scholarship showing the tradition of an Old Testament and Judaic Satan who is not all evil, a messenger of God the Father and not an autonomous agent, would indeed encourage readers to think that Woland acts for God.[8] The Apocalyptic aspect of the four dark riders in the night sky who comprise Woland's suite at the end become equated ultimately with the four winds of heaven, which are traditionally understood as messengers of God as well as the administrators of his justice. But Woland's actions and decisions appear autonomous, accomplished without consultation or orders, whether "good" or "bad." To be sure, he does not give, take away, or transfer "supernatural" power as a true usurper of divine authority would be able to do. However, nor does he act intelligibly as a special emissary for a particular purpose—that is to say, as a messenger bearing God's express command to the "natural" world. Thus he is neither a "vicar" nor a messenger.

AD HOC INTERPRETATIONS

The figuration of Woland as a parallel to the apocalyptic messengers is also ad hoc in the sense that it does not apply to other features of the character. It is comparable in this specific respect to the Christianized readings of Ovidian myths which held sway during the Western Middle Ages. Such interpretations often posited various referents for the same *énoncé* within the exegesis of a single narrative. In so doing, incidentally, they unwittingly imitated the very feature of Ovidian metamorphosis which posed the most portentous menace to Christian doctrine: the fact of an endless potential for further change which would point to a fundamental ontological instability. Allegories of this type often make it clear that they are, precisely, interpretations, not to be placed on the same footing as physical or objective reality. Assimilation of Bulgakov's text to various traditions does demonstrate precedents for the ambivalent character of Woland, who does justice and injustice variously, at the same time and at different times. But the literary fact of his existence ultimately remains untouched. Woland, who mediates (with his entourage) between the narrative levels of the novel, can make no stable sense to one seeking aprioristic authorization of prior spatio-temporal events. This is true for both "physical" realms, Moscow and Yershalaim.

"REALITY" AND THE CONTINGENCIES OF MATTER

Bulgakov created a Moscow which readers initially assume to be a self- evident, self-subsistent material world like that of modern journalism (with scrupulously noted landmarks), but whose incomprehensible supernatural twists come to problematize the stability of the entire world of the senses. Accordingly, the transmitter of the information that Woland claimed to have conversed with Pontius Pilate is the "unstable narrator" of the moment, Ivan Bezdomnyi. Events in space-time may or may not occur at the opposite extreme from being or truth. The very Muscovites under scrutiny tend to identify truth with matter, and readers are invited to behave analogously. However, Bulgakov's plotting undercuts such materialistic impulses (at random intervals, of course): matter emerges as potentiality, transferred to the realm of being as ephemeral, limited, and contingent.

Theologically oriented exegesis endemically courts the danger of reifying the very texts whose transparency it purports to be safeguarding, by persuading interpreters to conceive of mere textual parallels as things in themselves. As long as readers identify reality or truth with contingencies such as can be comprehended materially, they will achieve at best a partial understanding of Bulgakov's poetics and even of his truth claims. Treating exegesis as an objective correlative is ultimately a pursuit of relentless materialism, inadequate to the aims of the book. Conceding the suspension of ultimate "coherence" paradoxically brings us nearer to apprehending them.

REALISM IS NOT REALITY

The ontological difference in *The Master and Margarita* between history and myth, physical and poetic reality, emerges as largely illusory or conventional. What counts is the degree to which any form of being, or concept, embodies the nature of being, the act of existence. To that extent it is true, real, and actual; to that extent it has a life as part of spatio-temporal reality comprehensible within human limitations. Thus the interpretative, artistic, perceptual, spiritual, and emotive life are not rendered ontologically distinct from "history in itself." The irruption of the "supernatural" works to undercut the one-to-one correspondence between a picture of reality and something cognizable as reality itself. Those who—with the best intentions of clarifying mysteries—make no distinction between realism and reality are most vulnerable, as Bulgakov moves to subvert the assumption of sequences of self-subsistent events autonomous from any act of perception or mediation. By the metaphysics of the plotting alone, the determinate forms of the "supernatural" are all fiction, relatively unreal in comparison to pure awareness, which is the actuality or substance of all forms. Any attribute, anything that can be talked about or imagined, is a self-limitation of that being, so that in our processes of sifting out versions, say, of Woland, he approaches nonbeing, nonactuality, nontruth.

In other words, a thing emerges as true insofar as its form or identity is the very act of existence, awareness, or intellect itself. This quality is what attracts and delights those students of *The Master and Margarita* who have no intention of dissecting its mysteries, as well as those whose profession urges them to do so. It is accessible to them as a work which affords the experience of contingent forms (for their very instability) as qualifications of oneself, of whatever seems a noncontingent principle of one's own being. The book gives various forms to being which afford *glimpses* of being itself: it is a "revelation" in that it simultaneously reveals and re-veils being. Inscrutability or undecipherability are built into it for that very purpose. That the phenomenal world is a chaotic mixture that offers delusions to human perception is the obverse of the copresent hope of an entirely benevolent force working in the world. That force does not manifest itself in the sublunary world even by implication, except as a negative. Our sole connection to it would otherwise be Yeshua—a tenuous one even if Bulgakov's Yeshua more clearly manifested his divine nature.

YESHUA: SUBJECT TO WOLAND?

Woland moves often and easily in the world, whereas Yeshua—even to the last—does not come to earth again. Woland organizes worldly events (for good or ill), and Yeshua even consults with him at the end in order to obtain peace for his charges. Yeshua does not seem to have the unchallenged run even of his kingdom of light. As is well known, two of the possible titles Bulgakov had ideated for the novel about the devil were "The Great Chancellor" ("Великий канцлер") and "The Black Theologian" ("Черный богослов"), each bespeaking a functionary role for the chief character; yet it is Woland's book. To the end he remains obviously its principal agent. Near the conclusion of the book (chapter 29), when Woland condescends to explain to Levi Matvei that vice is necessary to offset virtue just as shadow is necessary to contrast with light, there appears the famous gnostic dictum: "What would your good do if there was no evil, and how would the earth look if shadows disappeared from it?"[9] As is known, the epigraph from *Faust* apparently responds to the question of Woland's identity: "I am part of that force which eternally wishes evil and eternally does good." This sequence is notably oblique in more than one respect, the most urgent one being not the discrepancies with *Faust* but the sheer lack of rationalizable necessity for the godhead to act as it did: neither light nor dark, good nor evil, are in any way "necessary" to the all-powerful. If anything, they are necessary to the human ordering of chaos. The Faustian epigraph could be interpreted provisionally, however, to show that Woland, very little displaced for the moment from Goethe's Mephistopheles, is beholden to a superordinate principle of divine goodness. Such an answer assumes that an expectation of God's *invisible*, uncognizable presence in this novel would be corroborated upon sufficient meditation.

YESHUA'S DIVINITY

It has often been observed[10] that Yeshua lacks the attributes of divinity. This is partly the product of overreaction to statistical norms of interpretation and is actually an overstatement—if Yeshua's healing ability and prophetic gift are taken into account.

To have made Yeshua *only* the good man who loses the struggle for good in the world—within the context we have described—would facilitate new, simple reifications. But Bulgakov leaves him a measure of divinity—an adumbration of it rather than a recollection (for indeed, at no stage does he call God his father). Thus the figure retains its function of pointing to the indescribable, as it could not do were the iconography overfamiliarized. To be sure, Yeshua is not alone as an index of divinity; even the soul of Pilate, if it contains a spark of light, is ready to be taken up into the moon and be further purified. But nothing in the potential being of Yeshua negates his ultimate alignment within the triune divinity which Bulgakov reinforces at the end.

That Yeshua resembles the Master—they have at times analogous innocence, analogous absorption in their great works, analogous singleness of mind—even belongs to the old topos of the artist as divine, making each of the two an imitation of *Deus artifex*. It is in the telling of the story by each individual that fallacies make their overt appearance. The Master uses Levi Matvei to underscore the fact of two competing stories, of more than one authority, of a "historical" creature who constantly eludes characterization. The problem that the Yeshua chapters are either chapters in a novel or chapters of a novel within a novel belongs to the same category as determining the truth or falsity of what is contained in various dreams. When confirmed, it is only by a hermeneutic house of cards constructed out of mutual corroborations. Even Pilate is vouchsafed some premonition of the future: he sees an image of Yeshua wearing a golden crown—perhaps the King of Heaven in glory. But this vision is disfigured by a contradictory element: the lower lip on Yeshua's face is pulled down in a deformed, infernal grimace, and an ulcer appears on his forehead. Pilate hears in his mind the golden trumpets of Caesar, which at that moment could represent either the eternal or the earthly king—or even both, in a momentary synthesis of linear "history." Pilate refers, ahead of time, to the "filthy informer Yehudah" ("грязный предатеь Иуда" [28]), a phrase Yeshua seems not to hear; then Yeshua prophesies the Kingdom of Truth, which Pilate shouts will never come. However, Yeshua may or may not exist as within Pilate's dream; even there he may or may not know of Yehudah's treachery. Readers are given the latitude to respond to Yeshua's prophecy of the advent of truth's kingdom in accordance with the instability of the truth-conditions, deferring to their own beliefs. But Yeshua's narrated behavior may be straightforwardly read not only as that of a naively good man, but also as that of his divinity. True, he seems to overlook the possibility of saving his life by dissimulating his statement about power. Yet in this very assumption of naiveté resides a precise proof of his acquiescence in the sacrifice to come. The writing keeps up an oscillation between the two natures, human and divine, so that the second person of the Trinity is foreshadowed while avoiding reification.

The play of sameness and difference (from the objectivized historical sources of scripture) means that things and events are defamiliarized—detached from the deceptive economy of "identification"—in the act of a subjective retelling. The use of the ancient Aramaic or Hebrew names for those who count in the Yershalaim narrative has the effect of displacing their cliché images. The term "Crucifixion" for the passion of Jesus is avoided entirely; Yeshua is 27, not 32 or 33 years old at that time; he is said to be from Gamala, not Bethlehem; his "surface structure" even minutely resembles Woland's in that he has a dark spot under his left eye, while Woland has a darker left eye. Furthermore, both Yeshua and Woland are at times taken to be mentally ill; it is on the ground of diminished responsibility that Pilate hopes he may have Yeshua spared legal punishment. But these surface resemblances in the eyes of the uninitiate also serve to distance Yeshua from their own customary associations. God is in the text, though not as we expect to meet him; therefore belief in him reestablishes itself freshly as a matter of free choice.

The twosome of Woland and Yeshua, the primary link between the novel's two narrative planes, is the figure which illustrates a collision between the representatives of two separate states of being—that "of this world" (be it Moscow or Yershalaim) and that which *points* to another, superior world (this despite the surface oppositions of Woland's deviousness and Yeshua's guilelessness). The enigmatic connection between Woland and Yeshua cuts across their rhetorical placement at seemingly opposite ethical ends of the providential order. Clearly, however, Woland's behavior cannot be characterized— even in the terms of portent and revelation that we have construed—as unambiguously evil, although what we are given of Yeshua's is indeed unambiguously good.[11] If we agree at least that the "proof of God's existence" to the inferior world has a "plus" value superseding its ultimate inaccessibility to reason, we have to acknowledge Woland as a part of it. From chapter 4 on, Ivan Bezdomnyi realizes that Woland's prediction of Berlioz' death (and its means) is a simple fact ("done"), and confirms that everything else spoken by the "mysterious professor" is also fact. But the proof therefore reposes with a falsely secure syllogistic rigor on the premise that Woland is always telling the truth. From this Ivan draws the meaning that he needs faith, not reason or ratiocination—and he is unwittingly correct. He has accidentally made a benign category mistake, but "'There's no need for any viewpoints,' answered the strange professor, 'he simply existed, and that is all.'"[12] Even the telling of the story is a deviation from the pure assertion of being.

THE "MANIFEST" OR RECOGNIZABLE IMAGE AS STOPGAP

It can happen anywhere that being is transfigured recognizably, because humans need images. Apartment 50 of Sadovaya Street 302b, Woland's local headquarters, accordingly becomes more than a microcosm of Moscow pettiness and material longings. It acquires a solemn depth as a supernatural place, a transfigured apartment with a dual relationship to the rest of the (infernal) Moscow cityscape. The mixture of trite ordinariness and miracle (for such it is) is a "take" on what happens in miracle tales. It is allowed to proceed untrammeled by blindness to the obvious and by the bureaucratic absurdities arising from cowardice. The vignette, for example, of Styopa Likhodeev's seeming to split in two (one Styopa is in Yalta while the other is in the Variety Theatre) underscores a legacy of fear and shame. At another level, though, even such alogisms as lend themselves most obviously to parody and ridicule can work to echo the paradox of Christ's assumption of a temporary, second, human nature. However, the world in which the Christ-event presented itself for interpretation is a land of shadows; for all human beings "all deception never vanishes." Even the intermittent moonlight, which vouchsafes insight to "lunatics," may be unbearable. When the cat Behemoth reveals his true nature to the Master and Margarita in chapter 24, the Master asks for permission to regard him and his entourage as a hallucination, and immediately Behemoth springs into his feline antics: "'And I certainly am like a hallucination! Note my profile in the moonlight.' The tom stepped into the column of moonlight and wanted to add something else, but he was asked to keep quiet, and he said, 'Very well, very well; I am ready to keep silent. I shall be a silent hallucination' and fell silent."[13] The Master's request for permission (of the apparent hallucination, to view it as one) is the paradox that defers a search for fixed meaning. The fixed truth is intolerable, for the presence of the divinity "in" this world would hammer home—or at least point unequivocally to—the divinity's indifference to creation. In an idealized world the skein of rampant dualisms would unravel at last, the knot of darkness loosen, the moonlight show itself as reflected from the sun. At that point of revealed transcendence the Manichaean splits would heal. But Yeshua only points to a further promise, that of Christ's dual nature.

YESHUA AS INDEX

But Bulgakov's working out of that nature in the world insists on the light projected by Yeshua's assumed human nature, on the strength of his sacrifice, humility, and love which can only partially or only indirectly mitigate metaphysical evil. If the divinity conceptualized in *The Master and Margarita* realizes his commands in the world without intrusion upon the free will of his own creatures, the net result emerges as an absence of power. For all his goodness, Yeshua does not possess the peremptory might that could even potentially bring order out of chaos.

To be sure, instead of insisting on absolute power and verity, a Christian persuader—as Yeshua is depicted *in potentia*—must remain part of the audience even while assuming temporarily what is objectively the role of teacher. Such power as the dictator might have over his audience is possible only if a great distance yawns between them. Some of the wavering reason exhibited by Yeshua fulfills this very function: he forgets things at times, or conflates them, or revises earlier statements. A Christian God "does not force, but asks" (Florenskii 1914: 324). Even the divinity approaches his creatures as if he were not omnipotent. That this is almost the precise restatement of a theologically ratified position does not affect, however, its particular relations to events and things in Bulgakov's novel.

The worlds of humankind—Yershalaim and Moscow—epitomize, seriously and farcically, the inability of humankind to relate to God. Significant exceptions occasionally cut through the implied generalization that humans cannot "know" God, implying rather that the constitution of such "knowledge" remains a mystery. In a sacred text the very inexplicability would be a positive argument for the existence of the bond. Thus the relation between God and man is there and not there at the same time. Transferring this conclusion to the structure of Bulgakov's masterpiece, the analogy helps to show why pieces are expressly constructed not to fit. As regards the plotting, the price of even an implied order would be a revealed manifestation of authority.

RATIONALIZING THE LACK OF FIT

The three persons of the Trinity now become relevant to the discussion, although these are scarcely, if ever, thematized (in accord with Bulgakov's demurral from rationalizing God). This suggestion does not contradict our argument against readings that derive proportional or inverse conclusions from theology. What has to happen instead is an effort to distance oneself temporarily from participation in the mysteries of Bulgakov's text.

Indeed, the Trinity itself has presented relatively few of the devout with either the desire or the occasion to analyze it. In the words of Karl Rahner, "Should the Trinity have to be dropped as false, the major part of religious literature could well remain virtually unchanged" (Rahner 1974: 11).[14] The theologian's opinion ensues from his evaluation of common religious experience: "Nowadays when we speak of God's incarnation, the ... emphasis lies only on the fact that 'God' became man, that 'one' of the divine Persons of the Trinity took on the flesh, and not on the fact that this person is precisely the person of the Logos" (ibid.). It has often been regarded as doctrinally probable that each of the divine persons, if God had freely so decided, could have "become man." A believer's understanding that the incarnation occurred need not be preceded by a fuller understanding of the three divine persons than that spoken for in the catechism. This implies that one may speak of them separately, and that agreement upon what the facts of the incarnation are has little effect upon agreement on the construal of the Trinity. Yet it is equally true that the psychologized Trinity of Augustine has provided us (as well as the thinker himself) with an enduring analog for the clarification of semiosis in the world. It is necessary to discuss the aspects of the Trinity separately, as well, in order to elucidate the idea that God has absented himself from the world of *The Master and Margarita*, although Yeshua has not.

This can be done, without attempting to draw a strict positive or inverse relation between Yeshua and any single detailed theological conception. One need only bear in mind the primary characterizations of the three persons as power (Father), wisdom (Son), and love (Holy Spirit). In Yeshua we see chiefly the human nature of the second person while intuiting little of his divinity, which would be understood as prior to his semblance in the world. Wisdom also irradiates various depictions of Ivan and of the Master. The third person, God as love, conventionally hypostatized by the Holy Spirit, may be understood as "present" chiefly through Margarita, who acts almost entirely out of selfless love for the Master. Love is manifest as well in the pairing of the Master and Ivan Bezdomnyi and of the Master and Yeshua— and even in the mercy of Ivan, Yeshua, and the Master (if his novel coincides with Bulgakov's) toward the arch-coward Pilate.

WISDOM AND POWER: BUT WHERE IS LOVE?

God as power, on the other hand, is evoked in the juxtaposition to Woland, whose own arguments rely chiefly on the unpredictability and insufficiency of worldly events as corroboration for providential authority. The uncontradictable "thereness" of events is the chief argument. When Berlioz is struck down, the text (which only later details the meticulous planning whereby Annushka drops sunflower oil in his path) presages some degree of collaboration between Woland and God—a God harking back to absolute authority, but working (if at all) through his agent and messenger.

A "logical" place to look for the role of the father is the case of Levi Matvei, who refuses to acquiesce in any rationale for why God does not put a stop to the sufferings of Yeshua "who had never in his life done the slightest evil to anyone" ("не сделавший в жизни никому ни малейшего зла" [174]). Having contemplated interfering with Yeshua's sacrifice on the cross by putting him to a speedier death, Levi Matvei curses the Old Testament God the Father alone. An accepting "theological" gloss would take Levi Matvei to task for not "realizing" that Yeshua "had to" be tested in his last agony "in order to" achieve victory over human death.[15] Yet none of this "inevitability" is ultimately accessible to reason despite the stopgap of rationalizing theology.

For to think of God openly as absolute power or quality is in effect to stop thinking about him. Absolute quality is unrealizable in itself. It is spirit, or the third person of the Trinity, its "law" written in the hearts of human beings, that encourages thinking about Christ. For spirit was given into the world as the gift which enables the interpretation of the advent of Christ (into the world). Philo Judaeus spoke (*avant la lettre*) of the divine Word as a bridge between God and the world, and also as the representative of humankind vis-à-vis the deity. Pauline theology unified the doctrine of the gift of the spirit, articulating a conception of Christ as the "second man" or second Adam who, by his righteous act in dying, ended the condemnation upon the first man (Romans 5, 12). Christ is then said to be the image of the invisible God. In the very early development, Tertullian already spoke in the second century A.D. of God and his word as the father and the son. However, fuller explanations generally manifest the difficulty of combining identity and distinction. As is known, in the arguments of various heresies God often appears to undergo division and dispersion. But the explanatory power of doctrine was reinforced by postulating a father who cannot be spoken of and a son and spirit who mediate in varying degrees between the deity and the world. Only the necessity of the father—of pure potential—has to be acknowledged in order for the system to work.

THE WORD AND THE "WORD"

The distinction among the three persons becomes conceptualized more clearly as concerning their mutual relation according to the analog of human language. Gregory of Nyssa argued (ca. A.D. 390) that just as our own words are not altogether the same with the mind that produces them, or altogether different, so it is with God and his word, which is both the same and distinct from him. The incarnation cognitively cut through the immanence of the Trinity: as in the writings of Augustine, stress falls upon the humanity of Christ and upon the resulting mediation between the world and the godhead. (The third person, or spirit, came to signify the fundamental lawlikeness of the Trinity taken all together.) The Nicene creed (A.D. 325) affirmed that the son is indeed of the essence of the father, a tenet subsequently kept in the Eastern church.

FATHERLESS HUMAN NATURE

Yet the character Yeshua has pointedly detached himself from his father. Perhaps in order to build into the structure a relentless duality for the other main characters, Bulgakov has removed that which was "built into" Christ by St. Paul and amplified by doctrinal tradition; there is no adumbration of Christos Pantokrator, the judge. We know Yeshua as a "member of the audience" with certain distinctive marks that can only point to an eventual assumption of divinity. Meanwhile the world can see itself only as fatherless, abandoned by supreme authority, subject to infinite deception, while the supreme repository of divine omnipotence—at all levels of the narration—is immutably remote, as when he distanced himself from the human nature of his son on the Cross.

The motif suggesting correlation between the end of the Yershalaim chapters and the end of the Moscow plot is a storm such as occurs at moments of world catastrophe like Yeshua's execution. If we suppose that this thunder and lightning connote the response of God—understood in his plenitude as the three persons—to the outer darkness of hell, still this brandishing of the father's ultimate weapon against rebellion creates no hiatus within the course of subsequent events. Yeshua instantiates a paradigm of sacrifice with no cataclysmic effect in the world. In partial likeness to Yeshua, Ivan Bezdomnyi tells the "truth" as he sees it, with no gain of power over evil.

Even if the parallels between Yeshua and other characters are comprehended as pertaining strictly to the human and not the divine nature of Christ, the neglect of his divinity (which is nonetheless signaled) is still not explained away. All of that which belongs to the godhead and is therefore immanent in Christ seems to have substantially withdrawn from earth, where Woland operates freely. Yet this is not absolutely the case, for as noted, wisdom and love do triumph at times. It is only power that is replaced in the action by Woland.

This is not to deny the occasional "presence" of comprehensive trinitarian symbolism in the text. For example, when Pilate interrogates Yeshua, the representations of all three persons of the Trinity are perceivable: Yeshua himself, an icon of the second person; the pillar of fire, which "stands" chiefly for the Father ("The Procurator raised his eyes to the prisoner and saw that a column of dust had caught fire next to him" ["Прокуратор поднял глаза на арестанта и увидел, что возле того столбом загорелась пыль" (28)]); the swallow, which is a symbolic equivalent of the dove or holy spirit ("At this moment a swallow darted into the colonnade, described a circle under the golden ceiling ... and disappeared behind the capital of the column. Perhaps it had decided to build a nest there" ["В это время в колоннаду стремительно влетела ласточка, сделала под золотым потолком круг ... и скрылась за капитель колонны. Быть может, ей пришла в голову мысль вить там гнездо" (27)]). It counts little, however, that these conventional symbols surround the scene, or even that Pilate does not seem to notice them. Bulgakov could be signaling that Absolute Being is inaccessible to human perception generally, while allowing readers to interpret some indirect "presence" substituting for it. That the godhead, and particularly the aspect of the father, or absolute causality, has withdrawn its help from earth is the point here, to be extrapolated from the force wielded by Woland. A representative has usurped, or "represents," a remainder of the Father's originary power to move events.

A LITERARY COROLLARY/ANALOGY
TO THE FATHER'S ABSENCE: PUSHKIN

If we seriously take into account the idea that *The Master and Margarita* is organized as a mirror of chaotic earthly actuality, then subsidiary elements in Bulgakov's text may be seen to underlie the sense of a creative power which has abandoned the earth. A corollary absence from the world within the novel is that of a principle of literary order. This is to suggest not that literary history (as recounted by the author, and not the literary history that would ultimately embrace him) could substitute for what cannot be answered by Bulgakov's treatment of the deity, but rather that the dearth of creative power in the sublunary world generally signifies the loss of the father.

The vector conveying this situation is Bulgakov's evocations of Pushkin, which have been analyzed in other connections by several scholars.[16] As in the play *Alexander Pushkin*, eventually retitled *The Last Days* (*Последние дни*), Pushkin does not appear in person but manages to "assert his ghostly presence all the more forcefully." (Bethea 1991: 192). The allusions to Pushkin in *The Master and Margarita* lead back to Pushkin's own works as points of reference, which in turn open onto the novel's broad thematics even when they seem trivial. The implicit allusion to Pushkin's *Mozart and Salieri*—the poet Ryukhin, sighting Pushkin's statue in central Moscow and deploring the Master's sheer luck—summarily evokes the supreme being of Russia's first great poet. As is known, Pushkin is inversely linked to Griboedov House—both as a part of a lost Griboedov (the playwright) and as a contrast to mass literature—when Ivan Bezdomnyi hears the polonaise from the opera *Eugene Onegin* blasting out of Griboedov House's open windows. And Ivan continues to be "tormented for some reason by the ubiquitous orchestra accompanying a heavy basso who sang of his love for Tatyana."[17] This marks Pushkin out as a lost ideal whose significance is experienced specifically in terms of his absence, even as a paragon, from the fallen literary world. The death of Pushkin and of good readings of him suggest a moment of Russia's fall from grace. And there is no counterportrayal or contrary example in the rest of the book. In chapter 15, Nikanor Ivanovich Bosoi, the building superintendent at Sadovaya, has often taken Pushkin's name as a kind of swear word, even though he knows nothing of the poet's works: "Nikanor Ivanovich before his dream had absolutely no knowledge of the works of Pushkin the poet but knew Pushkin the man intimately and several times a day pronounced phrases like 'So is Pushkin going to pay for the apartment?' or 'So, then, it was Pushkin that unscrewed the bulb on the staircase?' "[18] The name becomes a substitution for the unknown or inexpressible, like the name of the deity. And chapter 30, entitled "It's Time! It's Time!" ("Пора! Пора!"), with its freight of apocalyptic suggestions, and in which the final voyage and transfiguration of the Master and Margarita are revealed, takes its departure from Pushkin's late (1834?) poem: "It's time, my friend, it's time! My heart desires rest [peace]" ("Пора, мой друг, пора! покоя сердце просит"). The passage evokes a longed-for, still-absent resolution—and, moreover, one which never comes to make its nature explicit. In parallel with the secular god's having turned away from the world, cosmic creativity is also "otherwise engaged."

ABSENT FATHER, ABSENT ORDER—PRESENT MIRACLE

If God the Father is the source of potential order on earth, we are given every temptation to ponder the mystery of how such an order is constituted, and at the same time deflected from every provisional conclusion. Victor Terras has made the striking suggestion[19] that Bulgakov might be working "from scene to scene, or from conceit to conceit, without regard to the whole." Thus the plotting would represent an intermediate position whereby each scene or division would retain a separate "order." According to this intriguing idea, one might compare Bulgakov's rendering of events to the consecutive shufflings of a deck of cards in the hands of an expert cardsharp able to register the most recent result and proceed accordingly toward the desired contiguity relation. In a lead story entitled "How to Win at Poker, and Other Science Lessons," *The Economist* reports two relevant discoveries. The first is that in card games "in some systems the switch to randomness is abrupt. In other words, after six shuffles a pack is still visibly ordered. But after the seventh, it suddenly becomes random." The second is that "Card shuffling, when imperfect, is a good example of something called a 'Markov chain.' This is a process of change in which the future depends only on the present, not the past. For instance, what a shuffle does to a pack of cards depends only on the order they are in before that shuffle, not on how they got to be in that order."[20] From the perspective of chance, then, much of what happens seems to follow the designed randomness of card games.

Yet we also note the long-distance narrative causality whereby *The Master and Margarita*'s separate worlds—that of physical being and that of discourse—come together, just as its "locales" of Moscow and Yershalaim ultimately appear to blend into one great story. The form of *The Master and Margarita*'s wondrous construction—while allowing for readers' perception of chance—also allows for the parallel lines of disparate narratives to converge alogically, as in mathematical non-standard analysis, at infinity.

WOLAND SUBSTITUTES FOR THE FATHER

Alogisms are recognizable due to our inability to rationalize them; the author places the onus squarely upon his interpreters. The precedents for this hardly call for emphasis; as is well known, Bulgakov is an heir to Gogol. Yet Gogol believed, at the end, that the Devil ruled the world, hence the alogisms he builds into texts such as "The Nose" at every level in their very agreement point to the Devil's authority. Bulgakov adopts a compromised version of this dictum, in which Woland fills in for the father who has absented himself. Woland is power—but by default. He represents the monad that dominates all dyads, making the relentless dualistic structure ultimately yield—not to perfect unity under his rule but to an asymmetrical tilt that overrides the symmetry of oppositions and dyads. Thus the group of main characters consists of two dyads (Pilate and Yeshua, the Master and Ivan Bezdomnyi) plus one monad: Woland.

God is the absent third which would have mediated all of these dualisms, but he has turned his face—or, in other words, his attention—from the world. If we wished to take a leaf from Bulgakov's book, God would be imagined as a slightly British-looking gentleman "of the old school," in a bespoke suit, whose parting words while tipping his hat might be, "Woland, my fine fellow, the world is yours; I'm leaving it into your care. Do with it what you will." The playfulness implied here is not accidental or otiosely arch: the obverse side of the saddened nostalgia for originary power might be an enhanced sense of cosmic play.

What the world would look like without "shadow" remains hypothetical precisely because Woland is the "shadow" of the Father in the world—a metonymy for God insofar as he gives some form to divine omnipotence. The blanket statement that Woland is a "parody of God" (Ericson 1991: 18) does nothing to mitigate the extent of his power among human beings. At most one could posit the existence of a gap between material "realism" as exemplified by Woland's results in the world and a transcendental reality without palpable consequences in human behavior.

"ONE" AND "THREE": TRANSCENDENTAL REALITY

The assertion of a strong influence—but not a mandate—on Bulgakov's rendering of absence in the "Eastern emphasis on apophatic or negative theology" which "insists that we can only say that God is beyond all our definitions and speculations" (Zernov 1961: 236; cit. Ericson 1991: 26) is probably correct. Both Eastern and Western churches, however, may be said to rely upon at least a reluctance to iconize the father, as is manifest in the tradition of the Pseudo-Dionysus' *Treatise on Divine Names*.

We would like to propose here a possible further influence—and again, as no more or less than a semiotic blueprint of the figurative relations within the book—of the point in the Eastern creed which states that the spirit proceeds from the father, opposing the Western tenet that the spirit proceeds from the father and the son together. The effect of this particular bond between the aspects of father and spirit would conduce to our understanding of a greater degree of "absence," since even the immanent divinity of Christ would be "seen" to function less fully in the gift of the spirit (or law). It would not be the injunction against speculating on the Godhead *in toto*, but the directionality of the particular conceptual bond between the first and the third persons that would underlie the extra measure of negativity. For all that Bulgakov's rendition of the Yershalaim narrative concentrates on the incarnation and passion of Christ rather than on rational theology, it is not discordant with the complexity of his narrative plan to do justice to its underlying sophistication. As generations of non-specialist readers can attest, one need hardly be in possession of rational theology in order to experience this book viscerally. Theology does not even achieve articulation at this level; its arguments constitute barely a few of the text's explicit thematics (and, as noted from the outset, scriptural narrative tradition is no criterion by which to measure the proceedings in the novel). The premise that rational theology can provide an analogy to the workings of the human mind, however, is of use here, not because Bulgakov employs religious symbolism, but because the form of his plotting—and *not* its content—may be seen as analogous to the way theology works.

The spirit, called the gift of God, instantiates the mediating relation of the whole Trinity. It is this giving-and-acceptance that is impaired and distorted in a world that does not seek to understand and, even less, to replicate it. It is particularly with respect to the spirit that language (articulated at a very early historical stage and continuously shared by both churches) clarified God's gift of mediation to the world. The rendering in terms of being of the spirit has been understood throughout the history of the trinity as lawlike; it has not been subdivided by sectarian controversy or heresy, or by the doctrinal differences between the Eastern and Western churches. Spirit was given into the world as that which enables human interpretation of the advent of God into world history. We extrapolate—with a brevity that does not and need not do justice to the complexity of the whole conception—that what is lacking in the world (of *The Master and Margarita*) is the untrammeled and combined working of father and spirit, whether or not the son is made present and even understood as both immanent and eternal.

CONSEQUENCES OF THE TRINITARIAN ANALOGY
FOR BULGAKOV'S PLOTTING

The point here is not to ask whether Bulgakov intended this to come forward from the realm of rational theology but to posit a useful analogy between the particular "absence of God" and the novel's situational difficulties. We propose that the very lack of fit between the narrative pieces portrays the consequences of the self-removal of the father pursuant to humanity's non-acceptance of the gift of the spirit (and, concomitantly, of interpretation). Humanity in the novel has, so to speak, "returned its ticket."

Since according to doctrine the second person of the trinity does not "participate" in the procession of the third, or spirit, God's historical act of giving the Holy Spirit to the church (in the working-out of salvation history in the world) is also in particular an act of the Father and not the Son. If spirit, the most lawlike aspect of the Trinity, is understood to proceed from the Father alone, then the Christ figure, Yeshua, can appear among the denizens of the world without their being able to interpret his presence and draw consequences from it. The significance of this difference for the narrative of *The Master and Margarita* is that the son, iconized in his human nature and with his divine nature implied, can be made present as Yeshua at the level of earthly action without a commensurate "presence" of the other two aspects of the divinity. With father and spirit absent from the workings of history—manifest in the decisions humanity takes of its free will—the problematic dual nature of the son remains stranded in its actions, counterposed in turn to Woland. A "messenger" would be entirely dependent upon the will of the person who sends him. A vicar or substitute can take action either by applying the law or by using his own discretion in matters of which his Lord knows nothing. Woland's jurisdiction—like Yeshua's—represents a compromise, although it is securely installed within the course of events: is it at his own discretion or within the terms of the law that Woland acts as de facto representative of unrevealed divine power? The question is irresistibly prompted, the answer carefully crafted to remain insoluble. Acting simply as a new, catastrophic power which helps attest to the disappearance or loss of the father, Woland, with his familiar, "the best jester [literally: "tomcat"], who ever existed in the world" ("лучшим котом, какой существовал когда-либо в мире" [375]), plays tragicomically with pure human nostalgia for the authority of one origin, one sign, one meaning.

6

FRAGMENTS OF MEANING
IN SOLOGUB'S *THE PETTY DEMON*

Trepetov was always preparing to lead a simple life,
and with this goal in mind, he watched the peasants as
they blew their noses, scratched the backs of their
necks, and wiped their lips with the backs of their
hands. When he was by himself he sometimes imitated
them, but he always put off his simplification
[опрощение] for the next summer.[1]

Anyone who has read Tolstoy will immediately recognize the car-
icature contained in this capsule sketch as the special kind of ide-
alist characterized by Lyovin. What is not apparent, perhaps, is that
the passage refers to one Georgii Semenovich Trepetov, who is a
guest at another landowner's home in a different book, Sologub's
The Petty Demon (*Мелкий бес*). Trepetov "knew little and was an
incompetent doctor" (117 [X, 161]), and his interlocutor and host,
Kirillov, is an equally silly man. The occasion of their meeting fits
into a series of visits to townspeople which epitomize a whole way
of understanding the structure of Russian society. Two other au-

thors haunt this little episode: Chekhov (the doctor) and that most "estranged" (отрешенный) of writers, Gogol.

Not only do these authors leave echoes that linger indefinitely, but they communicate a sense of what it feels like to plumb the mysteries informing Sologub's major work of art. They help to convey the manner in which a book like *The Petty Demon* actually happens—as long as we consider their texts as fragments that are embedded as parts of a whole *context*. Inasmuch as Sologub's characters themselves have hardly any past to speak of, the presence of Russian textual fragments in their makeup confers a past upon them and allows us thereby to measure the distances that, taken together, constitute a "literary" history for them. We are discussing a novel that has a significant place not only in the ranks of Symbolist prose but in all of Russian literature. No less a critic than Mirsky judged it the best novel since *The Brothers Karamazov*.[2] To know more about how Sologub made his predecessors part of *The Petty Demon* gives us collateral information to help interpret it. As much as biographical data, such knowledge provides us with an effective way of entering the cultural consciousness of the author. The literary predecessor functions almost like a trope—the very detail that affords access to the individuality of a style or mind.

Given that the chief protagonist Peredonov's demons are ludicrous, it is surprising that relatively little critical attention has accrued to the Gogolian grotesque. Perhaps without conscious awareness that he was citing Gogol's own words, the critic Dolinin articulated in a classic essay the peculiar truthfulness of *The Petty Demon*: "Sologub has objectified himself, presenting us with an analysis which, although it deals *only with one side* [emphasis added] of his soul, is truthful to the highest degree" (1986: 133).[3] Gogol, of course, had projected in a letter that *Dead Souls* would constitute a world poem, but one that readers would perceive as markedly skewed: "All of Russia would appear in it, though only from one side" (Gogol 1940: 375).

In *The Petty Demon* reading functions allusively in various directions: as a metaphor for the pursuit or avoidance of knowledge; as a status symbol; as a marker of history or of the past; and, finally, as a clue to the varying assessments by its author of *The Petty Demon* in the context of Russian literary achievement.

The Petty Demon does not aspire to the panoramic canvas of *Dead Souls*, yet it is even more ruthless in its debasement of the whole of Russian society. Peredonov, the incompetent, perverted schoolmaster who seeks the post of schools inspector, functions as a microcosm of that whole. It is very much a part of his behavior to counterfeit knowledge of books he has never read; to lay claim to areas of expertise, such as child psychology, in which he shows the most marked deficiencies; and, in his entire person, to represent a disparagement of the professional and the functionary, the false littérateur and hypocritical pedant. Through this character, and often from the depth of his own terrors, the reader confronts a totally threatening environment. For Sologub, it seems, this encompassing darkness is even to include authors. Literature overtly includes itself in all that goes demonically awry. The novel plays with and torments its precursors. Writers no longer remain beyond reproach. To take account of the shifting presence of the most canonical Russian writers in *The Petty Demon* is to acknowledge that they have a place there as part of a possibly debased métier. References to them may alert us to a point of comparison, a heightening of distance, or a tragicomic rapprochement of remote points of view. Otherwise, by reminding readers of the whole context of another writer, Sologub shows how the present world hyperbolizes the past. At the same time, Sologub includes himself as the latest link in a chain leading from Pushkin to the Symbolists.

For example, where Gogol implemented certain procedures that Pushkin had used—such as producing sudden rapid shifts of viewpoint from narrator to some character, then another— Sologub takes off from the point at which Gogol had stopped.

The constant presence of chance is not only thematized in Pushkin but is made part of his narrative technique. Chance can include sudden, apparently inexplicable shifts of viewpoint. Vinogradov (1936) showed us the many faces of Pushkin's narrator.[4] And Gogol's extended similes are often based on the same kind of abrupt shift, acquiring a grotesque component from the puzzling nonsequitur that arises out of the ashes of a simple utterance. Sologub in turn adopts the technique of abrupt change with an absurdist twist. Characters often speak in Gogolian series that depend on sudden contextual changes: "'You have many enemies,' Liudmila tells Peredonov, 'they will inform on you, you will weep, you will die under a fence'"(325 [XXIX, 389]). Compare that with Bobchinsky's congratulations to the mayor's daughter in *The Inspector General:* "'Marya Antonovna, I have the honor of congratulating you! May God give you all kinds of prosperity, ten ruble bills [sic] and a little son just so ... big you can sit him on your hand. Yes sir: the little boy'll cry all the time-wah! wah! wah!'" (Gogol 1961: 305). Or a list of nearly epithetical attributes will appear skewed out of focus by a shift in the order: Peredonov, for example, imagines a spy hiding behind the wallpaper because there is room there for a "clever, flat, and patient villain" (284 [XXV, 344]).

One way of approaching the freight of previous literature in *The Petty Demon* is, of course, that of charting references, and they abound from beginning to end. Peredonov reads out in class a Krylov fable, *The Liar* (*Лжец*), which happens to describe him accurately. He displays ignorance of many writers, among them Chekhov. The Chekhov story *Man in a Shell* (Человек в футляре) centers on a character, Belikov, who could certainly find a place in *The Petty Demon*; Peredonov does not know this story. Peredonov's portrait of Mickiewicz seems to wink at him from the wall, whereupon he removes it and replaces it with one of Pushkin. Peredonov has already misidentified *The Bell* (Колокол, Herzen's newspaper) as a poem by Mickiewicz. These and similar examples deliver names and specific references, but at a less immediately accessible level we find allusions to famous texts. Verging on total madness, Peredonov imagines that a "snubnosed, hideous" peasant woman wakens him just as he is about to doze off and approaches his bed, muttering, then disappears "as though she had never existed" (347 [XXII, 413]). Her antecedent is, of course, the old peasant whom Anna Karenina sees standing near the tracks at the moment of her suicide, an apparition already glimpsed before in her dreams. There are passages that evoke frequently cited precursors, such as the one describing the house of the procurator Peredonov visits as the first in a Gogolian series:

> And truly, this house did have an angry evil look .... Both the wooden trim on the house and the roof itself had once been painted brightly and gaily, but time and the rains had made the color gloomy and gray. The huge and ponderous gates, higher than the house itself, as if their purpose was to repel enemy attacks, were always bolted.... Bare spots, vegetable gardens, and hovels were scattered all about ... all unpaved and overgrown with weeds. (100 [IX, 142])

According to Annenkov's memoir of Gogol (1934: 147), the description of Pliushkin's garden is the most reworked section of *Dead Souls*. It is a passage whose symbolism summarizes the collapse of all order, serving precisely for this reason as a corollary to the miserable sloth that characterizes Pliushkin himself. Sologub hyperbolizes this deadness into Peredonovism, adding to it a superordinate quotient of perverseness and stasis. As if this kind of concentrated allusiveness were not enough, Kirillov, one in the series of landowners, appears a "dead living person, as if his soul had been removed" (115 [IX, 159]). The text bristles with "speaking" names such as those of Mayor Skuchaev ("Boredom") and Tishkov, whose "secretiveness" actually consists in the fact that he talks only in rhymed couplets. These secondary references to Gogol, compounded with elements from other canonical authors, may help to prompt Sologub to insert the following nonsense into the mouth of Trepetov: "I don't know how thinking people can behave with such musty classicism ["служить затхлому классицизму"]!"(117 [X, 161]). In context, the remark ends up making a kind of sense as a slap at outdated, musty, false order and appearances.

The literary reminiscences surface as if to assure readers that nothing has changed in Russia since the time of Gogol, except for the worse. The more serious mood of Gogol's narrator is captured in a passage in which sound and sense crystallize into something poignant, then reemerge into the glare of the ironic grotesque. Liudmila and her sisters are singing folksongs together: "These sounds upon which the stress did not fall were drawn out especially painfully. It produced an extraordinary effect—the song would have induced fatal anguish in a new listener. ... O fatal anguish, resounding in the fields and in all places of our vast native expanse! An anguish personified in her wild fury [в диком галдении], an anguish which devours the living word in hideous flame, reducing once living song to mad wailing!" (162 [XIV, 210]). But this reflection on the living Russian word terminates in a grotesque dance by one of the sisters, who snaps her fingers and sways "motionless as the dead moon in its orbit" (163 [XIV, 211]).

No positive dialectic ensues from the mixing and sorting of older texts. *The Petty Demon*'s rhythm appropriates material only to cast doubt on the possibility of a future and the validity of a past. Momentary empathy with the pace of history comes to express itself in the dead beat of sloth. Not only is the dull sluggishness of Peredonovism the culmination of acedia in the Russian antihero, but it rules from beginning to end. Peredonov does not even react to what strikes him as funny at the beginning of the novel (ch. I, 11 [40]); the conclusion finds him muttering, in-coherent, and motionless, a state interrupted throughout only by aberrant, discontinuous movements. The same pace applies to the reading of Russian literary history that can be pieced to-gether from the embedded shards of reference and imitation. Gogol's presence reveals itself to be more pervasive and pro-found than a simple implicit comparison with a literary giant would indicate. In minute details of composition, Sologub com-ments through Gogolian modes and discontinuities upon a frag-mented world that finds its way into the very fabric of Symbolism.

Sologub, the extreme in a chain of "estranged" writers (after Pushkin and Gogol), most obviously reaches into narrative tech-nique as a corollary for confusion and withdrawal. Dolinin claims that no other author "so completely shuts himself and his world off from us with a more impenetrable wall" (1986: 124). He goes on to apply this idea to the structure of the novel: "We are presented not with a genuine sequence of events, as occurs in our lives, but merely with a formal or forced one, insofar as we unavoidably place everything in spatial and temporal order" (1986: 134). We might look for correlates in the German gro-tesque (Hoffman, Tieck et al.) as we examine Sologub's "objecti-fication" of characters and events. Yet unlike them, Sologub's "is not the kind of estrangement which is the product of reflection and philosophy. Rather it seems more likely that the starting point is a peculiar type of will ... which I would call centripetal" (Dolinin 1986: 125).

Dolinin's comments offer much food for thought, but we would like to take up the thread that binds Peredonovism not to lack of will—as first seems the case—but to the persistence of a *type* of will. Dolinin's psychological criticism seems to be play-ing Sologub himself as a kind of Gogolian character, since it is the result of an attempt to get at the author's psyche, to delve into the realm of his unconscious intentions. However, he uncovers not only Sologub's particular attachment to a discourse of desire but to the generative possibilities of the formal constraints of writing itself. Sologub's enlargement upon Gogolian grotesque delights in the elaborateness and intricacy of language for itself, in odd linguistic mannerisms, even in the use of rhythmic prose. Peredonov and his friends take humans for pigs. Volodin puns on *piatachok*, which means both small change and snouts, whereupon Peredonov hastily touches his nose to make sure he has a human face. The servant Klavdiia is called first Klavdiushka, then *diushka* ("pig" [dialectal]), in a flash-forward of verbal decline.[5] It is as if words carried an immanent will to fragmentation, a centripetal will.

Whereas in *Dead Souls* events develop from the main intrigue, in *The Petty Demon* they have no clear motivation but are strung in chains, wherein only the latest link may offer a clue to the next. The banality and trivial viciousness of the characters reflect the same traits in readers; as in Gogol's *Inspector General*, the text is to be a "mirror" of the reader.[6] But there ends the bond between them, for few are permitted to laugh at themselves as pictured in *The Petty Demon*. Readers become dupes, not accomplices, because they are even less able when reading Gogol to enter the closed microcosms than are the characters. Being at the endpoint of a missing trajectory, they are, again in Dolinin's words, "frozen symbols" (1986: 131). To achieve this kind of result implies a total embrace of the negative principle, the "one compulsory law ... a kind of categorical imperative 'not to act,' not to live with and among us, always to move in reverse motion" (1986: 125). In other words, Sologub involves his entire literary world in a program of negation that is not a relinquishing but a totalizing of the will.

As Fanger points out, the Gogolian grotesque helped give rise, via many stages, to Dostoevskian tragic realism: "However complex the relation of mainstream Russian realism to the prose of Gogol, there is another branch that goes directly from him to

Dostoevsky and from Dostoevsky to the symbolists" (1967: 125). To the many shared elements that others have discovered, we would like to add and concentrate on one for the particular development of *The Petty Demon:* the presence in the novel of a cycle of fear and sadomasochism. For Peredonov, fear and cruelty are concomitants, each stimulating the other. It is fair to say that there can be no eroticism without sadism in *The Petty Demon.* The mutual relationship helps to explain how even the tortured, such as children or animals, may themselves exhibit signs of evil or malevolence—for example, the cat, which is later doubled by the *nedotykomka.* Much of the sadism directs itself against children: schoolboys Peredonov torments in his capacity as teacher, or whose parents he induces to beat them; girls he imagines in humiliating sexual situations; Sasha Pyl'nikov, who seems to Peredonov like a girl; and so forth. As Rabinowitz remarks, "with few exceptions Sologub's stories read like elaborations of Ivan Karamazov's litany of child abuse" (1980: 344).

Indeed, the celebrated subplot of Sasha and Liudmila invites the comparison between the perverse aspects of their relationship and the episode in *The Brothers Karamazov* in which Alyosha and Lise Khokhlakova discuss her sadistic desires. "Both Sasha and Liudmila share a similar potential for such feeling" (Rabinowitz 1980: 79). Lise expresses her delight in murder; arson; child torture; and finally in her own propensity to evil, feeding upon itself. This chapter, actually entitled "Besënok" ("little demon"), provides a far more extended meditation on sadism than Sologub ever offers; but he draws from it liberally. Just as Lise enjoys the notion of a crucified child, Liudmila gloats over the thought of the drops of Christ's blood as he hangs from the cross. Like Peredonov, Lise sees small devils cavorting around her room that remain after she crosses herself, so that she reviles God aloud. The sexual stimulations of sadistic thoughts are already present: "Do you know," Lise tells Alyosha, "I should like to reap, to cut the rye? I'll marry you, and you shall become a peasant, a real peasant; we'll keep a colt, shall we?" (707 [pt. 4, bk. 11, ch. 3]). This is followed by her vision of herself spinning a young man like a top and then lashing him with a whip. In turn, Sasha and Liudmila vacillate between desire to possess and to inflict harm upon the other. Lise craves disorder; this makes her want to set fire to a house. And of course, in *The Petty Demon* a general conflagration puts a crematory end to an enormous social gathering at the ball. What *The Brothers Karamazov* states explicitly, however, *The Petty Demon* never articulates. "You take evil for good," Alyosha tells Lise, and the two indeed meet upon the ground of pleasure (708). Although *The Petty Demon* contains no extended meditation on cruelty and desire, these make so pervasive a dyad as to constitute their own metaphysical calamity. These corrupt desires can no longer be assigned to the sin of Cain or any original. They belong to an evil that can never be explained away by hatred but that has its own spontaneity, and is part-and-parcel of human desire.

Hence the famed Dostoevskian pity does not enter Sologub's text except as an external commentary: some miserable individual is compared to a "scalded puppy"; or the narrator will aver that even Peredonov searches for truth, as do we all, or pause to remark upon his estrangement from the natural order. Yet these instances are reported as encompassed by an evil whose opposing force can only be conjured up in language. We are reminded of Dolinin again, when he observes Sologub's "vague, unconscious terror of life in its entirety" (1986: 133). That complex of fear and pleasure built into the text forces its language to bear the marks of proliferating corruption, without offsetting compensation from any other universe of discourse.

Although *The Double* seems to represent most palpably the thematic presence of Dostoevsky in *The Petty Demon* (Koz'menko, in the 1988 Moscow edition [292]), numerous details also recall *The Devils*, from the coincidence of the word *bes* "devil, demon" to the nihilistic past Peredonov invents for himself as a source of anxiety and fear, to the masquerade ball in Sologub that recalls the one in *The Devils* for the benefit of governesses (cf. Erofeev 1985: 156). Both of the latter two events are disrupted when a crowd turns into a mob, and both celebrations are ended by a fire.

The terrible aspect of beauty, which became a subject for Decadence from Huysmans to Aubrey Beardsley, occupies considerable space in *The Petty Demon*. The chief locus is in the relationship between Sasha and Liudmila, with emphasis on her ambivalent appearance and desires. Much Grecian symbolism abounds concerning bare feet and legs and the freedom-enhancing properties of physical beauty. But the paragon of beauty's fearfulness and the rapacious demands that it makes upon the beholder is straight from Dostoevsky—from the effect on the Underground Man of the "sublime and the beautiful" to the famous passage in *The Brothers Karamazov* in which Dmitry discourses on how "a man of lofty mind and heart begins with the ideal of the Madonna and ends with the ideal of Sodom" (127 [pt. 1, bk. 3, ch. 3]).

Sologub enlarges upon several aspects of life that Gogol and Dostoevsky plumbed as deeply before him. The desecration of childhood as one might see it in Dostoevsky amounts to overt paedophilia in *The Petty Demon;* hellfire and the demonic move into the homes of commonplace people; political and moral denunciations and reprisals make up a regular feature of small-town life; the sluggish impotence of Gogolian society develops hypertrophic proportions. Strands from both authors run through the novel at an underground level. If *The Petty Demon* represents any view of recent Russian literary history, that view exhibits continuities but also discontinuities that attest to the contrasts among different periods.

No author is as entrenched in the text of *The Petty Demon* as Pushkin, and the remainder of what we have to say is largely devoted to him, partly because Pushkin has figured much less than Gogol and Dostoevsky in the study of Sologub's literary antecedents. To begin, Sologub entertained genuine and lasting admiration for what he saw as realism. His own intensification of themes of death, destruction, and madness may themselves be part of a hyperrealism—the exploration of inner reality, even if achieved through accumulations of trivial or hyperbolized details. The firm grounding in the realistic tradition initiated by Pushkin prompted Briusov to declare Sologub one of "the very few among the 'decadents' who is not removed from everyday reality ... [but] has preserved a vital, organic tie to the earth" (1904: 51). To this we would like to add that Pushkin is the liminal writer par excellence in respect of his place in literary history. He represents both the cultural past of Russia and the beginning of the modern world—drawing on the past to aspire to the future. In his works and in the eyes of subsequent authors, Pushkin marks a boundary of enormous significance for Russian literature.

No matter how firm our view of the mature Pushkin as a classical poet as well as a realistic prose writer, we must still acknowledge the importance of the supernatural and the fantastic in much of his major work. Besides *The Queen of Spades*, which we will discuss in detail, two of his other masterpieces, *The Stone Guest* (1830) and *The Bronze Horseman* (1833), which exerted a profound influence on Symbolist prose, make prominent use of supernatural events, to the point that the content of each hinges on them. Sologub implements the potential of the supernatural to portray randomness and chance, as was adumbrated by Pushkin. Of course, in Pushkin's case the intrusion of the supernatural (or the element of chance) subordinates itself to matters of epistemic import; in other words, to meditation on illusion as the limit of knowledge. The supremely significant limit is that between life and death, and it is in treating and testing this limit that Pushkin resorted to the supernatural. Gogol, of course, took his departure from that relation when he conceived *Dead Souls*;

and the establishment of illusion as the limit on knowledge was absorbed into Gogol's own fiction—into all the numerous instances in which the devil's work results in confusion. The inability to discriminate truth from fiction, the real from the unreal, is the condition Pushkin assigns to his protagonists, and ultimately to all mankind. It is no wonder, then, that *The Petty Demon* begins with an epigraph from one of Sologub's poems which depends and comments upon the quintessential instance of the supernatural, Pushkin's *Queen of Spades*.

In order to clarify our argument that *The Queen of Spades* wields decisive influence over Sologub's novel, some story telling is in order. We recall that the events turn around a card game. In a group of young officers at a party, one Tomsky remarks that he wonders why his grandmother never plays cards, considering that she has the secret of a series of three winning cards at faro. This grandmother, a countess, lived in Paris 60 years before and one night lost a great deal of money at cards. St-Germain, an adventurer, helped her recoup it by naming three cards that would win if played consecutively. She never used her secret again or revealed it to anyone (with one exception: a Pushkinian touch that has no subsequent issue). Among the guests listening to Tomsky's story is Germann, who wonders if he can get the secret out of the Countess. One day, he notices the old woman's companion, Lizaveta, and decides to court her in order to gain entree to the house. Lizaveta lets Germann know that one night she and the Countess will be out at a ball and tells him how he can get into the house in their absence. Germann follows the instructions, but rather than going to his supposed sweetheart's room he hides near the Countess' bedroom. When the old woman is left alone after preparing for the night, he questions her strenuously about the cards, pressing her and eventually pulling a gun on her, which causes her to die of fright. During the Countess' funeral service Germann steps up to the coffin, and just then it seems to him that she casts him a mocking glance, screwing up her eyes. That night her ghost visits him and tells him that he will win if he bets on the three, the seven, and the ace on consecutive nights. He follows her instructions at the house of a famous gambler and wins on the three and the seven, but on the third night, when he thinks he has placed his bet on the ace, he finds that a losing card—the queen of spades—is in his hand. It seems to him that she is screwing up one eye and grinning at him. He has lost everything he had and, in the epilogue, goes out of his mind.

Of the remarkable boundary shifts between the natural and the unnatural that characterize this story, Dostoevsky wrote (1959: 178):

> The fantastic must make contact with the real to such an extent that you almost believe it. Pushkin, who gave us almost all forms of art, wrote 'The Queen of Spades'—the summit of the art of the fantastic. And you believe that Germann really had a vision, one that is congruent with his world view. At the same time, at the end of the story, i.e., having read it, you don't know what to decide: did the vision emanate from Germann's nature, or is he really one of those who made contact with the other world, the world of evil spirits inimical to mankind? ... Now that is art![7]

The quotation that appears at the front of The Petty Demon, "I wished to burn her, the wicked witch," continues as follows: "But she called forth the evil words / I saw her, again living, / Her head all in flames and sparks. / And saying, I did not burn—/ The fire renewed my charms. / I take my body, nourished by the flames, / Away from the blaze to my sorcery. / And as I go the flame grows dim / In the folds of my magic garments. / Fool! You'll not find your hopes / In my mysteries" (351–52).[8] If we imagined this as the epigraph to The Queen of Spades it would call for no change. There you have it: Germann's threat against the old woman, her indestructible apparition, the burning of the playing-card queen, and its mocking resurrection. The final lines stress the hopelessness of Germann's illusion—that of winning, or of seeing the apparition?—and his being foiled by chance or a malevolent providence. Take the line, "The fire renewed my charms": Pushkin's Countess had been an eighteenth-century belle, and the old woman retains a certain misplaced (or displaced) sexuality. Here is something of the corresponding passage in Sologub's novel:

> With a crackle, mysterious pale red blossoms of flame unfolded and burned, black about the edges. Peredonov watched the flaming blossoms in terror. The cards warped and twisted and moved as though they wished to jump out of the stove. Peredonov grabbed the poker and thrashed them about. He was surrounded on all sides by minute bright sparks—and suddenly, in a bright and evil flurry of sparks, the Princess arose from the fire. (288 [XXV, 348])[9]

Sologub enhances the sadistic aspect of the unknown forces engineering the episode via another suggestion of sexuality: "Gloom took hold of him. It tickled him and laughed at him with cooing voices" (288 [XXV, 349]). Some of the taunting charm of the apparition remains.

These events should already be outlining a general resemblance to *The Queen of Spades*. The most apparent link between them does indeed consist in the old Princess. But our consideration of her part in the story will also result in the discovery of the other, deeper relations. Let us begin with the title: a playing card, which refers to the old Countess only indirectly, as a representation come to life in the hallucinatory imagination of the protagonist. The playing card is actually the last in a triplet of resurrections of the Countess, who is already dead when they occur, so that each appearance is connected with an error, mishap, or misinterpretation. The first occurs at the Countess' funeral when Germann thinks he sees her glancing up at him with one squinted eye. Since he reacts dramatically (falling into a momentary faint), this gives rise to the false rumor that Germann is the Countess' illegitimate son. The seemingly extra detail heightens a certain Oedipal aspect of *The Queen of Spades:* Germann muses on the possibility of becoming the Countess' lover, as does Peredonov the Princess'.

The second appearance, when the Countess reveals the secret of the cards, is preceded by a series of misconstruals by Germann as to the identity of the apparition: he first mistakes her for his orderly, then for his old nursemaid. The third and final appearance is due to the force of a power emanating from a super-reality. The Countess announces to Germann that she has come to him against her will, the emissary of a higher power.

From its initial publication, readers have associated the story with the general type of diabolism, and this view is in fact buttressed by an elaborate system of symbols, such as occult elements: the magic cards; the ghost of the Countess; the adventurer St-Germain, who pretends to be "the inventor of the elixir of life and of the philosopher's stone"; the "hidden galvanism" that seems to be rocking the Countess in her chair as Germann confronts her; and finally, of course, her apparitions, which cross all boundaries of reality and unreality, lower and higher realms. All events issue from a game of chance, faro, so that the supernatural becomes an expression of a higher level of chance.

The same interpenetration of the real and the supernatural creates something like "intermediate worlds," combining properties drawn from both. Even more importantly, the boundaries between possibility and impossibility are made to shift or are redistributed. One of the most effective means whereby Pushkin's tale crosses thresholds is the irruption of chance in the narrative. Germann's whole course of action is predicated on the illusion that the supernaturally obtained secret of the cards will guarantee his future happiness. But his undoing comes about as the result of an error based precisely on the irruption of chance into even this supernaturally derived system, at a higher level, just when success is nearest.

For if Germann had drawn the queen and the ace in reverse order, his queen would have won. This is quintessentially a matter of chance in a game of chance. There is no real explanation for Germann's having played the wrong card; the error itself occurred by chance. Since chance is equivalent to the absence of regularity, since it is the opposite of predictability, it is coherent with the supernatural, which becomes an effective way of representing chance. In Germann's case, chance emerges through that whole realm of the private, hallucinatory imagination which is opposed to reality.

Sologub in turn represents a far distant point in the progression toward a triumph of the aleatory. Everything in *The Petty Demon* conspires to let chance have its way: the near-total passivity and mutual suspicion among all the characters; the jerking, irruptive pace of their actions; even the chaos of the huge masquerade near the end, and the sudden shifts in sexual roles between Sasha and Liudmila. Here, too, the supernatural strikes us as wholly organic with the narrative, integrated with its form and content, crossing the limits of the real and the possible. Like that of Pushkin, the logic of Sologub's narrative world creates something like an "intermediate world" combining properties drawn from the natural and the supernatural domains; and as in Pushkin, the boundaries between worlds are made to shift. Statues come to life, for example, in *The Golden Cockerel* and *The Bronze Horseman*. But the typical context of an intermediate world is dreams or madness, both of which motivate events that would be impossible in ordinary life. Since dreams and hallucinations are part of actual human experience, they serve as a bridge connecting the real with the unreal, in a random, aleatory way.

Sologub's Peredonov, like Pushkin's Germann, ultimately goes mad. But *The Petty Demon* confronts readers with an entire maddened world. Where Pushkin concerns himself with boundaries, Sologub constructs alternate modes of seeing the natural through the filter of the unnatural, which he renders through metaphor or via erratic actions. The grotesque abounds: Volodin, for example, bears an uncanny resemblance to a sheep, and all kinds of sheeplike motions and expressions stick to him (20 et passim [XX, 55]). Or Rutilov tries to persuade Peredonov to marry one of his sisters, and while walking together they decide to pick one out right away (43–44 [IV, 79–82]). The *nedotykomka*—gray, elusive—whirls in and out of the narrative and finally becomes assimilated into the cat everyone habitually tortures, as well as to the old Princess: "She was a small ash-gray woman, covered with fading sparks: she wailed piercingly in a thin voice, hissed, and spat on the fire" (288 [XXV, 348]). Or demonism passes to Peredonov himself: "On an earth alienated from the heavens ... [he] looked on the world with the eyes of the dead, like some demon tormented in gloomy solitude by fear and sadness" (99 [IX, 141]). Dogs laugh at Peredonov while people bark at him (268 [XXIV, 326]). The inert world mocks him from a shared perspective of fear and sadism. As if a medieval world had lost its God but remained in possession of a profusion of signs, as Sologub has it, "that ancient Demon, the spirit of eternal disorder and aged chaos, rejoiced" (285 [XXV, 345]).

Pushkin resorts to the supernatural in dealing with the problem of knowledge and illusion, where madness is the extreme pathological transgression of their boundary. For Sologub the realms tend to blur together almost to the point of fusion. However, the pivotal event even of *The Queen of Spades* is about the failure of the boundary to hold. Germann threatens the Countess to get her secret, and again, upon losing the game, his cry, "*Starukha*" ("old woman"), echoing that threat, underscores the futility of his anger and desire. Germann's threat against the Countess had ultimately been powerless, so much so that even the intervention of supernatural forces that sent him her ghost had proven insufficient toward realizing his victory. The certainty first vouchsafed Germann has been falsified or disauthenticated. Peredonov, in turn, is moved about "by eternal forces, which, however, had no desire to bother themselves about him for long" (287 [XXV, 347]). The spuriousness that in *The Queen of Spades* constitutes an event in *The Petty Demon* is no more than a tired presupposition.

Each of the works we are comparing was composed against a background of an uncertain religiosity and a (partially resultant) attraction to demonism. Pushkin's attitude toward Russian orthodoxy seems to have been one of considerable and frequent vacillation, although he thoroughly assimilated the symbolism of the Eastern Church and infused his works with it. What can be distilled from his letters as well as his poetry concerning his views of religion and the Deity seems to be largely negative. With his marked preference for the negative mode, Pushkin may have been unwittingly retracing the path of negative theology by making infernal agents like the Countess substitute for the implied Deity. It is a direct index of what can be called his fundamentally denatured attitude toward religion that Pushkin hints at an unmentioned Agent for whom the playing cards stand as surrogates. When the Countess reveals the secret of the cards to Germann, she prefaces the magical formula with the explanation, "I have come to you against my will ... but I have been ordered to grant your request." She is evidently acting for a more powerful force, but its source and efficacy come into question.

The Petty Demon takes this kind of surrogacy much further: not only is the presence of a reassuring God denied to its characters and to their world, but the world that would function in the absence of vision is itself rendered profoundly suspect.[10] The notion of disharmony between nature and humanity, which is but one aspect of a huge Tolstoyan canvas, gives rise to a universe of dirty reflections glimpsed through filthy water (267 [XXIV, 325]).[11] Peredonov substitutes magic and superstition for religion. The *nedotykomka* turns up in church as well as at home. What is important is that with respect to religion no more or less than anything else, Peredonov's world represents a conflation of otherwise ordered things, in the absence of a unified faith in order.

We believe evidence exists to show that via his use of certain themes and plot developments, Sologub actually comments upon Pushkin's older, more ordered world. All these strategies crystallize in the figure—absent from the narrative proper but always a bone of contention—of the old Princess. That her name is Volchanskaya reminds us of Tolstoy's Bolkonskaya. That sole element "from another opera" already helps us to detach the source from its latest product. Note other details that follow or tally with *The Queen of Spades:* just as Germann works through the Countess' companion, Lizaveta, so Peredonov hopes to gain his end, the school inspector's job, through his mistress Varvara, who had once been employed by the Princess. But Sologub has taken the louche courting of Lizaveta and literalized it, concretizing it into a long-standing and sordid bond between Peredonov and Varvara, who generally loathe each other but stay mired in their relationship in the hope of future benefits. It is interesting that Pushkin also featured a seemingly extraneous detail in *The Queen of Spades:* remember the allusion to Chaplitsky, the only person to whom the Countess had ever confided the secret of the cards before Germann. He never appears again, nor do we hear any more of him. He seems as gratuitous or coincidental as the name "Volchanskaya/Bolkonskaya" in Sologub, as much a matter of meaningless coincidence.

Whereas Pushkin has the Countess exert her maleficent influence on Germann's fate through apparitions—as a corpse, or a ghost—Sologub uses the stratagem of a letter. From early on this document becomes the Princess' sole representative. In the second of the 36 chapters, Peredonov insists that Varvara get him a letter of recommendation from the Princess which would insure him the position of schools inspector. Varvara sets marriage as the condition of her cooperation in this scheme. Of course, no possibility exists that the Princess would ever write such a letter. So very soon Varvara and her friend Grushina conspire to forge and send Peredonov one of their own. They prepare the letter, in counterpoint to a crescendo of chaotic elements and the growing persecution mania of Peredonov. Varvara gives Peredonov the forgery. He fears deceit, demanding to see the envelope, and falls into a liminal state between belief and distrust, doubting the genuineness of the letter but showing it to everyone. Soon afterward Varvara quarrels with Grushina over the failure of the letter to convince even Peredonov, and they agree to compose a second one and mail it in a better envelope. At this stage the complement of literary references in the novel increases noticeably. A series of Gogolian visits to various townspeople unfolds, ending in chapter 11.

To this point the letter has already elicited or emphasized many of the main themes having to do with the manipulation of or estrangement from life, with the spuriousness overhanging the world. Specific literary references seem to mock the distance between the classic works and the one at hand. Peredonov never reads a book and is full of misinformation about authors. He does own piles of books, prominently displayed, including some by the radical writer Pisarev. These afford him the *frisson* of fear that they might be discovered by the police. Forbidden books assimilate themselves to other kinds of forbidden behavior, such as sexual behavior, which should be denounced to the authorities. And it is in chapter 20, where the sole reference to Pushkin occurs, that card-playing begins in earnest to represent Peredonov's doings. The portrait of Mickiewicz winks at Peredonov from the wall; he takes it down and replaces it with one of Pushkin. "After all," he thinks, "Pushkin was a courtier" (226 [XX, 280]). Peredonov then inspects a deck of cards as if to look for something: "They did not please him because of their large eyes. The last time he had played, it had seemed to him that the cards were smirking like Varvara" (227 [XX, 281]). He then punctures the eyes of the royal ones with a pair of scissors so that they would not stare at him, all under the "eye" of the author of *The Queen of Spades!*

The letter returns in the same chapter. At the card-playing club rumors about Peredonov have snowballed, and he begins to talk arrant nonsense. He has thrown out his forbidden books, his icons are now always lit, and there are even pictures of tsars on the wall. Peredonov plays cards in which he constantly sees mocking faces; he cuts them out over and over again. The queen of spades, especially, seems to grit her teeth at him when he plays. Meanwhile, Varvara has burned the first letter from the Princess in order to more conveniently replace it with the second one. Just as the cards had whirled around Peredonov, he dances with the new letter, which now promises him three positions as inspector, in his hand. Yet there is no expression on his face; his reaction to the hyperbole "was immutable like that of a wound-up doll, and there was nothing but a devouring fire gleaming life-lessly in his eyes" (235 [XXI, 289]). Furthermore, "the sound of his words had a weird indifference about them, as though he were a stranger and far removed from what he was doing" (238 [XXI, 293]). Now he scuttles about, accosting everyone with the letter in hand, repeating that he is to become an inspector. In inverse proportion to the paradoxical appearance and content of the letters, Peredonov's self-publicity becomes more and more blatant, his clinging to the document more desperate.

But inevitably the expected promotion does not come. With his mechanized faith in the spurious written words, Peredonov now comes to believe that the Princess must recently have become displeased with him. Varvara feeds his conviction that everyone is his enemy and lets slip that the second letter is a forgery, but now Peredonov is utterly given over to this fictitious document. The letter has become a fetish, first symbolizing and finally replacing the object of desire. Peredonov sees the Princess everywhere (just as Germann had seen the Countess) in his mind, imagines that she is in love with him, or has already been his lover and wants him back. Fearing that Peredonov will do something indiscreet with the letter, Varvara steals it from him in their bed, and he now feels more lost than ever. In proportion to the hyperbolic content of the letter (offering him three jobs), Peredonov multiplies his denunciations of enemies, for now it seems to him that Rutilov, Vershina, and the others all want to be schools inspector, and in the absence of the certifying document, spies seem to lurk everywhere. It is interesting that just when Peredonov loses the object upon which his entire imagined future depended, Pushkin's text engulfs Sologub's novel. On the crest of this wave Peredonov degenerates into unmistakable pathology. We see here the projection of the author's construction of the relationship between his text and its predecessor into the plot, transplanting *The Queen of Spades* into *The Petty Demon* as the mechanism that propels it toward its ending in a way that articulates a striking parallelism between the two works.

At this stage motifs from *The Queen of Spades* renew their force. Peredonov sees dancing knaves and eights and denounces the playing-card queens. He writes to the Princess, ecstatic with the imagined death-scent she exudes. "I love you, because you are cold and distant. … She's a hundred and fifty years old," he thought, "but she has great power. And this repulsion was mingled with desire" (287 [XXV, 347].

This scene truly gives us something to ponder. In Pushkin's tale the Countess appeared in five guises: first as a young, frivolous, but already thoroughly outdated beauty of the 1770s; then as a hideous crone of the 1830s (that is, contemporaneous with the story) who is trying hard to preserve her vanished beauty; then as a corpse, a ghost, and the queen of spades in the deck of cards. In each of these cases she incarnates the past. First she has a powdered wig, rouge, and elegant outmoded dresses that already represent a bygone historical period. This is to suggest that the Countess as a genuine erotic object is already replaced, in Pushkin, by the "letter." In other words, the literary vehicle is already, by the time of the story, the only medium through which the phenomenon of the desired Countess could possess any rational existence.

Given the precedent of the Countess and her treatment by Pushkin, Peredonov's Princess is indeed 150 years old. And note how the overture of his letter to her reaches toward the lost false document of her letter to him. It is as if the tradition of far-away love were the thing satirized. Any relation between the persons of Peredonov and the Princess emerges as entirely fictitious, links in a chain of false desire that atrophies under siege by words. Peredonov's delusion reaches a climax when he substitutes the letter for the Princess, just as Germann's did when he took the apparition for the Countess. Neither character understands that he is actually confronting two distinct levels of being.

As the end of Peredonov's sanity (if we can call it that!) approaches, the Princess seems to him "already here, near, very near—perhaps in this pack of cards. Yes, undoubtedly she was either the queen of spades or the queen of hearts" (288 [XXV, 348]). In a narrative leap, or jerk, Peredonov blames the deck for his confusion and burns it. It is then that as the cards curl and disappear, the Princess arises from the fire, gray like the *nedotykomka* and wailing like the cat. It is little more than an echo of this scene when Peredonov finally burns down the building containing the great masquerade ball, still clinging to the fiction of the Princess. Taunted by Vershina, he counters, "You lie. I burned her but I didn't finish the job: she spat on me" (346 [XXII,

412]), and we are returned to the epigraph of the book, in which the witch defies burning.

First in the letter and then in the pack of cards, the Princess is indestructible, as a sign of malevolent or random deities—and as a sign of the queen of spades. In both Sologub's novel and Pushkin's tale, with its demonism, triumph of chance, and detached style, an all-important text binds the deluded protagonist to an object of desire that will betray him. *The Petty Demon* hyperbolizes the suggestion latent in *The Queen of Spades* that texts are no more reliable than their agents, who are ultimately unfathomable. Pushkin's Countess was herself always a thing of the past and yet perennial, a terrible incarnation of the eternal feminine that arouses attraction and revulsion. In Pushkin desire is turned aside; in Sologub it is blocked and that block made permanent. Sologub creates a new reality entirely out of language and uses language, in turn, to undermine already posited realities. The spurious letter plays upon Sologub's representation of *The Queen of Spades*, whose context now consists of total negativity. Where nothing is natural, nothing can be certainly supernatural, and suspicion extends (in petty fashion) to everything. Even the frantic and uneven pace of actions and events concerning the letter mimes the abruptness and bewilderment of sheer chance. Amid such darkness Peredonov can only lurch from one viewpoint to another, always changing his evaluation of the letter.

The narrative of the letter epitomizes everything about Peredonov that is derivative and spurious. For him the letter has come to replace utterly the figure of the Princess, its presence and significance, so that the reminders of Pushkin's masterpiece seem at first reading to be no more than a mocking accretion of verbiage. Because Peredonovism debases language and counterfeits logocentric standards of value, it appears, again, that a world of texts is being dismantled. They are, however, actually being problematized, prised loose from absolute authority even as that authority is called to our attention. *The Petty Demon*, its devilishness no less for being domesticized, mocks the fetishizing of words for their own sake.

So many writers, books, and snippets of citations turn up in it as to put before readers a world of classic and recent Russian literature, all of it colored and distanced from us by Peredonovism. Sologub, clearly, looks not only to French Symbolism and the European cultural patrimony but to the Russian past. Unraveling the skein of authors who stalk these pages has been very much like trying to explain a joke.

If Pushkin's world already seemed to characterize itself by a kind of negative imperative, a pull toward the negative pole, that world remains a touchstone also of positive literary authority, a paragon, a *terminus a quo* that is being addressed by a newer yet more uncertain world. Germann's machinations appear straightforward, almost chivalrous, compared with the forgeries and falsehoods of which Peredonov is composed. But the writer of whom it is aptly remarked that he "creates a powerful image of a literally God-forsaken hole [отчуждение с неба] and its presiding spirit Peredonov"[12] surely recognized in Pushkin the detachment whose sublimity provided better contrast to his own than would the more overt alienation of Gogol. Hence the proper assessment of Sologub's novel in the words of Bely: "Gogolism tending to recolor itself into Pushkinism" (1934: 291).[13] To recognize the truth of Pushkin's presence in *The Petty Demon* and to evaluate and enjoy it, no written historical evidence is needed. Pushkin's intertextual authority is monumentalized in a literariness that betokens the formative power of literary events for generations to come. The traces left by writers, and especially by Pushkin, actually constitute a point of departure for, not a result of, interpretation: a hermeneutic, a means of finding a way into the book's nonverbal context, in which false ghosts walk in true dreams.

7

DIALOGISM AND POETIC DISCOURSE

Dialogism in contemporary discussions of literary theory is a term associated with the writings of the Russian critic M. M. Bakhtin, and almost exclusively with prose fiction. The concentration on prose to the exclusion of poetry follows from Bakhtin's own identification of "pure" poetry with the extreme opposite of dialogism, monologism. "The poet is a poet insofar as he accepts the idea of a unitary, monologically sealed-off utterance," writes Bakhtin (1981: 296).[1] In Bakhtin's view, the poet achieves his aim partly by transcending the inherently dialogic nature of language; the lyric poet privileges a single voice—his own—and strives to situate his discourse in a "utopian" realm purged of all external historical and social forces (Morson and Emerson 1990: 52–53). In this chapter we wish to show, on the contrary, how poetry remains importantly "dialogistic" despite Bakhtin's own prejudices, derived, perhaps, from the residual Romanticism that tinges all Russian scholarly writing of the first half of the twentieth century. We will illustrate this point with a survey of several kinds of poetic texts that are to be analyzed by examining the role of the (sometimes implied) addressee, the unheard "other voice" that provides part of the poetic context. We argue further that there is a productive way of looking at Bakhtin by comparing dialogism with Charles Peirce's concept of semiosis, the production and interpretation of signs. Lyric poetry is a sign system in the same sense that any literary work is. To the extent that dialogism informs semiosis (as Peirce himself argues), the analysis of lyric—as well as lyric itself—will be simultaneously "dialogistic" and semiotic.

We begin in an appropriately Bakhtinian mode with a sub-literary genre—book inscriptions. Two former high school friends meet after a hiatus of 30 years. One is a child psychiatrist, the other a professor of linguistics, and both have published books in their respective fields. Shortly after their reunion they give each other inscribed copies of their most recent books, and here are the inscriptions:

> Aug 14, 1986
>   Dear Mike
>   Some things in nature,
>   Like a seed, or a spore, or a friendship,
>   May appear to be dead.
>   But everything is there, in place.
>   All that is required is
>   A change of scene, of circumstances.
>   Lee [child psychiatrist]
>
>   For Lee,
>   whose kindness and forthrightness
>   are well-remembered from boyhood and
>   mirrored in the man.
>   Mike [linguistics professor]
>   23.VIII.86.

These two inscriptions fit within the definition of a "primary genre" as sketched by Bakhtin in his seminal essay "The Problem of Speech Genres" (1986: 60–100).[2] Bakhtin's main point is that any form of ordinary linguistic communication, whether oral or written, falls into generic categories—for instance, salutations, everyday exchanges between people in close social contact, etc.—and that these bits and pieces of primary generic material are the building blocks of the more complex ("secondary") genres that are involved in the literary use of language.

Another of Bakhtin's characterizations of utterances, in terms of their "addressivity" (адресованность), also extends throughout the entire spectrum of literary and nonliterary uses of language. Yet Bakhtin himself approaches an articulated typology of verbal art chiefly (if not only) in his considerations of the novel. The usefulness of his perspective to the literary scholar, we believe, extends to poetry as well, although it is relatively neglected by his critique of the univocal text. According to Bakhtin, addressivity is a constitutive factor of every utterance. In addition, "the various typical forms this addressivity assumes and the various concepts of the addressee are constitutive, definitive features of the various speech genres" (SG 98). Thus dialogism is simultaneously the condition of all language and a means of categorizing discrete types of discourse. All utterances presuppose potential responses; however, the different ways in which utterances elicit responses vary according to subject matter, context, and the situation, social position, and personal interrelations of the participants.

Every concrete utterance, for Bakhtin, is linked to others within a similar sphere or horizon of communication governed by addressivity. Specific examples of verbal art are to be studied in the light of kinds of addressivity as Bakhtin conceives them, with the aim of examining more closely poetic roles as played out on both sides of the text:

The addressee can be an immediate participant-interlocutor in an everyday dialogue, a differentiated collective of specialists in some area of cultural
communication, a more or less differentiated public,
ethnic group, contemporaries, like-minded people, op-
ponents and enemies, a subordinate, a superior, someone who is lower, higher, familiar, foreign, and so forth.
And it can be an indefinite, unconcretized other (with
various kinds of monological utterances of an emotional type). (SG 95)

This list contains four main types: immediate interlocutors,
differentiated collectives, less differentiated publics, and an unconcretized other. We will attempt to preserve the open character of the list in the spirit of Bakhtin's attachment to an "analytic"
history in preference to a "systematic" one (Todorov 1984: 92).
It is to be expected that hybrid "genres" will ensue from the attempt to locate them in kinds of reception.

The book inscriptions with which we began are, of course,
the printed reproduction of originals that were handwritten, the
immediate practical consequence of which is the unavoidable
loss of potentially significant information. Each of the writers
also would have relied on a wealth of knowledge about his partner in the exchange (personal history, specimens of earlier behavior, attitudes, expectations, etc.) which helped shape its
dialogic character. The process of interpreting these messages is
generally not intended as an exercise in cryptanalysis but rather
one of "reading the signs," much as a diagnostician might regard
a patient's symptoms or a detective clues—that is, in a process
defined essentially by inferences that are educated guesses.

The first inscription, dated "Aug 14, 1986," has chronological priority and is in a form that approximates poetry, for it appears in lines with initial words capitalized. In view of the fact
that the message is addressed to a linguistics professor—who, it

should be added, teaches language and literature—we can perhaps ascribe the poetic form to a desire on the psychiatrist's part to accommodate the verbal expression to his interlocutor's professional persona. This is one overt way of beginning to bridge the gap created by 30 years of non-communication, since it is a move in the direction of the addressee that is in one sense subordinative: the psychiatrist might be suppressing his habitually "scientific" speech mode, including a brisk matter-of-factness, in the interest of reestablishing a channel of communication. However, even this relatively minor phatic feature provides a nutshell illustration of the essence of dialogism, because the text (in its linear form) has been constructed with the author's representation of his addressee's persona, against which the purport of the form is to be perceived and evaluated. The opening "Dear" may be regarded either as an expressionless token, a purely conventional epistolary feature, or as a word that has been energized by the impulse to overcome the circumstances of temporal disjunction between the former friends. Note that this opening need not have been deployed by design: it is enough that this otherwise debased word still retains the potential of giving rise to an interpretation with an emotively revivified meaning.

With a written text, punctuation marks may be significant in ways other than the conventional one of signaling syntactic and intonational boundaries,[3] and the first inscription seems to contain instances of this. The absence of a period after the abbreviation of the month ("Aug") and of a comma after the addressee's name ("Dear Mike") may be seen to cohere with an attitude that chooses to dispense with redundancies and gets to the core of signification without unnecessary formality. "Aug" is after all immediately recognizable as an abbreviation without the redundant period. And since "Dear Mike" is set off from the body of the inscription by space, why duplicate the function of spacing with a comma? The absence of these marks is a sign of a certain insouciance, an eschewal of formality devoid of function.

But there is a relative absence of punctiliousness on the part of the first transcription's author in yet another respect: randomness of punctuation. Yes, he does omit the appropriate marks in the two cases just discussed, but he also does not fail to put them in their appointed places in the body of the text. Why? Besides randomness as a value, perhaps the reason behind the completely conventional punctuation in the body of the inscription is conditioned by the fact that, despite its looseness, it is still intended as an assimilation to poetry, a more formal mode of discourse. It is one thing to countenance randomness or spontaneity or informality as a value, but to omit punctuation in a poem that is being offered up as part of a dialogic appeal would be to risk overstepping the boundaries of behavior concerning which the author has no secure knowledge due to the hiatus in the friendship. Looseness here could be taken as an insult, an outcome incompatible with the affective goal of the transaction—a gift, moreover a gift "made" with one's own "hands."

In view of the placement of the date and the recognizable epistolary character of the opening, the author of the first inscription obviously intended to have his message take the form of a letter. Since letters as a matter of custom occasion or invite a response, one implication of this particular generic choice might be that the psychiatrist expected something in return from the professor, an expectation that was duly fulfilled nine days later when he was presented with his friend's own inscribed book. But the author of the second inscription does not follow formal suit: his message is not epistolary. As a sign inhering in a pervasively dialogic context, this fact may indicate something about the second writer's own habits with regard to the form of the inscription genre; or it could signify that he does not wish to assimilate himself to the first writer, thereby maintaining a measure of independence or contrariness that might be characteristic of him generally, not just as an ad hoc reaction occasioned by the particular circumstances.

There is one accommodative trait, however, that betrays a solidarity between the writers. The second inscription is not a poem, but it does resort to a syntactic parallelism of sorts ("well-remembered ... and mirrored") that seems to be an acknowledging bow in the direction of the first inscription's avowedly rhetorical stance, a stylistic response that lends itself without difficulty to identification as being induced by dialogism. The reaction is determined both as to form and content by the utterance that elicited it.

All kinds of inferences could be drawn from the relative lengths of the inscriptions. The wordiness of the first is not just the result of the enchained repetitions ("like a seed, like a spore, or a friendship"; "everything is there, in place"; "a change of scene, of circumstances") but of a general mind-set that requires a broad canvas. In orienting himself toward the genre of the book inscription, the first author has superimposed onto it the genre of the friendly letter, hence the length of the utterance as part of its form. This superimposition of one genre on another articulates a dominance relation between them: the letter is a friendlier form with a greater emotive value than a plain inscription. In reestablishing contact with his boyhood friend, the psychiatrist has apparently chosen to stress friendliness in an indirect reference to their shared past. This attitude makes the first inscription more personal in tone, signifying an affect that appears to be missing from the answering inscription.

The second inscription is notable not only for its relative brevity but also for its unwillingness to respond in kind. What seems to be valued by the second writer is not what may remain *from* the past (cf. the first text's "everything is there") but what is remembered *in* the past. The primary focus for the second writer is their shared boyhood. By totally ignoring the assimilation of relations between people to that of natural phenomena so prominent in the diction of the first text, the author of the second is evidently responding in a very different voice. The dialogue, then, only represents a convergence in a limited sense, and the antiphonal quotient is much stronger than might be apparent at first glance. The psychiatrist, in line with his textual espousal of randomness, explains the rekindling of an old friendship as the work of chance. All that something appearing to be "dead" needs in order to be resuscitated is "a change of scene, of circumstances." The element of chance is heightened by the semantic indeterminacy of the bland phrases chosen—clichés, really.

These inscriptions belong essentially to Bakhtin's first type of addressivity involving immediate participants. They also instantiate his concept of primary or "preliterary"—more accurately, "subliterary"—genres. Here it happens that the partners in the exchange of utterances are actually in close spatio-temporal proximity to each other and to the occurrence of the speech act, so that the example can be said not to refer at all to Bakhtin's three other kinds of addressivity.

In its simplest and purest form the dialogic character of utterances is represented by those that typically *require* a response (verbal or non-verbal). Questions, commands, and varieties of appeal fit this category. The latter two kinds—grammatically, imperatives and vocatives—are subsumed by Jakobson's so-called conative (better: hortative) function of language oriented toward the addressee (Jakobson 1960: 355).

Extended appeals that resort to commands at crucial points are manifested by folk-literary formulas that are among the most ancient known examples of verbal art: incantations or magic spells (Toporov 1969: 11). Among the Indo-European languages, texts that allow the reconstruction of an Indo-European poetics of magic spells are particularly well preserved in the Slavic area, of which a good representative for our purposes is Russian. In Russian these incantatory utterances (*заговоры* or *заклинания*) were most frequently employed to rid human beings of disease or its symptoms, including the evil eye (Bogatyrev 1956: 256). The pronunciation of a spell was accompanied by movements or gestures that were among the repertoire of folk medicine (such as subjecting a sick person to a steam bath while incanting). The close link between ritual and verbal performance can be seen in the frequent iconic relation between word and act, as when some part of the content of the incantation is simultaneously acted out by the utterer. Here the movements or gestures are just as much units of discourse as are the words.

The imperative mode is the typical grammatical vehicle for spells, and the addressee is commonly anthropomorphized, so that a disease, for example, is appealed to as if it possessed human powers of volition (Bogatyrev 1956: 258–63). From the dialogic standpoint one can begin to understand such instances as being directed to an addressee that constitutes the projection of the human utterer, either ad hoc or in alignment with ritual protocols established by the community. The addressee can "answer" even if nonhuman by performing the action being commanded or requested in the magic formula. The folk in Russia in fact commonly spoke of disease in the same terms as of a human actor. These incantations are therefore paradigm cases of the first category of addressivity.

There is a natural connection between magical spells and incantations and the more familiar modern version, prayer. Whereas incantations have to be uttered in at least a whisper if not aloud to be considered effective, prayers can be said silently. The addressees, however, are somewhat analogous in that incantations are addressed to an object which the addresser wishes to move by words, as does a prayer addressed to God. Despite their differences, incantations and prayers both exemplify Bakhtin's first category in that they are addressed to an immediate participant or interlocutor. In the context of a religious community, where people gather to pray together, the private is commingled with the public in such a way as to produce the hybrid of first and third categories, now including an "ethnic" or "like-minded" group.

The genres just discussed have explicit addressees. This puts them in contrast with the most familiar and nonpareil religious text, the Bible. Without entering into the complex matter of all its forms of address, it is instructive to note that the kind of dialogism informing biblical discourse emanates from its feature of formal parallelism of verses, which itself constitutes *interior* dialogue. Among modern investigators of Hebrew poetics, James Kugel and Robert Alter have shown that parallelism is only part of the picture, and that the apparent dyads of lines in parallel actually shape a paronomastic and cumulative series (Alter 1965, Kugel 1981). In Kugel's particularly felicitous terms, the speaker is saying not "A = B" (as, according to Kugel, Bishop Lowth would have it) but "A—what's more, B." This situation corresponds nicely to Bakhtin's idea that utterances complete each other in the sense of filling out the discourse, a non-additive accumulation of meaning. In this example from Jeremiah 12 (New International Version), "Why does the way of the wicked prosper? / Why do all the faithless live at ease?," the parallel words lead the reader to meditate on one colon in the light of the other through the combined similarity and divergence of meanings. Regardless of what one makes of the second colon, the relationship between the two cola is what constitutes dialogism. The relation itself, however, is an implicit third element that is often not brought out in analysis.

Each of the three examples of poetic dialogism that follow here falls within Bakhtin's first category, that of immediate interlocutors. The extent to which they differ, however, in terms of their participation in more public and general kinds of social interaction, is particularly instructive with respect to the potential development of each individual poetic current, and to the involvement in each of ideological material in the broad sense.

While all dialogues according to Bakhtin are composed of utterances, they are also situated in communicative contexts that create a spirit of contrast or (even) rivalry. One of the consequences is a certain amount of disharmony, even an agonistic movement among utterances. Remembering this along with the precise *Wörter und Sachen* backdrop may help us demystify one of the most famously enigmatic fragments of Heraclitus:[4]

> ou xyniasin hokōs diaferomenon heoutoi homologeei palintropos harmoniē hokōsper toxou kai lyres.

> (They do not comprehend how a thing agrees at variance with itself [literally: how being brought apart it is brought together with itself]; it is an attunement turning back on itself, like that of the bow and the lyre.)

This fragment is typical of Heraclitus' *forma mentis* in that it begins with a negation ("They do not comprehend") that seems to be a polemical retort to and denial of some prior position held by others. This immediately engages dialogism as a constitutive principle of the form of Heraclitus' utterance (in just the Bakhtinian sense). Leaving aside the phrase "at variance with itself" for the moment, what is crucial to the interpretation of the whole fragment is the combination *palintropos harmoniē* (backward-turning structure/attunement/connection). The original sense of *harmoniē* seems to have been joining or fitting together, and that is the way it is used by Homer and Herodotus among others in the context of carpentry or shipbuilding. But *harmoniē* also has from the beginning a figurative meaning— "agreements" or "compacts" between hostile men (as in the *Iliad*)—from which it can move to the connotation of reconciliation (personified, for instance, as the child of Ares and Aphrodite in Hesiod's *Theogony*). Finally, *harmoniē* occurs in the familiar musical sense of the "fitting together" of different strings to produce the desired scale or key.

The notion of overcoming strife or conflict associated with *harmoniē* suggests a possible connection with the institution of poetic competitions in early Greek literature, in which a contest between choirs is basically a contest between poets.[5] Although there is no overt description in Homer, other sources provide a clear idea of the trajectory that a poetic competition followed: first, an exchange of metricized philosophical questions and answers; next, completion of a couplet begun by an opponent; finally, recitation of complete verse passages. (A modified example of this procedure is available in Aristophanes' *Frogs*, in which accuracy is sacrificed to comic effect.) From the viewpoint of a reconstructed Indo-European poetics it is interesting to note the relevance of the Vedic Indian tradition (Dunkel 1979: 254–64). The Rig-Veda contains information about numerous bitter rivalries between families of poet-priests who competed with each other for a god's favor by means of invocations (simultaneous or sequential), or by testing each other via metricized pieces of theological or philosophical wisdom.

The comparison with Vedic is instructive because both Vedic and Greek texts employ the terminology and imagery of war or battles in describing verbal jousting (as in the *Iliad*). On one hand, there is a somewhat paradoxical relation for Homer between talking and fighting, as if these two actions were diametrical opposites that are conjoined to signify the totality of possible modes of action (*Il.* 1.258, 2.202, 9.53–54). On the other hand, they imply each other through the common factor of prowess. The presence or absence of prowess in one action may imply the same in the other (e.g., *Il.* 2.337–38, 13.7278). In verbal conflict both occur simultaneously, as in a quarrel, a council, or a poetic competition. A martial vocabulary thus comes to be applied to verbal conflict.

When Heraclitus says of *palintropos harmoniē* that it is "like that of the bow and lyre," one can take it as a description of physical events that apply to these two "instruments" with respect to the movement of a string in each case: the string returns to a state of rest after being drawn or plucked, and harmony is thereby reestablished (Robinson 1987: 116). Although this explanation is not countermanded by any other and does not itself contradict any figuratively oriented one, still the fragment might be more generally explicated by referring it to the cultural circumstances of a poetic competition.[6] It would, in other words, represent a Heraclitean figuration of the polyphonic nature of speech—and, by extension, of men and the world—all of which are in their essence defined by a form of conflict that requires an ultimate resolution. If one were to say (with Kahn) that Heraclitus is the first great master of artistic prose, then he might also be called the first polyphonic author.

For modern readers (let alone for Heraclitus) the word *palintropos* could allude to the figurative meaning of bow and lyre in virtue of its use of -*tropos* ('turning') to configure tropes or metaphors. "A thing at variance with itself" would be a particularly apt and profound way of describing the ontology of a trope, in which the opposition of figural and literal meaning must simultaneously be present and resolved.

A text of this sort requires the same approach one would take to poetry. The specific context of a poetic competition as a working hypothesis may even have helped penetrate its ideological purport. The idea of a contest or polemic seems to vie with the lyric impulse. There is, however, a marked contrast between attitudes such as this in the Western and Eastern poetic tradition.

Whereas the Heraclitean "contest" involves the two contenders or contending parties directly in dialogue, it also gathers into its purview a "differentiated collective of specialists" in a given cultural communication scenario. It seeks in secondary degree to elicit the response of those in the know and simultaneously to enhance group solidarity among them. Our second example of verbal art, Japanese linked verse, similarly engages the two categories while emphasizing the first, but it lacks the overtly agonistic element. *Renga* (literally, 'linked songs') and *haikai* ('ribald harmony') are related poetic forms unique to Japan that reached their apogee in the fifteenth and sixteenth and the sixteenth and seventeenth centuries, respectively; both have histories spanning several centuries into the modern period.[7] The upper unit of a renga stanza is three lines, the lower unit two. The poems were typically composed by two or three poets at a single sitting, working in alternation to compose a given number, which can be in the thousands but normally runs to one hundred stanzas. The form of the renga had already been set by the Kamakura period (ca. 1185–1382). Its successor, the haikai, usually runs to 36 stanzas but is otherwise composed of exactly the same stanzaic unit. Many of the renga masters were priests by training, since priests could function ideally as intermediaries between the classes within a rigid system, enjoying a social freedom that combined with literary strength and the respected status of teacher. Renga poetry "became a craze" *(JLP 13)* around the time that famous practitioners like Sōgi (1421–1502) or Bashō (1644–1694) were in their ascendance. Early on, poets increased the resonance and meaningfulness of their craft by incorporating allusions to other poems (as well as to prose classics). Thus intertextuality prospered on many levels.

Renga are linked in a continuity at each point of juncture but are otherwise discontinuous. The same stanza may, for instance, first be spoken by a man in connection with its predecessor and be altered by its successor to be spoken as by a woman. Often the meanings conveyed are changed quite drastically. There are many means of joining the links which do not touch. The renga stanza has related but distinguishable existences: (1) as an individual poetic unit; (2) as a stanza combining with its predecessor to make a single poem; and (3) as a stanza combined with successors to make another single poem.

A given stanza possesses nothing integral with any other stanza. Only the initial stanza, called *hokku* (which later became the well-known *haiku* form), has no predecessor; only the last stanza has no other added to it. Linkage is effected in many ways: parts can be determined by the method of setting them down on folded sheets of paper; they can be defined by topics that may run beyond two stanzas or be repeated for seven or a hundred; they can be linked by a "rhythm" derived from music. The stanzas making up linked semantic integers, each with two others, also possess semantic integrity as part of a whole sequence, where wholeness derives not merely from immediate connection but from sequence otherwise meaningfully conceived. That is to say, linked poetry is a kind of plotless narrative that follows the curve of feeling and response.

The importance of sequence and response comes from the poetics of Japanese classical literature. "If Western poetics originated in the Greek encounter with drama … Japanese poetics (like Chinese) derives from encounter with lyric poetry" (*JLP* 5–6). Linked poetry is one particularly conspicuous example of a fundamental lack of interest in mimesis or representation in East Asian literature, in which respect it contrasts most openly with Western literature (Miner 1981: 376). It is fitting that the two central terms of classical Japanese poetics characterize the axioms of affectivity and expressivity: "'Kokoro' means heart, mind, or spirit—the human capacity to be affected and to understand. 'Kotoba' means words, languages, signs, or techniques—the human capacity to make known to others what has been gained by the kokoro" (*JLP* 6).

The renga's inner narrative of feeling seeks to elicit a response, which propels it forward. Some sequences even begin with the lower, or two-line, part of the stanza—as if already to open with a response. An original poem could lead to a poetic response centuries later when recalled by another poet. So compelling is the response accorded a great poem that a long series of poems might be generated from it. The practice presumes that proper reply—adequate expression—testifies to proper capacities for being affected. Being moved and being led to expression define poetic activity. The cries of animals and bird songs could move one to respond with a poem, just as would the prior poem of a friend. For such reasons the essential character of extended literature is in fact assumed to be responsive sequence. "Matters such as being subject to an Elizabethan humor or a ruling passion or *idée fixe* do not enter" *(JLP* 7). The consistency of human character is to be found not in a dramatic consistency but in the capacity to respond appropriately.

The factor making linked poetry genuinely feasible is multiple authorship at a sitting, which requires not only that all poets participating be capable of creating good poetry but that they know each other's ways well enough to do so together.[8] The naturalness comes from affective stimulus, which derives in turn from a world view conceived in largely Shintō or Buddhist terms, where other animals and even spirits were considered to be susceptible to feelings, and birds expressed themselves in song. There is some resemblance to the Western medieval conception of a whole world perfused by signs. Japanese linked poetry, however, does not consist, as Western poetry often may, of expostulation and reply but of more subtle continuances and sequences posited on the very incompleteness of a poetic process. The openness of such a process is both maintained and governed by the very great number of rules of composition.

Even those formal traits that are easily accessible to Western readers enhance the fluidity of renga. When looking at the examples below, note that the translator has deliberately omitted punctuation, partly because it would compromise the polysemy within one stanza that is gained by an absence of boundaries. Here is the most famous renga opening from the collection called *One Hundred Stanzas by Three Poets at Minase (Minase Sangin Hyakuin):*

Yuki nagara	Despite some snow
yamamoto kasumu	the base of hills spreads with haze
yube kana	the twilight scene
	(JLP 185)

Yoshimoto, one of the greatest renga masters along with the author of the above example, Sōgi, wrote that connection is the poetry of renga. The following example by Kyūzai shows two kinds of connection:

Monofu no	Mount Tonami
tate o narabaru	standing like shields aligned
Tonamiyama—	by warrior hands—
nami ni katabuku	into the waves there slowly slips
yumihari no tsuki	the moon curved like a full drawn bow
	(JLP 22)

The assonance and consonance in *tonamiyama/nami ni*, together with the military imagery, constitute the two kinds of connection. The greatest of the renga masters, Sōgi, distinguished between poems of words (*kotoba no haikai*) and poems of thought (*kokoro no haikai*), a distinction somewhat similar to Quintilian's *figura sententiae* and *verborum* ('figure of thought/speech'). For the Japanese, however, *kotoba no haikai* would prove practically untranslatable because it is based on wordplay. Here is a stanza from a poem of thought by Sōgi:

Namida oba	The tears let fall
oni mo oto suto	show that even demons weep
kiku mono o—	by the sound one hears—
—kawara no ame no	—upon the roof tiles the rain
akatsuki no koe.	gives forth the voice of dawn.
	(JLP 39)

Linkage between juxtaposed units results from topical similarity or affinity of mood; from a more precise relation of diction and imagery; or the return of certain motifs. In each case the immediately contiguous units constitute the dialogue.

The renga as a poetic form differs fundamentally from all Western types of linked poetry (like the sestina or the "crown of sonnets") in that the links are made exclusively by stanzas in juxtaposition to each other. By contrast the Western forms are irradiated by one plan.

These Japanese lyric series are motivated without the overt idea of a contest though they do make response to external stimuli and occasions. They lack the rhetorical thrust of persuasion or an aspiration to dominance, in part because there was no tradition of public speaking in Japan to promote the development of oratory. Perhaps the most vivid contrast we could find in the West is that of Provençal troubadour lyric.

The Provençal lyric, especially in its earliest known manifestations, typifies much of the agonistic stance represented by Greek poetic contests. However, the contrastive focus of much of the poetry applies not only to the immediate participant-interlocutor (as often does occur explicitly) but to the kind of interior dialogue found in biblical parallelism and less obviously in prayer. The poems polemicize within themselves and often proceed from *sic-et-non* ('yes-and-no') types of argumentation. Such internal disagreement engages the opinions of a "differentiated collective of specialists," Bakhtin's second category, but also comes to include his third: a "more-or-less differentiated public, ethnic group, contemporaries, like-minded people." Even poems that seem obscure to modern scholars confronted with the task of uncovering their references must be understood to discuss the concerns of illiterate and carousing lords and ladies, or the political wrangles of their times. The personal interrelations of the poet and his implied audience range over a whole listening public. At the same time the corpus of poems retains, in the large, its unity as a cultural artifact, thereby evading Bakhtin's fourth category of participant, the "undifferentiated, unconcretized other."

The first known troubadour, William of Aquitaine (Guillem Comte do Peiteus), already seems to be polemicizing with an opponent represented through another, prior poem or set of poems when in his mysterious riddle he announces that he will make verse out of absolutely nothing:[9]

Farai un vers de	I will make a verse of
dreyt nien:	absolutely nothing;
Non er de mi ni	it will not be about myself
d'autra gen,	or other people,
Non er d'amor ni	nor about love or
de joven,	youth,
Ni de ren au...	or anything else...

(APT 2)

This little incipit repudiates what appear to be conventional topics in antecedent Provençal verse.

It makes little difference whether the argumentation seeks to persuade the listener to love or war, but simple exhortation is almost never enough. From the outset the poet answers an implied opponent, who may be in the most obvious case another poet, or a coveted woman, but more subtly a whole set of values in which something is found either sufficient or wanting. Another of William's poems begins:

Pos de chanter m'es	Since I feel like singing,
pres talentz,	I will make a
Farai un vers,	verse, for I feel grief:
don sui dolenz:	but I will not obey
Mais non serai obedienz	

(APT 9)

The reference is to the obedience engaged in by a servant of love, who makes himself the humble follower and his lady a lord.[10] Even the ethic of courtly love itself is based on a reversal.[11]

Of course, troubadour poetry is replete with works that express joy or nostalgia or delight in a new spring season. But even in such cases most of the poems open against the counter pull of a difficulty overcome, or a distaste for the present. Many begin with a series of negatives, for example the following, by another of the earliest and likewise instantly communicative troubadours, Jaufre Rudel:

No sap chanter qui so non di,	He cannot sing who utters no note, nor
Ni vers trobar qui motz no fa make	verses, who says no words, nor
Ni conois de rime co•s va	does he know how rhymes should go,
Si razo non enten en si.	unless he feels the whole form within himself.
Mas lo mieus chans comers' aissi	But my song begins as you will
Com plus l'auziretz, mais valra,	hear, and will really be worth something.
a a.	

(APT, 35)

Like the composers of renga, these troubadour poets have been moved to response, and they expect to be judged by the quality and aptness of the response they evoke in turn. But the stimulus is not in nature, or not in nature alone. Their verse enters from the start into a rhetorical crossfire. The practical background of much of this yields plenty of actual rivalry and mutual insult among troubadours, which played itself out in actual courts and jockeying for material security and aristocratic patronage. These realia also affect the proliferation of verse satires by poets about each other.

Both rhetorical argumentation and sheer delight in oppositional word-making occur in concert with external rivalry, as happens in the genre known as the *tenso* (< L *contentio*). It is like the Latin *conflictus* in the sense of being a debate poem, but the *tenso* is composed by two or more poets in succession—like the renga.[12] It is constructed as a dialogue, maintaining the same rhymes and meter throughout. The poem may have a rigorously debated subject matter but could instead consist of a running exchange of insults. Among the poets who indulged in the latter and extended the form (together with his partner) to include eight full sonnets was Dante. Other poets debated such standard subjects as the value of love, the active versus the contemplative life, and so on.

Many poems were composed by single poets in the form of a *tenso*; these include one between God and a renegade monk. The *tenso* form shows its filiation with the *conflictus*, which was composed by one person. The spirit of scholastic disputation often takes over even those poems that have an amorous subject, and it is then related to the fiction of the Court of Love. Sometimes two contenders will present their opening views for judgment by a patron or beloved woman, or one will take a *sic-et-non* attitude and switch positions in midair.

Some *tensos* begin in the midst of things, taking into account an already assumed position on the part of the person being challenged by the opening speaker. Here is an example by Raimbaut d'Aurenga in which the subject is the superiority or inferiority of difficult versus easy poetry:

Ara•m platz, Giraut de Borneill,	Now I'd like to know, Giraut de Borneill,
Que sapcha per c'anatz	why and wherefore

blasman	you go about blaming
Trobar clus, ni per cal semblan.	hermetic [closed] poetry.
Aiso·m digaz	So tell me why you value
Si tan prezatz	something that is so
So que es a toz comunal;	common to everyone that
Car adonc tut seran egual.	it makes everyone equal.

(APT 72)

Giraut de Bornelh answers this strophe by appealing to the practical benefits and larger audience accorded to accessible poets:

Seign'en Lignaura, no•m coreill	Lord Lignaura, don't quarrel with me if
Si qecs sti trob'a son talan.	everyone finds his own way according
Mas eu son jujaire d'aitan	to preference. I can judge so far:
Qu'es mais amatz	whoever composes in a light, easy way
E plus prezatz	is more loved and valued; and don't
Qui•l fa levet e venarsal;	turn that against me.
E vos no m'o tornetz a mal.	

(APT 72)

The tenso is indeed a fit genre for debaters about the proper degree of specialization for the lyric. What these two are discussing refers directly to the latitude of their projected publics. The poem constitutes not only a professional argument aired in private but a debate within the area of specialists that could be overheard by the public at large, which could then take sides, completing the circle. Rather than give voice to a desire for concord, the tenso vents feelings of conflict and hones the rhetorical skills of antagonists, in this case of poets with contrasting attitudes toward the larger public. Western lyric tradition, at least in the Romance-speaking countries, continued throughout the Middle Ages to encourage frank and open debate concerning the nature of its public, an area of strife that came to involve even the famous question of the very language to be utilized for poetry. Japanese verse by comparison evinces no tension between the learned and the plebeian, the smaller versus the larger public. In addition, whereas Provençal lyricists came to imitate openly certain canonical models, even to the extent that prompted parody and satire, the intertextuality of Japanese linked verse is more organic, springing from the verbal level itself as links gradually joined the chain. The continuance of certain rhyme sounds from poem to poem—by the same or different lyricists—did not, in Provençal lyric, betray a comparable degree of group solidarity among the participants. While a more detailed comparison of the two traditions lies beyond the scope of this chapter, it should already be clear that these features, along with the concomitant of a larger or smaller public, greater or lesser intimacy and unity, emerge forcefully in the light of Bakhtin's concept of addressivity.

Posing the question of the addressee has helped clarify important differences between two poetic traditions, but beyond this Bakhtin's own discussion of dialogism in the novel, viewed together with the question of addressivity, promotes an understanding of the very nature of lyric communication. His conception of the "superaddressee" (надада́ресат), to which we now turn, shows that dialogism is not confined to the realia of a relation between two things but always presupposes a third. This may come down to the construal of a dyadic relation by a third "participant," the superaddressee. At the outset, it is the theological derivation of the concept that provides access to it:

> The person who understands inevitably becomes a third party in the dialogue. ... Any utterance always has

an addressee ... whose responsive understanding the author of the speech seeks and surpasses. This is the second party. ... But in addition to this second party, the author of the utterance, with a greater or lesser awareness, presupposes a higher superaddressee, whose absolutely just responsive understanding is presumed, either in some metaphysical distance or in distant historical time. ... In various ages and with various understandings of the world, this superaddressee and his ideally true responsive understanding assume various ideological expressions (God, absolute truth, the court of human conscience, the court of history, and so forth). (SG 126)

The superaddressee can be construed as a kind of virtual third that ultimately eclipses the addressees with which we have been dealing. This third element is what allows utterances to be integrated into a contexture, in a process that involves matching bits and pieces, very much like the one we utilized in the discussion of the two book inscriptions. To match utterances in dialogistic movements also means to complete them at least provisionally. While Bakhtin takes utterances to be complete in some fundamental sense in order that they may function as discourse units, literary utterances compose a much lesser quotient of "completedness" (*завершенность*) than those that belong to the primary genres of ordinary communication. What this implies for interpretation is that the polyphony characteristic of actual literary utterances always carries with it the dynamic process of mutual completion, through which meanings grow cumulatively toward fuller understanding.

We would like to propose a fifth category of addressee for lyric poems: the first person speaker ("the lyric I") himself. This is no sophistry: the dialogic character of semiosis has as its limiting case communication between two participants that are no more than the self of one moment appealing to another or deeper self for assent, different phases of the ego.

On the scale of worldmaking poems, the outstanding example of this category is that of Dante, who conversed and polemicized in *The Divine Comedy* with the former self, and the text imaged forth in his other self-commentary, *The New Life*, and (as is well known) in all of his works. The projection of character in the *Comedy* substitutes various phases of one ego for each other in a tireless questioning that eludes simple classification of author/character. Each self becomes a partner in the activity of being.[13] Yet the series is cumulative, not additive; progresses toward semantic exhaustiveness; and continues potentially far beyond the text. In his book on Dostoevsky's poetics, Bakhtin also noticed this feature and singled out Dante as the only writer whose "gift" as a polyphonist is equal to that of his hero (Bakhtin 1984: 30).

Human beings have a fundamental desire to have their utterances interpreted (or "heard," as Bakhtin put it [SG 163–64]), which makes intentionality of discourse inalienable from the dialogic character of communication. One might wish to say that words are tokens of intentionality by virtue of their interpretability. But it is obvious that words in and of themselves have no intentionality whatever. By themselves they are "thinglike" (SG 164).

A way out of this problem might be to propose that the intentionality of both words and interpretations is due to the relation of one to the other. This would locate intentionality squarely where it belongs dialogically—in the semiotic process (semiosis) rather than in any of its constituents (Short 1981: 204). When it comes to verbal art in particular, we can also conclude that the locus of intentionality is neither in the author nor in the reader—least of all in the text—but rather in the matching, converging, or "fitting together" (*harmoniē*) of utterances.

Bakhtin's advocacy of a third element (the superaddressee) helps integrate dialogism into the larger context of literature as a kind of semiosis—the word the modern founder of sign theory, Charles Sanders Peirce, used to mean both sign action and sign interpretation. One of the foundational ideas behind Peirce's theory is that all thought (which for Peirce is a kind of semiosis) is dialogic, by which he aligns himself squarely with Plato (W1:172):[14]

> It is first of all needful, or at least highly desirable, that the reader should have thoroughly assimilated, in all its parts, the truth that thinking always proceeds in the form of a dialogue—a dialogue between the different phases of the ego—so that, being dialogical, it is essentially composed of signs, as its matter, in the sense in which a game of chess has the chessmen for its matter. Not that the particular signs employed *are* themselves the thought! Oh, no, no whit more than the skins of an onion are the onion (about as much so, however). One selfsame thought can be carried upon the vehicle of English, German, Greek or Gaelic; in diagrams, or in equations, or in graphs: all these are but so many skins of the onion, its inessential accidents. Yet that the thought should have *some* possible expression for *some* possible interpreter, is the very being of its being... . (4.6)[15]

On Peirce's view, to be a sign is to have, actually or potentially, some more or less definite function in a dialogue. The requirement that there be at the least a potential reference to an utterer and an interpreter in order that the full understanding of a sign be possible commits Peirce simultaneously to the dialogic character of semiosis and to the conception of sign theory as a theory of communication (Brock 1975). This conception necessarily involves a third element in sign action, relating, representing, or mediating between sign and object, which Peirce calls "interpretant" (a term he coined). Semiosis is in effect the process of something being interpreted as a sign of something else, which presupposes a triadic relation between sign, object, and interpretant consisting in the *potentiality* something has for being so interpreted (corresponding to Bakhtinian "openness").

According to the Bakhtinian formulation, "in the process of generation, the content being generated also generates" (Medvedev and Bakhtin 1979: 95). In an analogous sense, poems are always situated in a series of semioses defined by preexistent poems and the newly generated resonances between them and their predecessors. The telos of this process, whether it be called dialogism or semiosis, is understanding. Lyric poetry, like any literary discourse, is composed of signs which create in the mind of an addressee "an equivalent sign, or perhaps a more developed sign," as Peirce defines the interpretant (2.228). As noted by a recent commentator, the dialogic act may be seen to comprise three elements: the *dialogic object* (the telos of communicative interaction), the *dialogue* proper (the social and historical interchange determined by the dialogic object), and the *communicational interpretant* (Hardwick 1977: 96), which would describe for readers of poetry the state of temporary resolution or tentative closure determined by dialogic interaction (Kent 1989: 224–25). We conclude that the Bakhtinian idea of dialogism is subsumed by and productively amplifies the concept of semiosis, and that the communicative aspect of lyric is fundamentally dialogistic despite Bakhtin's relegation of pure poetry to the category of monologism.

8

PUSHKIN'S POETIC MENTORS

LOMONOSOV

Although much has been written about Pushkin's views of Lomonosov and of his possible indebtedness to Russia's "first lyric poet" (as Pushkin himself called Lomonosov), a completely satisfying assessment of the relationship may be permanently out of reach.[1] Perhaps one fundamental reason for this situation is the contradictory nature of Pushkin's pronouncements concerning Lomonosov, whose predominantly negative tone and content have inclined Pushkinists to give the whole matter rather short shrift. One might rationalize Pushkin's negative reaction to Lomonosov's poetry by remembering that Lomonosov's baroque sensibility clashed with Pushkin's classicist educational background and resultant taste in literature; Pushkin, for example, had little use for the "frenetic" school (Victor Hugo, Jules Janin, et al.) of his own time, since it was too "baroque." The baroque style of sharp contrast, blatant overstatement, ornamentalism, "metaphysical" (i.e., "far-fetched") imagery, and the rest simply did not appeal to Pushkin.

We can hardly understand Pushkin's critical stance in this age of Lomonosov's renewed appeal to us as modern readers without recourse to literary-historical reasons. The simple passage of time allows us the luxury of a considerable historical distance from Lomonosov that was denied to Pushkin, in many ways a man of the eighteenth century. In the same way Belinsky, as perceptive a critic as any, said that he could not understand Derzhavin. It is obvious that Derzhavin was for Belinsky in the same limbo as Lomonosov was for Pushkin: not close enough to appreciate as a contemporary, not far enough to evaluate with historical detachment.

Chronologically, Pushkin's critical comments are extant in his letters and articles beginning in 1824.[2] In the poetry we have reactions starting a decade earlier that are, moreover, positive. In fact Pushkin's debut as a published poet, "К дгругу стихотворцу" (To a Poet-Friend) (1814), written when he was still a student of the Lycée, contains the following lines (echoing Batiushkov's "Мои пенаты" (My Penates) [1811–12]):[3]

Меж тем как Дмитриев, Державин, Ломоносов,
Певцы бессмертные, и честь и слава россов

(Whereas Dmitriev, Derzhavin, Lomonosov,
Immortal singers [poets], the honor and glory of the
    Russians)

During this early period when Pushkin's literary outlook is dominated by an adherence to the positions of the Arzamas society (particularly Zhukovskii and Batiushkov), he refers in "К Жуковскому" (To Zhukovskii) (1816) to Sumarokov's envy of Lomonosov in the following terms:

Ему ли, карлику, тягаться с исполином?
Ему ль оспоривать тот лавровый венец,

В котором возблистал бессмертный наш певец.
Веселье россян, полунощное диво?

(How can he, a dwarf, contend with a giant?
How can he dispute the laurel wreath
In which our immortal poet became brilliant,
The joy of Russians, the northern miracle?)

The first discursive mention of Lomonosov is contained in a "Note" Pushkin wrote in draft form in 1824 that was prompted by Bestuzhev's article in Полярная звезда (Northern Star) entitled "A Glance at Russian Literature in 1823." Pushkin here refers admiringly to Batiushkov as "Счастливый сподвижник Ломоносова" (Lomonosov's Fortunate Partner) (*PSS* 7: 15). In a letter to Bestuzhev from May–June 1825 *(PSS* 7: 115) Pushkin argues (contra his addressee) that Russia possesses a literature

> but it is criticism that we lack. That accounts for the reputation of Lomonosov (I respect him as a great man but, naturally, not as a great poet. He understood the true source of the Russian language and its beauty; that is his main contribution).[4]

The most extensive discussion of Lomonosov from this period comes about midway through Pushkin's reaction to Lémontey's introduction to the French translation of Krylov's fables, which Pushkin published in 1825. Pushkin criticizes Lémontey for a number of mistaken notions, among them the latter's views of Lomonosov. Pushkin's "corrections" amount to a substitution of his own characterization (*POL:* 122–23 = *PSS* 7: 21–22):

> At times, in the case of a few born poets, poetry is the single passion that engulfs all the attention, all the efforts, and all the impressions of their lives; but when

we begin to study Lomonosov's life we shall find that the factual sciences were always his main and favourite pursuit, while on the other hand the writing of poetry, though at times a recreation, was for him more often a dutiful exercise. In our first lyric poet we looked in vain for flaming fits of passion and imagination. His diction, even, figurative and picturesque, owes its chief merit to its deep grounding in written Slavonic, and to its happy mingling of it with the vernacular. That is why his versions of the psalms and other close renderings of the exalted poetry of the Scriptures are his best works. They will remain eternal memorials of Russian literature; we will for a long time to come have to learn our poetic language from them.

Finally, in an article written between December 1833 and April 1834 and planned as a running commentary on Radishchev's celebrated *Путешествие из Петербурга в Москву (Journey from Petersburg to Moscow)* (1789), Pushkin carries out (in an eponymous chapter) what might be thought of as his most sustained criticism of Lomonosov (*POL*: 346–47 = *PSS* 7: 191):

Lomonosov was a great man. ... He founded our first university. Or, rather, he was himself our first university. But in this university the Professor of Poetry and Rhetoric was no more than a meticulous official, not a poet inspired from above, nor an orator with the power to fascinate. ... In Lomonosov there is neither feeling nor imagination. His odes, modeled on those of German poets of his day who have long since been forgotten even in Germany, are tiring and bombastic. His influence on literature was harmful and it is still felt to this day. An inflated style, preciosity, an aversion for simplicity and accuracy, the absence of any national characteristics and of any originality, these are the marks left by Lomonosov.

In spite of these harsh judgments that come toward the end of Pushkin's life and have for that reason been considered definitive, there is also little doubt that Pushkin imbibed much from Lomonosov and knew Lomonosov's poetry exceedingly well.[5] Echoes of Lomonosov have been detected in the battle scenes of *Poltava*, in many important loci of *The Bronze Horseman* (*Медный всадник*), and generally wherever Pushkin takes up the theme of Peter the Great, as he does in lyric form, for example, in "Стансы" (Stanzas) (1826; "В надежде славы и добра ... " [In the hope of fame and kindness/goodness]).[6] An article (Lebedev 1987) dealing with Lomonosov's impact on nineteenth-century Russian poetry goes through some of these instances of "creative borrowing" (e.g., the resemblance of the first poem of Pushkin's cycle "Подражание Корану" [Imitation of the Koran] to Lomonosov's "Ода, выбранная из Иова" [Ode Selected from Job]) and provides a more general perspective in which to measure Lomonosov's legacy. There are according to this analysis three levels or aspects (at a minimum) of historical influence. First, a particular theme can be traced to Lomonosov, as exemplified by the reworking of Horace's "Exegi monumentum" that is undertaken initially by Lomonosov (1747) and then in turn by Derzhavin (1795) and Pushkin (1836).[7] Second, there are cases of direct imitation or stylization; Pushkin's "reminiscences" of Lomonosov in *The Bronze Horseman* (as analyzed by Pumpianskii 1939) are a particularly subtle and important instance. An ironic counterpart is provided by Pushkin's well-known (and self-glossed) parody in the beginning of *Eugene Onegin* (V.25) of Lomonosov's lines "Заря багряною рукой..." (The dawn with its crimson hand ...) (cf. Gorodetskii 1962: 36).

The third aspect of Lomonosov's penetration is clearly the most significant. At a deep structural level far removed from the mechanical replication of words or phrases, one finds an orientation toward poetic diction that is tantamount to a functional isomorphism or homology, to the creation of a "Lomonosovian element." As in the case of Griboedov or Krylov, poets who recur to particular locutions originating in these classic predecessors may betray no conscious awareness of their literary provenience. This is the condition that seems most aptly to characterize Pushkin's "debt" to Lomonosov.

In a great poet like Pushkin, of course, all three aspects of Lomonosov's legacy tend to be utilized simultaneously. The famous "Клеветникам России" (Slanderers of Russia) (1831) is a good case in point, being the poetic apogee of the "Russia and the West" theme established for Russian belletristic literature by Lomonosov (Lebedev 1987: 309). Beyond being the thematic progenitor and providing the type of poem (the ode) that serves as its stylistic model, Lomonosov constitutes the repository from which Pushkin (consciously or not) draws the lexical means and the syntactic wherewithal for his own version.[8] This example is a particularly good illustration of the fact that Lomonosov's poetic formulas and characteristic diction, so striking in their tropological exuberance, lend themselves to an effortless incorporation into a different stylistic register without losing their recognizably individualistic traits. Pushkin, with his consummate talent for transformation of poetic material, accomplishes just this feat in the last stanza of his "В часы забав иль праздной скуки" (During Times of Games or Empty Boredom) (1830), which according to Lebedev (1987: 302), recalls Lomonosov's "Ода на прибытие..." (On the Arrival ...) (1742):

Твоим огнем душа палима
Отвергла мрак земных сует,
И внемлет арфе серафима
В священном ужасе поэт.
(Pushkin)

(Seared by your fire the soul
Rejected the darkness of earthly worries
And the poet listens to the seraphim's harp
In a sacred horror)

Священный ужас мысль объемлет!
Отверз Олимп всесильный дверь.
Вся тварь со многим страхом внемлет,
Великих зря Монархов Дщерь...
(Lomonosov)

(A sacred horror enshrouds one's thought!
Almighty Olympus has opened the door.
All creation listens in great fear
Watching the daughter of the Great Monarchs ...)

As a further test case for the validity of the third aspect, that
of functional parallelism, we would like to offer a brief analysis
of Pushkin's "Муза" (Muse) (1821), which has to our knowledge
never been discussed in this context.

В младенчестве моем она меня любила
И семиствольную цевницу мне вручила;
Она внимала мне с улыбкой, и слегка
По звонким скважинам пустого тростника
Уже наигрывал я слабыми перстами
И гимны важные, внушенные богами,
И песни мирные фригийских пастухов.
С утра до вечера в немой тени дубов
Прилежно я внимал урокам девы тайной;
И, радуя мена улыбкою случайной,
Откинув локоны от милого чела,
Сама из рук моих свирель она брала:
Тростник был оживлен божественным дыханьем
И сердце наполнял святым очарованьем.

(In my youth she loved me
And handed me a seven-barreled flute;
She heard me with a smile, and lightly
Along the sonorous slits of the empty reed
I already played with my weak fingers
Stately hymns inspired by the gods
As well as peaceful songs of Phrygian shepherds.
From morning to night in the mute shade of the oaks
Assiduously I listened to the mysterious maid's lessons;
And making me happy with a chance smile,
Having flung aside the tresses from her lovely forehead,
She took the flute from my hands herself:
The reed was enlivened by divine breath
And filled the heart with sacred charm.)

This poem belongs to an important group of lyrics from the years 1820–21 connected with Pushkin's stay in the Crimean town of Gurzuf on the Black Sea. With a couple of exceptions they evoke the context of classical antiquity, and ultimately found their way into Pushkin's first volume of verse among a cycle entitled "Подражание древним" (Imitations of the Ancients). Actually, despite this designation the poems are not imitations proper; they are, however, all in alexandrines and exhibit the kind of imagery typical of the way Pushkin and his contemporaries understood ancient poetry.[9] The spirit of classical verse is captured in this kind of poetry through its mythological allusions and the evocation of a pastoral ambience reminiscent of ancient Greece. The idyllic setting of "Muza" underscores Pushkin's fondness for memories of his first steps as a poet during his student years at the Lycée (cf. the introductory stanzas of *Eugene Onegin* VIII, with its similar imagery). The idealized picture of this time in his life would often serve Pushkin with material for the realization of the theme of "first poetic trials."

"Muza" is certainly a poem belonging to a "high" style, but it is curious how this level is pointedly balanced off by neutral vocabulary, with the result that both the nature of the muse and the nature of poetry end up being characterized as a complexus of the earthly and the divine. The poet's first lessons involve playing both solemn hymns ("гимны важные") inspired by the gods and peaceful songs ("песни мирные") of Phrygian shepherds. The fife or flute is designated now by a Church Slavonic word (*цевница*), now by a neutral Russian word (*тростник, свирель*). What to a Romantic sensibility would constitute linguistic commonplaces of adjectival qualification (*немая тень* 'mute shade' and *дева тайная* 'mysterious maid') is simultaneously not voided of a mythopoeic content that lurks just beneath the platitudinous surface. Particularly the phrase *тайная дева*, with the conventional figuration of poetry by allusion to its mystical or mysterious origins, has the potential to conjure up a mythological or hieratic context. At the same time this mysterious maiden with her "divine breath" is endowed with quite mundane attributes and described as performing decidedly "human," even flirtatious, actions: she bestows a casual (*случайный*) smile on her pupil and takes the flute from his hands with a toss of her "tresses." Even the closing phrase "святым очарованьем" can be understood at once as ordinary or special: *святой* as a debased epithet in the Romantic lexicon (of the sort "Молчит его святая лира" [His sacred lyre is silent] ("Поэт")), in which the meaning "sacred" is at best faintly redolent of religious semantics; or in its primordial, sacral sense. In the same way *очарованье* has both a hackneyed connotation ('charm,' giving rise to the flirtatiousness aspect of the muse) and its latent content of sorcery (cf. *чары* 'charms/spell', *чародей* 'sorcerer').

More to the point of a possible functional parallelism, the figural torsion involved in a juxtaposition like *немая тень* 'mute shade' is just what Lomonosov was infamous for, and what Sumarokov lampooned (see Serman 1966: 182–90). It is features of Lomonosov's style like this that "allow us to see in him the initiator and the precursor of Romantic poetry in the years 1800–1810" (Serman 1966: 190), i.e., those years immediately preceding Pushkin's entry onto the literary scene, and marked by poetic production having such a far-reaching impact on his own style (owing chiefly to Zhukovskii and Batiushkov). The same can be said to a lesser extent of *звонкие скважины* 'sonorous slits' with reference to this combination's figural appropriateness and "Lomonosovian feeling." None of this even begins to touch on the instrumental(!) metonymy that lies at the core of the poem's semantics—a tropological gambit so familiar from Lomonosov's odes.

The emphasis on linguistic repertoire placed in the service of poetic diction seems to be the most pervasive trace of Lomonosov in Pushkin. This view accords well with Tynianov's assessment that "while recognizing Lomonosovian principles of the literary *language*, Pushkin decisively rejected Lomonosov's literary *principles*. ... He perceived Lomonosov's language detached from Lomonosov's poetry" (Tynianov 1929: 156, cit. Serman 1966: 251; cf. Vinogradov 1935: 41).

All the same, the Lomonosovian ode represents the epitome of the genre for Pushkin, and when he has occasion to resuscitate the eighteenth-century odic style, as in *Poltava* and *The Bronze Horseman*, it is just there that his debt to Lomonosov becomes most palpable. As Pumpianskii (1939: 114) points out, however, "Pushkin does not develop the odic theme creatively but rather 'cites' it... . Pushkin's odisms [одизмы] from *Poltava* to 'Памятник' ['Monument'] are simultaneously a resurrection and a dethronement of the classical eighteenth-century tradition: herein lies the profound dialectic (i.e., the leading) contradiction in Pushkin's attitude toward the legacy of eighteenth-century poetry."

It is no happenstance that resonances of Lomonosov sound out most conspicuously in literary material that has to do with

Peter the Great. Indeed for Pushkin, Lomonosov and Peter seem to go together almost as an inevitable coupling of Russian cultural history. In the extended meditation on Lomonosov cited earlier, Pushkin speaks of "Lomonosov's all-embracing genius ... the great Peter's illustrious fellow worker [partner]" *(POL*: 122; "о всеобъемлющем гении Ломоносова...сподвижника великого Петра" [*PSS* 7: 21]). Pushkin's image of Lomonosov, in other words, rests on an analogy between Peter as the founder of the Russian state and Lomonosov as the originator of Russian poetry.

The common element of origins is not all. The historical dimension that is projected from these beginnings in the eighteenth century takes on the aura associated with anything stamped "classical." In one astute critic's words, "Lomonosov's system is the primary source for the understanding of Russian classicism, and Lomonosov is the first symbol of the classical tradition that proved to be viable for almost a century."[10] The interesting thing, of course, is the great distance separating the "classicism" of Lomonosov from what is otherwise considered the paradigm case (e.g., Sumarokov). Pushkin evidently valued, as a practical matter of poetic technique and his strictures notwithstanding, the *concordia discors* inhering in the striking juxtapositions of linguistic material and the resultant heightening of metaphorism.[11] It is not only the creation of new cultural institutions but the determination (and ability) to yoke together historically incompatible entities, combinations not sanctioned by tradition or precedent, that is so characteristic of Peter and defines his unique role. The perfect corollary of this parallelism follows: just as Peter in *The Bronze Horseman* is irretrievably consigned to Russia's past, so Lomonosov's whole literary outlook and manner as cultural givens are only resurrected in order to be set aside.[12] This, we believe, is the true meaning of Pushkin's expressed attitude toward Lomonosov as his most formidable native literary predecessor.

The account of this relationship has its human epilogue. Among the products of Pushkin's greatest burst of creativity, the autumn of 1830 he spent in Boldino, are some elegiac distychs in a classical vein. One of these poems, "Отрок" (The Youth), paints a verbal miniature of Lomonosov's youth:

Невод рыбак расстилал по брегу студеного моря;
　　Мальчик отцу помогал. Отрок, оставь рыбака!
Мрежи иные тебя ожидают, иные заботы:
　　Будешь умы уловлять, будешь помощник царям.

(A fisherman was laying out his net on the shore of the
　　frigid sea;
A boy was helping his father. Youth, leave the fisherman!
Other nets are awaiting you, other concerns:
You will capture minds, you will be a helpmate to tsars.)

The time of the poem's composition coincides with a general resurgence of interest in Lomonosov, which helps to explain its rather late appearance in Pushkin's oeuvre. The publication between two covers of Gnedich's translation of the *Iliad* in 1829 prompted a poetic tribute from Pushkin three years later ("С Гомером долго ты беседовал один..." [You alone conversed with Homer for a long time]) and was evidently the culmination of a prolonged period of close attention to the whole poetic ethos of classical antiquity as filtered through its (mainly French) eighteenth-century revival.

There is a "myth-making" aspect to this bit of verse that is consonant with the predominantly mythological context of Russian "anthological" poetry in general. Lomonosov's life and works had, by the 1830s, congealed into a legend, and it is this myth's historical origins that are thematized in Pushkin's elegiac distych. The impression of a quasi-Lomonosovian style suggested by the poem's archaic lexicon (*брег* 'shore', *отрок* 'youth', *мрежи* 'net', *уловлять* 'capture') and its stylized tenor is reinforced by textual knowledge that the first draft actually had "Будешь ловитель умов, будешь подвижник Петру" ("You will be the capturer of minds, you will be Peter's helpmate") as its last line (Grigor'eva 1981: 149; cf. Il'inskaia 1970: 220). The infusion of a prophetic element heightens the sense of mythic purport, aided by the pointed seriation (as in "Muza") of synonyms from the neutral Russian and the Church Slavonic lexical strata (*невод/мрежи, мальчик/отрок*). The folkloric mode alluding to Lomonosov's peasant background is bodied forth by *студеное море*[13] and ought to be reckoned as part of a semantic counterpoint pitting not only Church Slavonic against neutral, and folk vs. literary, but literal against figural ("Мальчик отцу *помогал*" vs. "будешь *помощник* царям"; *мрежи* 'nets' vs. 'snares, entrapments'; *ловить рыбу* 'catch fish' [implicitly] vs. *умы уловлять* 'capture minds').

One way of summing up the significance of Pushkin's poetic tribute is to regard "Otrok" as a complete icon of Pushkin's image of Lomonosov. The constituents of this icon are: (1) Lomonosov's humble provenience; (2) the fact that he answered the call ("Отрок оставь рыбака!") and was therefore not to be equated with run-of-the-mill professional littérateurs;[14] (3) his distinguishing traits as (a) an intellectual/scientist ("Будешь умы уловлять") and (b) a figure of great civic significance ("будешь помощник царям"). There is also a significant absence with respect to the structure of Pushkin's icon: no mention whatever is made of Lomonosov as a writer, reflecting Pushkin's own severe indictment ("египетский суд") of Lomonosov as a poet not "inspired from above" ("не поэт, вдохновенный свыше").

However that may be, there is finally no doubt about Pushkin's high regard, bordering on reverence, for Lomonosov the man.[15] Even as he was censuring Lomonosov the poet, Pushkin continued to manifest a supervening admiration for Lomonosov's deep-rooted independence of spirit by implicitly contrasting him with the majority of eighteenth-century Russian writers who paid obeisance to the monarch and his/her court:

> Lomonosov, born to a low estate, did not think of elevating himself by means of impudence and familiarity toward persons of higher status (even though his rank entitled him to be their equal). At the same time, however, he knew how to stand up for himself and placed no value on the patronage of his benefactors or his own welfare when it came to his honor or the vindication of his favorite ideas. Hear how he writes to the very same Shuvalov, *the representative of the muses, his lofty patron,* who attempted to joke at his expense. "Your excellency, I do not even wish to play the fool before my Lord God, let alone any potentates."["Я, ваше высокопревосходительство, не только у вельмож, но ниже у Господа Бога дураком быть не хочу."] (*PSS* 7: 196)

When in the last years of his life Pushkin found himself in a similarly onerous position at court and in high society, he characterized his own unbending will to resist injustice in a letter to his wife (of 8 June 1834) by quoting Lomonosov:

> They look on me now as a serf [холоп] with whom they can deal however they wish. Disfavor is easier to bear than contempt. Like Lomonosov, I don't even want to be a fool before my Lord God [Я, как Ломоносов, не хочу быть шутом ниже у Господа Бога] (*PSS* 10: 381)

The complexity of Pushkin's attitude can finally be understood as a sign of Lomonosov's merit as a man and as a poet. For Pushkin, Lomonosov's stature as the founder of Russian poetry and the Russian literary language is rife with ambiguity, mirroring the ambivalence of his perception of Peter the Great. We may concur in the judgment that "Pushkin sees the main value of Lomonosov's poetry not in its own merit but in its constituting the foundation of all our poetry" (Lebedev 1987: 297). This understanding is the key to resolving the tension between Pushkin's negative pronouncements and his frequent recurrence to Lomonosov's language and ideas in his own poetry.

PETRARCH (VIA BATIUSHKOV)

Although much has been made of Pushkin's recurrence to Dante's *Divine Comedy*,[16] the potentially more significant influence on Pushkin's style of Petrarch has been all but totally neglected.[17] As we will try to show, this is a matter that goes far beyond mere citations of Petrarch, which are few but memorable.[18] In *Eugene Onegin* (I.XLIX) Pushkin identifies the language of love with that of Petrarch:

Ночей Италии златой
Я негой наслажусь на воле
С венецианкою младой
То говорливой, то немой,
Плывя в таинственной гондоле;
С ней обретут уста мои
Язык Петрарки и любви

(PSS 6: 25)

(Of the nights of golden Italy
I will enjoy the languor freely
With a young Venetian woman,
Now talkative, now mute,
While floating in a mysterious gondola;
With her my lips will find
The language of Petrarch and love.)

A little later in the same chapter (I.LVIII), Pushkin envies Petrarch for his ability to assuage the torments of the heart and win fame by singing Laura's praises:

> Любви безумную тревогу
> Я безотрадно испытал.
> Блажен, кто с нею сочетал
> Горячку рифм: он тем удвоил
> Поэзии священный бред,
> Петрарке шествуя вослед,
> А муки сердца успокоил,
> Поймал и славу между тем:
> Но я , любя, был глуп и нем.
>
> *(PSS 6: 29–30)*

(The mad alarm of love
I experienced joylessly.
Blessed is he who combined
The fever of rhymes with it: he thereby doubled
The sacred delirium of poetry
Following in the footsteps of Petrarch
And calmed the torments of the heart
And caught fame by the way:
But I, loving, was foolish and mute.)

The last *Onegin* citation of Petrarch is the epigraph to the sixth chapter which comes from a fusing of lines 49 and 51 of the *canzone* (XXVIII) dedicated to Giacomo Colonna:

> La sotto i giorni nubilosi e brevi
> Nasce una gente a cui l'morir non dole.[19]

In one of the *Belkin Tales* (1830), "Метель" (The Snowstorm), Pushkin characterizes the love of his romantic heroine Mar'ia

Gavrilovna for the Hussar colonel Burmin by commenting, "One couldn't say that she flirted with him; but a poet, noticing her behavior, would have said: Se amor non è, che dunche?" *(PSS* 8: 84). This recalls (with the mistaken "dunche" for *dunque*; see below) the first line of one of Petrarch's most famous sonnets (CXXXII), "S'amor non è, che dunque è quel ch'io sento?" ("If it is not love, what then is it that I feel?"). Finally, perhaps the most easily remembered mention of Petrarch occurs in the second line of Pushkin's metapoetic "Сонет" (Sonnet): "Суровый Дант не презирал сонета; / В нем жар любви Петрарка изливал" *(PSS* 3: 214) (The severe Dante did not contemn the sonnet; / In it Petrarch poured out the fire of love). Along with "Поэту" (To a/the Poet) ("Поэт! Не дорожи любовию народной" [Poet! Do not value the love of the people]) and "Мадона" (Madonna),[20] this exhausts Pushkin's sonnet production, all of which occurs in 1830. The last of the three is particularly significant because it exemplifies Pushkin's profound thematic assimilation of Petrarch. Drawing upon a tradition of ecphrastic sonnets whose most influential exemplars were by Petrarch (LXXVII and LXXVIII), Pushkin's "Madonna" echoes Petrarch's use of the painting to emphasize the permanence of love: "Одной картины я желал быть вечно зритель, / Одной" (One painting I wished to be the eternal viewer of, / One) (ll. 6–7), just like "Et sol ad una imagine m'attegno" (CXXX, l. 9; [And I keep myself to one image]).

It is highly likely that Pushkin did not come by his knowledge of Petrarch accidentally. We know from Modzalevskii's inventory of Pushkin's library that it contained many books in Italian and two multivolume histories of Italian literature, by J. C. L. Simonde de Sismondi and P. L. Ginguéné. The latter devotes the entire second half of volume 2 (pages 334–566) to Petrarch, illustrating a substantial discussion of his poetry with the original Italian and accompanying French translations that amount to 22 sonnets and 9 *canzoni* (cf. Rozanov 1930: 124). Pushkin's development of a poetic language devoid of baroque opacity, of vulgarisms or didacticism can be traced to the influence of Petrarch via Batiushkov, who not only tried to write poetry "in the Italian style" but actually introduced Petrarch's poetry to the Russian reading public in an 1815 essay which appeared in Number 7 of the journal *Вестник Европы* [*European Messenger*] the following year. Pushkin expressed his admiration for Batiushkov's verse in a number of explicit ways, among them the only case of extensive literary-critical marginalia we possess in Pushkin's own hand, to part two (containing the poetry) of his copy of Batiushkov's *Опыты в стихах и прозе* (*Experiments in Verse and Prose*, 1817).[21] In a number of instances Pushkin uses the word *гармония* ('harmony'), and it is clear from the entire context of these comments that by this word he means something about the sound structure that approximates the language of Ariosto and Tasso, as well as Petrarch.[22] There is no doubt that Pushkin shared Batiushkov's admiration for the mellifluousness of Italian and decried the barbarousness of Russian, as was expressed by Batiushkov in a letter to Gnedich from 1811 (Batiushkov 1886/ III: 164–65):

> Guess what I am beginning to get angry at? Do you know at what? At the Russian language and our writers who treat it unmercifully. As it is, the language is somewhat faulty, a bit tough, and smells of the Tatars. What about the *y* [sound]? What about the *shch*? What about the *sh, shii, shchii, pri, try*? Oh, barbarians! But so be it! I'm sorry that I'm angry at the Russian people and its speech. I just was reading Ariosto, breathing the pure air of Florence, enjoying the musical sounds of the Ausonian language, and speaking with the shades of Dante, Tasso, and the sweet Petrarch, from whose lips every word is rapture!

These are the sentiments that underlie Batiushkov's project to reform the language of Russian poetry. Pushkin acknowledged Batiushkov's role when he wrote in a fragment from 1824 (Lebedev et al. 1978: 63; *PSS* 11: 21): "I agree that ... Batiushkov, who was considered a comrade-in-arms of Lomonosov, did for Russian what Petrarch did for Italian."

Although the phonic aspect is clearly at the forefront of Batiushkov's and Pushkin's advocacy of Italian as a model for Russian poetic language, Petrarch's importance is by no means confined to it. Before analyzing in detail several Pushkin poems for their implementation of a Petrarchan harmoniousness, we wish first to survey in brief the most salient ways in which Petrarch exerted a substantive impact on all of European poetry.

It is difficult to think of any figure in the history of Western lyric poetry who dominated his world of letters as Petrarch did, or one who was more persistently imitated. Petrarch's fame was as wide as Europe: for the distinction of his writing, his belief in Rome as the rightful capital of a unified world, for his faithfulness to study and writing and the innovative yet unstartling quality of his lyric, and for his precocious historical awareness of the reality of epochs past and yet to come, Petrarch founded his own standard. The fact of his renown makes for the further difficulty of isolating his direct influence from that of scores of epigones who followed him in France and Italy and who were well known to Pushkin. Even in their own day, Petrarch's sonnets and *canzoni* were not especially "original": the sonnet form had been invented about a hundred years before Petrarch used it, and the "song" was essentially an Old Provençal form. But Laura, for Petrarch the incarnation of earthly beauty, with implications of the heavenly, the inspiration to virtue and poetic glory, was the first world-class perennially, warmly desirable lyric beloved. She inspires, obsesses, and distracts, and finally comes close to signifying life itself, tempting but transient, exhilarating but spiritually dangerous, even despondent. What Petrarch did with the

traditional troubadour tradition of love lyric was to give it un-
equaled refinement of expression and bring to the contemplation of sexual love (with all its paradoxical potential of joy and
anguish) a tenderness, melancholy, devotion, and longing that
make up a particularly Petrarchan moment of truth, one of such
emotional appeal and such psychological validity that for all its
occasional preciousness of expression (a feature incrementally
augmented by his imitators), this truth has become part of the
Western psyche.

Petrarch's *Canzoniere* consists of 366 lyric poems whose
order is loosely chronological except for the sharp line between
poems written "during Laura's lifetime" and those composed
"after her death." The dates of the poems' composition run
roughly from 1330 to nearly the end of Petrarch's life (1374), and
he continued polishing and revising them into his last years.
A number of them have acquired a historical importance that
flattens their impact: there is the sonnet of paradoxes, the cata-
logue-sonnet, the lyric of My Lady's Perfection, the neopla-
tonizing lyric, all dear to literary historians and salon versifiers.
Their status as landmarks in the panorama of letters and sentiment places undue strain on the reception of many of the poems.
Happily, many more where the poet tells of his love of solitude,
his secret crises of faith, his grief and spiritual conflict, his sol-
ace in poetry, obliterate the centuries and speak their own language to each poet and each reader.

Since the poems speak not so much of external events as of
psychological experience, what Petrarch has to say is almost
uniquely untranslatable: his effect depends entirely on his manner of saying what he has to say. Aside from his creation of the
modern lyric lover and the latter's predicament, Petrarch's
poems are largely imageless. Without his cadences, his mastery
of placement, his speaking syntax and phonetic control of flow,
they vanish unappreciated. The mastery of syntactic and grammatical relations over other aspects of their subject matter is still

insufficiently studied, as is the phonetic substance of their prosody. The Slavist reader of this chapter will have begun at this moment to comprehend something of the kinship of Petrarch and Pushkin. It is our aim to trace the main lines of this relationship in a comparative study of the two poets, demoting for the purpose the literary-historical intervention of petrarchists and the host of petrarchists *après la lettre*, to whom modes known to us as quintessentially Petrarchan were intertwined in what was simply the only lyric idiom available to them.

The problems attendant upon this comparative analysis are mainly three: first, to establish that there exists a store of images, emotions, and associative clusters assimilated by translingual experience from Petrarch to Pushkin;[23] second, that this experience, though mediated by numerous petrarchists, remains typified by Petrarch's unique contribution; third, to find an accurate measure of the poets' common craft. Is the quality of the bond between Petrarch and Pushkin intractable to measurement or even simple discussion? Our concern is not allayed by the awareness that both poets make use of a classical patrimony. It is no wonder that in translation Petrarch easily sounds generic, Pushkin flat.[24] Where Petrarch yields to display is exceptional; in Pushkin it is virtually nonexistent, with the result that the poetic lexicon seems quite obvious. Common metaphors turn up, such as the one Petrarch uses for a lover, Pushkin for a poet, of dragging one's life through a desert:

Petrarch (XXXV):
Solo et pensoso i più deserti campi
Vo mesurando a passi tardi et lenti

(Alone and filled with care, I go measuring
the most deserted fields with steps delaying and slow.)

Pushkin ("Пророк" ["The Prophet"]):
Духовной жаждою томим,
В пустыне мрачной я влачился,—

(PSS 3: 30)

(Tormented by a spiritual craving,
I wandered abjectly in the desert)

But the example proves to be one overworked by petrarchists.[25] No imported line or citation can prove accountable for the uncanny poetic effect shared by these two poets. Rather than a mere transcultural petrarchism, we are faced with a similarity of what strikes at cognitive and aesthetic values, which is the core of style.

Petrarch and Pushkin have in common a detachment or self-distancing from the subject matter of love, which is actually highlighted by the lyric first-person speaker. Generalities such as these lend themselves to demonstration at the stylistic and syntactic levels. Expressions of doubt concerning the intensity of the emotion being vented emerge from a simple lexicon, limpid diction, and easily penetrable circumlocution, as in the following Petrarchan ballad (LV):

Quel foco ch'i' pensai che fosse spento
dal freddo tempo et da l'età men fresca,
fiamma e martir ne l'anima rinfresca.
Non fur mai tutte spente, a quel ch'i' veggio,
ma ricoperte alquanto le faville,
et temo no'l secondo error sia peggio.
Per lagrime ch'i' spargo a mille a mille,
conven che 'l duol per gli occhi si distille
dal cor, ch'à seco le faville et l'èsca:
non pur qual fu, ma pare a me che cresca.
Qual foco non avrian già spento et morto
l'onde che gli occhi tristi versan sempre?
Amor, avegna mi sia tardi accorto,

vòl che tra duo contrari mi distempre;
et tende lacci in sí diverse tempre,
che quand' ò più speranza che 'l cor n'esca,
allor più nel bel viso mi rinvesca.

(That fire, which I thought had gone out because of the cold season and my age no longer fresh, now renews flames and suffering in my soul. They were never entirely extinguished, as I see, those embers, but somewhat covered over; and I am afraid that my second error will be the worse. In tears that I scatter by thousands and thousands my sorrow must flow forth through my eyes from my heart, which has in it the sparks and the tinder, not merely as it was before, but, I fear, growing. What fire would not have been put out by the floods that my sad eyes are always pouring forth? Love, though I have been tardy in seeing it, wishes me to be untuned between two contraries; and he puts out snares of such different temper that, when I most hope that my heart can get free of them, then he most enlimes me again with that lovely face.)

This poem, chosen at random, happens to approach closely in subject matter Pushkin's "Я вас любил" (I loved you once). A speaker-lover takes account of the replenishment of fiery suffering in his heart, never quite extinguished despite his hopes. The syntactic arrangement in the first tercet holds in suspension the resolution *rinfresca* 'refreshes', which seems to oppose *spento* 'burnt out' but forms a communality of rich rhyme with *fresca* in the preceding line. In line 4, *spente* again echoes line 1. The following stanza speaks of a typically in-between state qualified by "from what I see; so far as I can tell": the amorous sparks had been only "somewhat" (*alquanto*) covered, not quite extinguished. The possibility that the "second error" may be graver than the first is distanced by *temo* (I'm afraid that...), and the last line of the stanza, beginning "no pur qual fu" ("not just what it was"), could go either way. But the lover decides for growth, not decline, again filtering the resolution through the self-analytical "it seems to me" *(pare a me)*. The remainder of the poem shows the lover caught between contraries (line 14) and the repertoire of Petrarchan "imagery"; *foco* 'fire' (again *spento!*), *onde* 'waves', *occhi tristi* 'sad eyes', *lacci* 'lures', *speranza* 'hope', *bel viso* 'beautiful face' scarcely distract from the paronomastic, hence intensely interrelated, rhymewords. All of these are either descriptive, quasi-metaphoric verbs (*distempre* 'disturbs', *cresca* 'grows', *rinvesca* 'entangle anew', now echoing its first use as a noun in line 10) or past participles (*morto* 'dead', *accorto* 'noticed'), or the lone noun *tempre* 'moods' which saps some force from the rhyme with *distempre*. Note the semantic correspondence of *spento* in first rhyme position with *spente* (line 3) and *morto* (line 11, the beginning of the final stanza). Petrarch's favorite rhyme of *veggio* 'I see' / *peggio* 'worse', an intransitive verb with an adjective, mutes the *faville* 'sparks' that it envelops, not to speak of the inexpressive hyperbole *a mille a mille* 'in thousands' and the final *distille* 'be distilled', which effectuates the dispersion of the sparks.

In Pushkin's "Я вас любил" (1829; *PSS* 3: 188) every assertion of love is either beset by doubt (i.e., lack of certainty) or the expression of an implied counterfactual. The first two lines ("Я вас любил: любовь еще, быть может, / В душе моей угасла не совсем;" [I loved you once: perhaps that love / Has not been snuffed out completely]) only assert a love with reservations. The last two ("Я вас любил так искренно, так нежно / Как дай вам Бог любимой быть другим" [I loved you so sincerely, so tenderly / As God grant that you be loved by another]) establish an equivalence which is simultaneously a covert negation: the sincerity and tenderness of the love can only be matched in the subjunctive universe of a wish, a state which has no present and at best an unsure future.

These are the ways of talking about love that foreground emotion merely as an instrument of self-knowledge, whose value in itself is sure to outlast the love they describe. Therefore, both Petrarch and Pushkin neutralize the incidental changes that would otherwise mark the passage of time. Both poets merge the events of psychological time into continuous flow interrupted only by a punctuation resembling that of ordinary speech. Whereas Petrarch is more "precious," Pushkin more sociable (as in the last line), each abstracts from the changeability of external life only those subjects that may connote eternal value. No images as such are present. In Pushkin shifters, in Petrarch the most general common nouns, make up a linguistic continuum that neutralizes the difference between signifier and signified, due to the relative lack of a referential (conceptual) component. As pointed out by Jakobson *(SW* 2: 705), the combination of a strong emotive connotation with a "scantiness or absence of the referential, conceptual component" is most apparent in musical semiosis. At some distance from that extreme lies the musical quality of Petrarchan language.

Pushkin and Petrarch resemble each other in several more global respects which have to be considered elastically. The following points are meant to be taken only as a suggestive listing and concentrate on Petrarch as a shorthand obviation of lack of space; almost all of Pushkin's poetic oeuvre could easily serve as terms of comparison (cf. Vinogradov 1941: esp. chapters 1 and 4).

❡ Petrarch's innovation of a modern psychological idiom is in great measure a work of reduction, of what one of his most perceptive readers has called "unilingualism" (Contini 1964: xii). Petrarchan vocabulary is restricted with few and significant exceptions to terms with a high specific degree of "poeticity"; to terms which cohere amongst themselves to form vague-sounding but closely allied semantic fields; and to terms denoting "eternal objects" in a closed circle abstracted from the mutability of history.

Di pensier in pensier, di monte in monte
mi guida Amor, ch'ogni segnato calle

(CXXIX)

(From thought to thought, from mountain to mountain
Love guides me; for [I find] every trodden path)

Anima, che diverse cose tante
vedi, odi et leggi et parli et scrivi et pensi;

(CCIV)

(Soul, who sees so many different things,
and hears and reads and speaks and writes and thinks)

❦ Nature as such is scarcely if at all present in Petrarch. Generic natural description appears chiefly as a foil for human sentiment ("Chiare, fresche e dolci acque / ove le belle membra / pose colei che sola a me par donna"; [Clear, fresh, sweet waters, where she who alone seems lady to me rested her lovely body]; CXXVI).

❦ Petrarchan concepts rarely contravene a general "naturalness." His diction, essentially modern, contains few archaisms. Pushkin's economy shows even less convolution.

❦ Related to the above three points is the attenuation of force in all parts of speech.

• Nouns tend to be general and common, forming circumlocutionary phrases and frequently puns or paronomasia, as in sonnet X, to Stefano Colonna (head of a powerful Roman family, father of Giacomo; cf. n. 19):

Glorïosa columna in cui s'appoggia
nostra speranza e 'l gran nome latino [etc.]

(Glorious column on whom rests
our hope and the great renown of Latium.)

• Adjectives often carry substantial value. They are more like epithets than like predicates (*gran desio* 'great desire', *be' pensieri* 'good thoughts', *dolce fume* 'sweet light', *amate rive* 'beloved banks'), thereby avoiding declarative statement.

• Verbs are often metaphoric and rarely active (*et questa spene m'avea fatto ardito* "and this hope has made me bold" [XXIII. 103]; *cose ne la mente scritte* [things written in my mind; XXIII. 92]; *Se 'l sasso...tenesse vòlto...le spalle* ['If the rock kept its back turned'; CXVII. 1–4]). Verbs are almost inevitably nonviolent, just as substantives are often "unactualized" (Contini 1964: xxiii), abstracted from action. Both poets make abundant use of verbal nouns (Petrarch: *Il cantar novo e 'l pianger delli augelli* [The new singing and the weeping of the birds at daybreak make; CCXIX]).

• One important means whereby Petrarch avoids effects of mincing courtliness or effeteness is his essentially litotic rhetoric, as in the line, *Primavera per me pur non e mai*, which is litotic in the most general sense (It is never spring for me = I am always unhappy; it is always winter in my soul) and works through substitution, thus conforming to what Contini characterized as "evasiveness" (1964: xxxii).

• Evasiveness is quintessentially characteristic of both poets. Among its means are the placement of the strongest word first in a line, as in the above example; the judicious use of enjambment to neutralize rhyme (thereby capturing the quality of mellifluous prose); and adherence to a lexicon that displays internal coherence more than, or at least as much as, external reference. Unsurprisingly, these features coalesce into what Contini terms Petrarch's "rhythmic dominant" (1964: xxxii).

• A semiosis approaching that of music does not, however, preclude certain dominances of subject matter. Among these is an intensely personal, confessional tone of intimacy with readers that was introduced into modern Western poetry by Petrarch but finds its way into Russian poetry with the advent of the Pushkin pleiad. Cf. Petrarch: "Quand'io mi volgo indietro a mirar gli anni...i' mi riscuoto, et trovomi si nudo..." (When I turn back to gaze at the years...I shake myself and find myself so naked... . CCXCVIII).

• Confidentiality and the attenuation of force, especially in love lyric, lead to a world of human psychologism, in which human feeling is related to the external world by an imputation of similarity that transcends simple procedures like the "affective fallacy" in nature. Jakobson's judgment (*SW* 2: 704) that the poet simply neutralizes differences and boundaries via "the interplay of the two dichotomies contiguity/similarity and factual/imputed, admit[ting] a fourth variety of relation, namely imputed similarity" is particularly applicable to Petrarch and Pushkin alike.

• A religiosity approaching the ineffability of human love appears in both poets, although certainly not bequeathed by one to the other, as was the "religion of the beloved" with its antecedents in Italian and Provençal poetry for Petrarch, and in petrarchists for Pushkin. Petrarch's "lay" religion, somewhat surprising against the cultural background of late medieval Italian poetry, would be unremarkable in international lyric after 1800; but both Petrarch and Pushkin are remarkable for their invocation of God as a touchstone of poetic consciousness, which always has some point of tangency with religious feeling. Petrarch's God sometimes hovers as a monitory presence, but outside of structures and systems: this God consoles tedium and relieves fatigue, in fact constitutes a psychological theme. Pushkin, who is often accused by critics, including theologians, of being blasphemously insouciant about God and godliness, often invokes God as a necessary commonplace petrified in linguistic phrases (e.g., as in "Не дай мне Бог сойти с ума" [God forfend that I go out of my mind]). God signifies through a poetic consciousness of reality and of the relationship between human beings and their universe. For both Petrarch and Pushkin, religion cannot function as an empirical correlate or even a verifiably reliable instrument for understanding the world. Both poets expose the uncertainty of human knowledge as an insuperable barrier to man's boundless conceit and impossible aspirations.

• Both Petrarch and Pushkin incorporate a mythology of the shade (cf. Senderovich 1980). *Ombra* is a typically Petrarchan word, referring polysemously to the state of the soul after death and/or pastoral coolness, or darkness and shadow of a protective kind. Allowing for mediation of this topos by such poets as Byron or Foscolo, Pushkin nonetheless achieves a specifically Petrarchan effect: his sonnet on the sonnet ("Сонет") begins by comparing Dante and Petrarch and contains the Petrarchesque line "Под сенью гор Тавриды отдаленной" (Beneath the shadow of the mountains of distant Tauris).

• Both poets achieve a fundamentally aristocratic tone with a light touch (cf. Driver 1989: chapter 2). Although they share a fascination with antiquity and possibly have certain Roman models in mind (notably Ovid and the elegiac poets Propertius and Catullus, unmediated for Petrarch but mediated for Pushkin by elegiac moderns such as Parny), this interest does not begin to account for their aristocratic temperament, not least because antiquarianism and ruins were ubiquitously fashionable in Pushkin's time throughout Europe. Analogously, the Petrarchan topic of fleeing the public, contemning the crowds, delighting in exclusivity and solitude, had become so commonplace by Pushkin's time as to vitiate Petrarch's innovation of it. Such themes are not constitutive of the aristocratic tenor of Pushkin's lyric.

• The development of a diaphonously clear poetic language devoid of baroque (*après la lettre*) opacity, vulgarism, or overt didacticism was a common aim of both poets. Contini's remark that Petrarch was possessed of a classicism that filtered through romanticism would apply as well to Pushkin. Literary history has borne out the analysis in these poets' respective influence on the language of lyric.

A literary-historical perspective on the relationship between Pushkin and Petrarch necessarily returns us to Batiushkov, Petrarch's champion in Pushkin's Russia. In his marginalia to Batiushkov's *Опыты* (Experiments), Pushkin is lavish in exclaiming "прелесть'" ('marvelous') and "прекрасно" ('beautiful'). Consider the ninth strophe of the poem "К другу" (To a Friend):

> Нрав тихий ангела, дар слова, тонкий вкус
> Любви и очи и ланиты;
> Чело открытое одной из важных Муз
> И прелесть—девственной Хариты.

> (The quiet character of an angel, the gift of speech, refined
>   taste.
> Eyes and cheeks of love,
> An open forehead of one of the stately muses
> And the delightful appearance of a virginal Charide)

This is marked with a vertical line along the right margin, and the first two lines elicit the following from Pushkin (Lebedev 1987; 306, *PSS* 12: 267): "Italian sounds! What a miracle worker this Batiushkov is." The entire seventh strophe is accompanied by the ejaculation (ibid.) "delightful [прелесть]!—what is more, everything is a delight," and the last nine lines of the whole poem are marked with a vertical line; underneath Pushkin adds (Lebedev 1987: 307): "A strong, complete, and brilliant poem." Batiushkov's "Радость" (Happiness), a free translation of the eighteenth century Italian fabulist Casti's poem "Il contento," garners the following comment (Lebedev 1987: 319): "This is

Batiushkovian harmony." Underneath the famous "Тень друга" (Shade of Friend) ("Я берег покидал туманный Альбиона" [I was leaving the foggy shore of Albion]) Pushkin writes (Lebedev 1987: 301): "Прелесть и совершенство—какая гармония!" (Delight and perfection—what harmony!).

By way of concluding this chapter, we want to examine some of these Batiushkovian *loci* from the point of view of their sound pattern and attempt to ascertain what in particular could have given rise to Pushkin's exultation over their "harmony." The methodology is the same as the one applied to Shakespeare's Sonnets in chapter 1. By the criteria for sonority established there, the ninth strophe of "K drugu," which is especially relevant because of the phrase "звуки итальянские [Italian sounds]" in Pushkin's characterization, the sonority and obstruency quotients are .190 and .095, respectively. Now, if we analyze all of "Ten' druga," using 14-line spans as convenient units (because of their direct comparability to the sonnet), we get the distribution shown in figure 1:

Figure 1					
Lines	Syllables	SUs	SQ	OUs	OQ
1-14	157	43	3.65	13	12.08
15-28	157	53	2.96	17	9.24
29-42	158	48	3.29	14	11.29
39-56	165	38	4.34	13	12.69

It is interesting to note that at the extremes, there is a relation of complementarity between the two types of units: the greatest sonority (.296) is balanced off by the highest ratio of obstruency (9.24), and the lowest obstruency (12.69) is complemented by the lowest sonority (4.34). In fact, there is a uniform progression in the relation between the two quotients: as the sonority decreases, the obstruency also decreases, which means that there is overall a constant maintenance of sonority even when the obstruent quotient rises.

Pushkin actually outdoes Batiushkov in the sonorousness of his verse. His "Muza," analyzed earlier, is of special interest here as well because Pushkin is reported to have said, when asked in 1828 by N. D. Ivanchin-Pisarev why he had chosen to write these particular verses into the latter's album, "I like them: they are redolent of the verse of Batiushkov [отзываются стихами Батюшкова]" (Maikov 1895: 222).

This poem is striking for its high sonority. Over a span of 173 syllables it has 58 sonorant units and only 11 obstruent units, yielding a sonorant quotient of .335 and an obstruent quotient of .064. The very high degree of sonority, which is the result here of both indicators acting in concert, can be appreciated more palpably by looking at the figures for three other well-known Pushkin poems in the same stylistic vein: "Я пережил свои желанья" [I have outlived my desires; 1821], "К *** ("Я помню чудное мгновеье")" [To *** ("I remember a miraculous moment"); 1825], and "Что в имени тебе моем" [What's in my name for you; 1830]. Figure 2, while showing that these three are all much less sonorous than "Muza," also reveals that they are still significantly more sonorous than poems examined from (1) the production of Pushkin's lesser coevals; and (2) three eighteenth-century predecessors.[26]

What stands out in these figures is the consistent tandem relationship between the two quotients in Pushkin—but not in the other poets. The extreme example of this is in "Muza," which achieves the highest sonority quotient (.335), as well as the lowest obstruency quotient (.064). The rest of the sample exhibits intermediate values for all the poets including Pushkin, but it is only in Pushkin that these two quotients *combine* in one poem to render the poem maximally sonorous.

Naturally, due to the difference in structure between Italian and Russian,[27] a Petrarch sonnet like CXXXII, from which the mangled opening line is taken by Pushkin and inserted with-

Figure 2			
	Syllables	SQ	OQ
Pushkin			
Muza	173	.335	.064
"Ia perezhil"	102	.206	.127
K***	192	.297	.099
"Chto v imeni"	136	.287	.140
Gnedich	139	.209	.072
Kiukhel'beker	209	.215	.100
Glinka	119	.118	.143
Viazemskii	176	.301	.136
Kozlov	140	.279	.129
Ryleev	119	.160	.143
Odoevskii	119	.203	.109
Lomonosov	112	.250	.098
Sumarokov	147	.259	.116
Derzhavin	136	.147	.096

out attribution in "Metel,"[28] has a far more dispersed obstruency quotient (.033), though its sonority quotient (.278) is comparable to that of our Russian examples. But a Petrarchan imprint in Pushkin ought never to be discerned merely in the comparability of these quotients. In Pushkin's "Èkho" (1831), for example, the quotients .146 and .083 are in and of themselves neutral with respect to the phonetic structure, but the sound is definitely an echo of the sense (cf. Ward 1975):[29]

Ревет ли зверь в лесу глухом,

Трубит ли рог, гремит ли гром,

Поет ли дева за холмом—
На всякой звук

Свой отклик в воздухе пустом

Родишь ты вдруг.

Ты внемлешь грохоту громов,

И гласу бури и валов,

И крику сельских пастухов—

И шлешь ответ;

Тебе ж нет отзыва…Таков

И ты, поэт!

(PSS 3: 276)

(Whether a beast roars in the empty forest
Or a horn blows or thunder thunders,
Or a maid sings beyond the hill—
To any sound
Your own response in the empty air
You generate suddenly.
You listen to the roll of thunderclaps,
And the voice of the storm and the waves
And the shout of village shepherds—
And send your answer.
But to you there is no response…Such
Are you, poet!)

As the ligatures show, the constant sound reversals throughout the poem diagram both the symmetrical nature of an echo as an acoustic event and the asymmetry between the echoless poet and all of the other producers of sound. This is just the sort of orchestration with which Petrarch's poetry is synonymous.

9

THE MEANING OF METER

Whether meter has meaning is part of the larger question whether the content of verse is represented iconically in its form, a question as old as the study of poetry itself. Aristotle answers it affirmatively in the *Poetics* (1459a.31–1460a.4):

> As for its metre, the heroic has been assigned it [the Epic] from experience; were anyone to attempt a narrative poem in some one, or in several, of the other metres, the incongruity of the thing would be apparent. The heroic in fact is the gravest and weightiest of metres—which is what makes it more tolerant than the rest of strange words and metaphors, that being a point in which the narrative form of poetry goes beyond all others. The iambic and trochaic, on the other hand, are metres of movement, the one representing that of life and action, the other that of the dance. Still more unnatural would it appear, if one were to write an epic in a medley of metres.... Hence it is that no one has ever written a long story in any but heroic verse; nature it-

self... teaches us to select the metre appropriate to such a story. (1941: 1481–82).

Dante echoes this view when he reserves the longer, syntactically more developed verse line for poetry of weightier content (*De vulgari eloquentia* II. v. 10). In Russian literary history one is reminded of the famous competition among the three great eighteenth-century originators of literary verse in Russia, Trediakovskii, Lomonosov, and Sumarokov, which involved the unprecedented procedure of each poet submitting his translation of Psalm 143 to the judgment of the reading public.[1] In the commentary preceding the translations Lomonosov argues that each of the two binary meters, iamb and trochee, has an emotional color that is appropriate to it, each a subject matter that it implements and an aesthetic character (including genre) toward which it gravitates owing to the meter's own formal nature. According to Lomonosov the iambic foot is endowed with "nobility" since it contains a "rise" from an unstressed to a stressed syllable ("стопа ямба...имеет благородство, для того что она возносится с низу в верх"); hence the iamb is fit for use in heroic verse and in the ode. The trochee by contrast involves a "drop" from a stressed to an unstressed syllable, hence is deemed by Lomonosov to be proper to elegiac poetry. Trediakovskii takes the opposing view in this debate, denying that either iambs or trochees have a meaning uniquely and naturally appropriate to them, while Sumarokov sides with Lomonosov. (The point of the competition, as all three poets emphasize in their prefatory remarks, is not to see who can compose the best translation but to settle a controversy of theoretical poetics.)

Jumping now to the twentieth century, the issue of the "semantics of meter" has been given prominence in the work of the leading contemporary Russian metrist, M. L. Gasparov, who considers meters and their variants to have what he calls "semantic aureoles" ("семантический ореол"), a designation which appears to have been inaugurated in a slightly different form by Vinogradov (1959: 28).[2] Gasparov insists (e.g., at 1976: 358), however, that meters have no "organic" meaning. Indeed, he adduces the very pronouncements of Lomonosov on the semantic values of iambs and trochees as a paradigm case of "rhetorical exaggeration" (ibid.) to be contrasted with the enlightened attitude of modern scholarship, which can no longer countenance such excesses. In Gasparov's view the only legitimate area of investigation is what he terms the "historical" relation between metrical variants and the semantic matter they encompass. Through continued use over time certain variants become associated with a specifiable range of genres, themes, and semantic substance. Citing John Hollander's concept of "meter as emblem" (1959), Gasparov recognizes (1979: 283) that meters may become "emblematic" of a fairly concrete poetic content, typically when the history of the meter or variant is marked by a particularly prominent poem (e.g., the five-foot trochee through Lermontov's famous "Выхожу один я на дорогу ..." ["I walk out onto the road alone ..."]). The representative character of some aspect of poetic form is, of course, not limited to meter and may include rhyme and stanzaic structure, among others.

The notion that meter is devoid of organic meaning has a deceptive appeal. Gasparov's position is based on the conviction that direct, one-to-one, ahistorical correlations between form and content cannot be made out in poetry. But this objection dissolves as soon as we shift to a *strictly relational* and generally more abstract concept of correlation, and examples of iconicity in its chief subspecies, that of diagrammatization (relations mirrored by relations), are everywhere to hand. One of the most straightforward cases is that of the angrammatization of a riddle's answer in its phonic substance (Gerbstman 1968). Dante's invention of *terza rima* with enchained rhymes in the *Comedy* is in perfect alignment with the conceptual leitmotif of a *poema sacro*, the indissolubility of the Trinity. Pushkin created and implemented the fourteen-line stanza in *Evgenii Onegin* because this long form mirrors the work's peculiarity as a novel in verse, a genre "organically" requiring extended narratorial cadences. The history of the sestina, perhaps the most closed poetic form of Western literature, which spans more than eight centuries (from its invention by the troubadour Arnaut Daniel through modern practitioners like Auden), shows that the asymmetrical disposition of rhyme words always diagrammatizes a whole set of asymmetrical content elements including this fiendishly difficult poem's tropes.[3] At an even more abstract level of analysis, consider the difference between Russian literary and folk poetry in respect of the constraints on rhyme that each canon imposes. In masculine closed rhyme, for example, the range of allowable final consonants is much wider in proverbs and riddles than in "imaginative" verse (Shapiro 1978: 364). This trait can be seen as an indicator of the generally more restricted nature of poetic structure in literary production (a view borne out by the entire tradition of philology) as compared with the less-regulated one of folklore, metrically as in many other respects. In a similar vein of abstraction, Pushkin's turn toward the end of his life from poetry to prose (cf. Èikhenbaum 1923) is accompanied by a shift away from canonic metrical forms to freer ones like those of "Песни западных славян" ("Songs of the Western Slavs") (cf. Trubetskoi 1963: 59). The iconicity inherent in these examples is less straightforward but nonetheless palpable.

These examples are, to be sure, not strictly metrical in the narrow sense of Gasparov's observations, which is not to say that metrical ones do not exist. An obvious case is hypermetrical stressing for semantic emphasis (cf. Laferriere 1980: 431–34 where phenomena of this sort are called "the *semantic effects of metrical deautomatization*" [431]). But even this common example leaves the matter of the iconicity of metrical variants (as realizations of "verse design" rather than "verse instances"— more on this distinction later) untouched, and here at least Gasparov's insistence on the nonorganic, conventional (qua historically determined) character of the meaning of meter seems to be justified.[4] In the face of what would appear to be the exclusively historical determination of the semantic content of specific metrical variants like the Russian amphibrachic trimeter (Gasparov 1982) or the trochaic pentameter (Vishnevskii 1985), perhaps we would do well to abandon the search for "intrinsic content" as a will-o'-the-wisp of research into metrics. The rest of this chapter is devoted to spelling out the reasons why we should do no such thing.

Progress in this area of poetics has been thwarted, we believe, because the seminal insights of the two most prominent Russian structuralists of the interwar period, Trubetskoi and Jakobson, have never adequately informed the research agenda (their own included). Starting at least as early as 1930 (see Trubetskoi 1975: 182), the idea arises that "linguistic values, not bare sounds, are the building-blocks of verse, and the role that prosodic elements fulfill in a given linguistic system is decisive for verse" (Jakobson SW 5: 148). Much later this idea is amplified to the point of an assertion that "the constituents of the poetic meter are *relational concepts*...and the relations concerned are not mere contingencies but *genuine oppositions*" (SW 5: 574, emphasis added). It is clear from Trubetskoi's formulation of the problem (in a letter to Jakobson dated November 11, 1930) that these linguistic values are *markedness values* (cf. SW 5: 574). Because of its crucial importance to our analysis we translate the relevant passage in extenso (Trubetskoi 1975: 182):

> In normal linguistic consciousness the symbol of the archiphoneme is the passive (unmarked) phoneme of a given correlation. Thus, for instance, for every normal Russian the symbol of the correlation *t/ t'* [unpalatalized/palatalized *t*] is, of course, not *t'* but *t*. For a normal Czech the symbol of the correlation *a/a* is

[short] *a*, not [long] *ā*. So that if from this point of view one approaches the stress correlation in Russian, then it is easy to be convinced that the unmarked member of this correlation is not the unstressed but rather the stressed vowel, since it is just the stressed *u, a, i* that serve for every normal Russian as the symbol of the correlation *ú/u, á/ a, í/i*. In other words, the stress correlation in Russian is expressed not as the opposition of "stressedness: unstressedness" but as the opposition "unreducedness:reducedness" [of the vowels. ...I think that the understanding of the essence of the stress correlation in Russian allows one adequately to explain the fact that in Russian versification metrical schemes are constructed on the normalization of the placement of unstressed (reduced) vowels: the iamb—the meter where all odd syllables are unstressed; the trochee—the meter where all even syllables are unstressed; and the ternary meters—meters where a pair of unstressed syllables is repeated at an interval of one syllable.

The notion that stressed and unstressed syllables in Russian verse are evaluated unequally (aside from any phonetic consequences) is anticipated in Trubetskoi's earlier review (1923–1924: 456) of Jakobson's *О чешском стихе* (*On Czech Verse*) (1923), in which Trubetskoi treats the unstressed syllable as the sole unit of measurement of metrical time in Russian verse ("in Russian prosody...the unit of measurement is the unstressed...syllable...for a Russian the sole criterion of rhythmic time is the short unstressed syllable"). Fourteen years later in his study of Pushkin's "Pesni zapadnykh slavian," Trubetskoi succeeds in formulating a more substantial statement of his analysis of Russian versification—as a result of his own major advances during the interim (Trubetskoi [1937] 1963: 56):

...in most theories of Russian versification the highly essential feature of basic linguistic oppositions on which contemporary "phonologists" have worked especially is lost sight of, namely the privative character of these oppositions.

Under privative opposition in the most general sense we understand the opposition of the presence of some feature to the absence of that feature. In certain sectors of language (e.g., in morphology) a special kind of privative opposition dominates: the obligatoriness of the feature is opposed to its non-obligatoriness. ... And it is just this kind of privative opposition which plays a decisive role in metrics (particularly in Russian). The statement that "Russian versification is based on the alternation of stressed and unstressed syllables" is not quite accurate. In actual fact the alternation is between either "obligatorily stressed" and "non-obligatorily stressed" or "obligatorily unstressed" with "non-obligatorily unstressed" syllables.

Trubetskoi then goes on to give his own definitions and resultant classification of traditional Russian meters, line-ends, and line-types by number of feet.[5] "What is most curious (and lamentable) in view of his explicitly phonological framework is the fact that Trubetskoi refrains from applying his own notion of markedness ("the privative character of linguistic oppositions") to the analysis of metrical units.[6] It is this dangling thread that we now propose to take up, limiting ourselves to canonic ("classical," traditional) Russian verse forms.

Meter, as Trubetskoi points out (1963: 58), belongs exclusively to the domain of *langue*, hence any discussion of the *values of metrical units* must necessarily be understood as pertaining to *verse design* rather than to verse instances (cf. *SW* 5: 573, 587). It is in this light that Russian binary meters are to be evaluated as unmarked vis-à-vis their marked ternary counterparts.[7] These two basic types of Russian meters are opposed to each other in precisely the same sense that the term and the concept of opposition are endowed with throughout language and culture (recall *SW* 5: 574). Strictly speaking the opposition is between binary and non-binary meters; this statement of the terms is not only more precise (as well as being more consistent with the privative character of opposition) but more accurately reflects the fact that: (1) "free" or "non-classical" verse forms (including the so-called strict stress-meter forms known in Russian as *dol'niki*; see Tarlinskaja 1993) are also to be admitted to the canon; and (2) these forms (particularly *dol'niki*; see Gasparov 1984: 254–55) are known to have a decided affinity with ternary meters in their statistical realizations.

It is especially important to understand that the unmarkedness of binary meters emanates not from any statistical properties of ordinary language or from their implementation in poetry.[8] Markedness belongs primarily to form and not to substance. We must consequently examine the ontological structure of the terms of any opposition in order to comprehend their markedness values. It is at this point that we need to recur to Trubetskoi's determination of the value of stress in Russian and its pertinence to meter (1975: 182).

Russian stressed syllables are unmarked and unstressed syllables marked. Applying the idea (Michael Shapiro 1980b) that multiply marked units (i.e., units containing more than one marked component) are of a greater degree of markedness than singly marked units or unmarked units, it becomes apparent that binary meters are by definition composed of units (here: feet) that contain one fewer marked component—the unstressed syllable—than are ternary meters, which invariably have no fewer than two unstressed syllables in their verse design aspect.

In fact we would claim that it is the unmarked value of binary meters and the marked value of ternary meters that underlies and accounts for their relative frequency in the history of Russian poetry (or English, for that matter). Binary meters are more frequent primarily because they are the unmarked member of the opposition binary vs. non-binary, where the marked term's compass includes ternary meters as a basic variant. Relations at the level of paradigmatic structure are mirrored diagrammatically at the level of textual distribution—poetic texts being identical in this respect with those of non-poetic speech (cf. Shapiro 1983: ch. 2).

Exactly the same relational analysis applies to rhyme types in binary meters, that is to rhymed line-ends that are traditionally called masculine, feminine, and dactylic depending on whether there are (1) no syllables after the last stress; (2) one such syllable; or (3) two unstressed post-tonic syllables, respectively. The fundamental opposition is that between masculine and non-masculine rhyme types. Masculine rhymes are unmarked in virtue of the fact that they are constituted by a stressed syllable (the unmarked value of the syllable for syllable type) and have no post-tonic unstressed syllables (the marked value for syllable type). Bearing in mind the principle of multiple markedness (multiply marked units, etc.), we come to the conclusion that within the marked category of non-masculine rhymes the feminine subtype is less marked than the dactylic because it has one marked (unstressed) syllable whereas the dactylic has two.

It is instructive to confront this purely structural characterization of rhyme types with their historical development in Russian poetry. In the eighteenth century masculine rhymes were not resisted until Lomonosov broke through this essentially alien prohibition imported from Western Europe (Gasparov 1984: 83). Dactylic line-ends were totally impossible in French poetry and hence taboo as well (although they were not unknown in their unrhymed version; Gasparov 1984: 84). The other major restriction was against the adjacent repetition of rhyme types (again, imported from France) which meant that there had necessarily to be an alternation of masculine and feminine rhymes (закон альтернанса) wherever both cooccurred in the same poem. Exceptions to this "law of alternation" were felt very keenly to be exactly that (like Lomonosov's famous "Лицо свое скрывает день ..." [Day hides its face...])—but not, nota bene, when they occurred in the (marked) genre of the literary song, as attested to by numerous examples from Sumarokov's rich production that display "blanket" (*сплошные*) masculine or feminine rhymes throughout.

The subsequent history of this aspect of Russian rhyme is characterized by a decisive shift away from such external restrictions (Gasparov 1984: 146). Aided by Zhukovskii's orientation away from French models toward English and German ones in which blanket masculine and feminine rhymes (non-alternation) were allowed, the first phase of this evolutionary process (from ca. 1816 through the end of the 1820s) saw the introduction of lines with exclusively masculine rhymes, followed in the 1830s by blanket feminine rhymes. Dactylic rhyme came last, again through the agency of Zhukovskii's metrical innovations of 1822–1824 (Gasparov 1984: 148). This progression is consistently accounted for by Gasparov (cf. 1973: 144ff.) as a series of disparate (but not unconnected) events conditioned by purely literary factors such as the powerful stylistic impact of a particularly striking poem (e. g., Karamzin's "Il'ia Muromets" [1794] in unrhymed [!] four-foot trochees). Without disparaging the importance of literary-historical precedents it should also be noted that the development under discussion only becomes *coherent* when viewed in terms of the structural characteristics of the rhyme types themselves apart from the historical record. On this analysis it is no accident, therefore, that the unmarked rhyme type of masculine was introduced first, when blanket rhymes constituted an innovation. This innovation was followed in order by the introduction of blanket feminine rhymes and then by dactylic—that is to say, first by the less marked type and then by the most marked type of the three. It does not seem far fetched to claim that the historical drift in this process was governed by a telos, itself defined by the markedness values of the entities as they evolved. That telos was the propagation of the diagrammatic relations between the values of the rhyme types and their contexts of occurrence in the historical record.

An analogous determinant can be observed in relation to dactylic rhyme as a special case. To anticipate a more detailed account later, here it must first be stipulated that within binary meters iamb is unmarked vis-à-vis trochee (for reasons to be set out below). When Zhukovskii translated Joan of Arc's monologue from Schiller's *Die Jungfrau von Orleans* in 1820 and published it in 1822–1824 together with a translation of some verse from Byron, he utilized dactylic rhymes where the originals had none (Gasparov 1984: 148). Gasparov draws (to reiterate) a direct causal line between the introduction of dactylic rhyme here and the "the memory in Russian poetry [of that period] of Karamzin's 4-foot trochees" (ibid.). He also sees the Karamzinian stylistic influence as the answer to the strictly metrical puzzle concerning the resort to trochaic verse at the very apogee of the iamb in Russian poetry (Gasparov 1973a: 144). Our addendum here would be that the trochee as the marked binary meter is more apt to be the *context* of dactylic rhyme for reasons of structure rather than literary history. In the marked context of trochaic verse it is the marked rhyme type (here: dactylic) that is to be expected in accordance with a general process known as markedness assimilation whereby marked units cohere (are congruent) with marked contexts and unmarked units with unmarked contexts. There is nothing preordained or absolute about this process or the principle governing it. It is nonetheless a real structural tendency in a systematically teleological sense. This understanding of the tendency toward coherence or congruence between contexts and units as applied to the history of Russian rhyme also explains why by the 1850s and beyond, when they cease to be exotic rarities, dactylic rhymes are utilized overwhelmingly in trochaic and dactylic verse (Gasparov 1984: 194), the maximally marked members of their respective metrical categories, binary and ternary (see below).

The issue of the value of meters within the two chief categories of binary and ternary is among the most vital that we wish to address in our analysis. Before getting into details there is one principle of structure that must be mentioned before all others, which we call *the principle of marked beginnings*.[9] All units of poetic structure, we believe, conform to this principle of organization absent certain countermanding conditions. Since texts also have middles and ends, for the relational force of this principle to be assessed one must also recognize the value of these contexts as positional entities. Endings are marked along with beginnings except that they are of a lesser degree of markedness than are beginnings. Both beginnings and endings considered jointly can be thought of as *margins* and opposed to middles (*nuclei*) as marked to unmarked positions together with the substance comprising them.

With the principle of marked beginnings as a backdrop we can now look anew at the traditional syllabotonic meters of Russian poetry. Taking iamb and trochee first and bearing in mind that unstressed syllables in Russian are marked and stressed syllables unmarked, we arrive at the evaluation of iamb as the unmarked and trochee as the marked binary meter. If the values of the meters are seen as conforming to the principle of marked beginnings, then the meter that begins with a marked syllable conforms more closely to the principle than does its opposed counterpart, with its initial unmarked syllable. Iambs begin with an unstressed (marked) syllable and are thereby unmarked; trochees begin with a stressed (unmarked) syllable and are thereby marked.

Ternary meters are amenable to exactly the same analysis

except that there are two oppositions within this category, which is itself the marked member of the opposition (see above). The category of ternary meters subdivides into dactyls on the one hand and amphibrachs and anapests on the other. Dactyls are the most marked member of the category because they have a stressed syllable in initial position (of the foot), i.e., the number of unstressed pretonic syllables is zero. Amphibrachs are more marked than anapests but are unmarked vis-à-vis dactyls, whereas anapests are unmarked vis-à-vis both dactyls and amphibrachs, the criterion of markedness being the number of unstressed syllables in the foot before the tonic: the fewer pretonic unstressed syllables, the more marked the foot and hence the meter.

That there are two distinct criteria involved in evaluating types of meters—as well as an order of their application—should not be overlooked. In the opposition of binary and non-binary meters the binary meters are evaluated as unmarked by the principle of multiple markedness. In the case of the opposition between subtypes within binary and ternary meters the operative criterion is the principle of marked beginnings in the first instance and the principle of multiple markedness secondarily.

Let us now juxtapose this purely structural scheme to what is known about the behavior of Russian iambs and trochees, using Laferriere's excellent inquiry (1979) as a guide. The statistical prevalence of iambs over trochees (as well as all other meters, for that matter) is widely recognized and amply documented (Zhirmunskii 1975: 46; Gasparov 1974: 50–62). The iamb's supremacy is a direct outcome, on our analysis, of its unmarkedness; correspondingly the marked status of trochees within this category is mirrored statistically by its relatively restricted frequency (ditto, incidentally, for English; see Hascall 1971: 225).

The phenomenon of hypermetrical stress, defined as "a lexical stress in non-ictic position" (Laferriere 1979: 96),[10] can be understood from this perspective too. To get matters straight we have to realize that the *incidence* of stress in non-ictic position is marked but that the *stress itself* is an unmarking of the syllable on which it falls, owing to the fact that unstressed syllables in Russian are marked and stressed syllables unmarked.[11] This differential concept can be applied, for instance, to hypermetrical stressing of the specific sort in which the ictic position is also realized in the same foot. Such a stress is certainly marked, but the syllable on which it falls is rendered unmarked (changed from marked to unmarked status) by virtue of shifting from what would otherwise (metrically) be an unstressed syllable to a stressed syllable. In Russian binary meters the incidence of hypermetrical stress (in strictly literary genres; see Laferriere 1979: 97 et passim) is less frequent in trochaic than in iambic lines, a trait it shares with English verse (Newton 1975: 137). The statistical disparity is particularly pronounced in the first foot (nearly 30 times as frequent in iambs as in trochees). The differential concept of markedness as applied to Russian linguistic stress in a metrical context accounts for hypermetrical stressing in iambic more frequently than in trochaic verse by virtue of the congruence between the unmarked value of iambs and that of stressed syllables. With regard to the prevalence of hypermetrical stress in the first foot it is the incidence of such stress evaluated as a marked occurrence that is congruent with the marked value of initial feet in conformity with the principle of marked beginnings. These are further instantiations of markedness assimilation as an explanans of the fact of congruence or coherence between units and contexts.[12]

This markedness analysis also has a bearing on the long-standing controversy over the exact terms in which the restriction on hypermetrical stressing (запрет переакцентуации ['prohibition against transaccentuation']) is to be stated. In a reprise of this issue Gasparov (Kholshevnikov 1984: 174–78) joins Kholshevnikov (1984: 68–73) in setting aside Jakobson's claim (1973; cf. *SW* 5: 584) that the exemption of monosyllables from this restriction is to be explained phonologically, as the result of the neutralization of distinctive stress in words with only one syllable (cf. Laferriere 1979: 98–99, who also disagrees and cites Gasparov 1973b: 409). Gasparov's argument leans principally on the observation that hypermetrical stress can also occur in disyllables—specifically in ternary meters—which makes the phonological properties of monosyllables irrelevant to the problem of "transaccentuation" (Kholshevnikov 1984: 176). The examples that illustrate the problem from the standpoint of Russian ternary meters (omitted from consideration by Jakobson 1973) and cited by Gasparov (ibid.) are revealing (the meanings are irrelevant):

PERMISSIBLE LINES
1. В чác отлива на илистом дне
2. Ты возьми мою [moiú] руку, товарищ
3. Я опять мою [móiu] руку под краном

IMPERMISSIBLE LINE
4. Я мóю себе руку под краном

All these lines are anapestic with hypermetrical stress: on a monosyllable in 1 and on a disyllable in 2–4. For the sake of comparison consider also the following minimal pair of iambic lines (Jakobson 1973: 242; cf. 1969: 29):

PERMISSIBLE
6. С нéй убежать мечтал гусар

IMPERMISSIBLE
7. С нéю бежать мечтал гусар

Gasparov (Kholshevnikov 1984: 177) reformulates the rule governing Russian syllabotonic verse in several parts that take account of ternary as well as binary meters:

1. Verse consists in the alternation of strong and weak positions;
2. the syllabic span of strong positions is 1 syllable, of weak positions—1 syllable in binary meters, 2 syllables in ternary meters, and 1–2 syllables in *dol'niki;*
3. the last strong position is occupied by the stressed syllable of any word;
4. the remaining strong positions may be occupied by either stressed or unstressed syllables of any word; and
5. weak positions may be occupied either by unstressed syllables of any word or by the stressed syllable of any word *that does not extend* beyond the boundaries of the weak position it occupies [emphasis in the original].

He then adds:

> The definition is exhaustive at this point; further details (about what variants occupying which positions are preferred or avoided) are expressed in relative rather than absolute terms—"constants," "dominants," and "tendencies" (introduced by R. Jakobson as well).

Gasparov's final wording is an attempt to reduce the several parts of his version of the "rule of Russian verse" to the following formula:

> Russian syllabotonic verse is verse in which there is a regularized alternation of positions that may and those that may not be occupied by the stressed syllables of words *that have no restriction on the placement of word boundaries.*

Granting Gasparov's further point that this formula has the advantage of accurately encompassing the syllabic as well as the tonic side of the designation of Russian verse as "syllabotonic," we would nevertheless urge a different wording that is consistent with our whole analysis:

> Russian syllabotonic verse is verse in which there is a regularized alternation of marked ["weak"] and unmarked ["strong"] positions that may or may not be occupied by the unmarked ["stressed"] syllables of words whose marked ["unstressed"] syllables *if any* can only occupy a marked position.

This formulation offers all the essential advantages of Gasparov's final version and, we believe, goes a significant step further by integrating Russian verse theory in a uniform conceptual framework that embraces contexts and units *at all levels of analysis,* not just the metrical.[13]

The superiority of an integrated framework can be tested further by a reexamination of two of the staples of the statistical analysis of Russian verse, the so-called "basic laws concerning the fulfillment and non-fulfillment of ictuses" (Laferriere 1979: 114).[14] By this is meant: (1) the tendency of the Russian verse line to avoid stressing contiguous ictuses starting from the obligatorily stressed final ictus and working back toward the beginning of the line; and (2) the tendency of the first ictus to be omitted, thereby making the second ictus more "stable," i.e., more likely to be realized.[15] As Laferriere astutely points out (1979: 116) these statistical tendencies "relate less to the line's *primary rhythm* (the succession of weak vs. strong ictuses) than to the line's *secondary rhythm* (the succession of feet)."[16] However, in either case these statistical data have not to do with verse design but with the cumulative distribution of verse instances, which means that they are silent about the foundations of Russ-

ian verse theory and speak volumes about the empirical consequences of the theory's constitutive principles.

From the perspective developed earlier, in fact, it is evident
that the two contiguous ictuses at the end of the line (the ultima
and the penult) are subject to dissimilation as an indirect result
of the principle of marked beginnings, whose relational corollary is that endings are less marked vis-à-vis beginnings while
remaining marked overall vis-à-vis the unmarked value of middles. In the case of the Russian verse line the penultimate ictus
is a "middle," i.e., a medial unit. But *in its relation to* the ultimate
ictus, which is unmarked both in virtue of its status vis-à-vis beginnings and its invariable stressedness, the penult is opposed to
the ultima, hence its evaluation as marked.[17] The statistical consequence of this evaluation is the tendency for the penultimate
ictus to go unrealized, i.e., for there to be an unstressed (marked)
syllable in this position.

Similarly it is the principle of marked beginnings that accounts for the statistical tendency of the first ictus in the line to
go unrealized. This marked context is congruent with the realization of the marked unit—an unstressed syllable.

Looking beyond these well-known cases one can grasp not
just their secondary, derived nature as the empirical stuff of
poetry (both rhythm and rhythmic/metrical variants are to be
subsumed under this rubric) but the equivalent hierarchical status of that hoary pillar of poetic construction, parallelism.[18]
Whether in verse or music or any fundamentally temporal
medium, parallelism bears the same relation to form as do the
statistical data to the principles of structure (design) of which
they are the empirical outcome. Principles and laws (as Peirce
observed many years ago) are never the cumulative total of their
instances and are never exhausted by them. Applying this foundational idea to the matter of parallelism and to parallelistic construction in verse, we realize that these are part of the
content-substance of poetry; but that this aspect is *simultane-*

ously transcended by the aspect of content-form, which is the one that pertains directly to meaning, to the formation and growth of symbols.[19] Jakobson's oft-cited definition of the poetic function (1960: 358) entails his own dictum regarding the equalization (equal realization) of all the units of poetry, but it has not been sufficiently well understood that this is valid only at the level of content-substance. The supervening formal nature of his and Trubetskoi's concept of markedness ("intrinsic content") is borne out by the *unequal evaluation* (asymmetry) of the units themselves, including metrical units, and in their being correctly defined as *oppositive* as well as binary and relative.

Trubetskoi advocated extending to metrics his fundamental insight into the asymmetric nature of linguistic oppositions ([1937] 1963: 56). A resumption, after a lapse of more than half a century, of the research program prefigured by the methodological implications of his ideas promises to yield a new and definitive understanding of the meaning of meter as part of poetic structure.

10

WIMP ENGLISH

With the contemporary shift away from traditional work requiring brawn to the epicene service economy relying on brain power, dexterity, and "good customer relations," there has been a concomitant change in speech patterns whereby directness and plainspokenness are regularly being avoided in favor of indirection and blandness. These patterns are especially typical of public pronouncements and the speech of persons who must take care to be as neutral or noncommittal as possible.

This kind of speech can be called *Wimp English*, a designation coined by Marianne Shapiro. In this chapter we would like to describe some features of Wimp, particularly as a variety of American English, but not only, given the dominance of American speech patterns in the English-speaking world.

Despite the fact that elementary handbooks of forceful writing routinely warn against its use, one of the most entrenched means by which blandness is achieved is the use of the passive instead of the active voice. The passive necessarily means a diminution in force because agents are always grammatically less central than subjects, quite apart from changes in syntax; cf.

Miss Smith paid attention vs. *Attention was paid by Miss Smith*. But there are at least three other grammatical means of achieving toothlessness.

The first is the use of the modal *would* after the first person singular pronoun with verbs such as *hope, think, imagine*. The combination—*I would hope*—is so commonplace that one tends to forget its peculiarly blunted character: *I would hope that Jane would pay her debts* is so much more circumspect than *I hope that Jane pays her debts*. Politicians, managers, bureaucrats, and flak-catchers of all stripes, including academics, are often heard uttering such locutions. In an interview concerning the film version of Tom Wolfe's novel *The Bonfire of the Vanities*, the director, Brian De Palma is quoted as saying: "the book caused a tremendous furor when it came out. I would hope that the film would have [sic] the same furor" (*New York Times*, December 16, 1990, p. 42). The effect of the *would* here is to distance the speaker from hope: not only is he afraid to hope that the film will have the same success as the book but even to allow himself the hope. The catachresis of the verb *have* with respect to *furor* (signaled by our *sic*) only underscores the pusillanimity. This is linguistic "wimpishness" par excellence.

A second feature of Wimp English is the use of the participle or deverbal adjective, particularly adjectives in -*ive*, plus *of* instead of the verb, e.g., *They were admiring of her coiffure; we are very supportive of his initiative* (cf. Hamp 1988); *This trait is indicative of a certain mentality; They are desirous of the public's approval*; etc. The adjectives, being stative, are necessarily attenuated vis-à-vis the finite verbs with which they are correlated (or derived from) because as nominalized verbs they lack the main property of a transitive verb: its transitivity, specifically its ability to govern the *direct* object.

Nominalization also entails the further consequence that the sentence will be longer, often leading to convolution, hence a further attenuation of semantic directness. Another likelihood is that a sentence built on an adjectival construction like *is indicative of* will be a simple (subject-predicate) sentence, although possibly "swollen by parentheses and modifiers" (Wells 1960: 216). The combination of parataxis and extended length has the effect of deflecting semantic force.

Thirdly, and most intriguingly, there is a relatively new feature of Wimp English. On 27 July 1990, Michael Shapiro was sitting in the Manhattan office of the American Automobile Association and overheard a woman say to an agent, "My dilemma, if you will, is that…" Now, judging from the context, *dilemma* was being used in a perfectly straightforward way: the woman had only a limited amount of time in which to visit two destinations and had to make a choice. The use of a somewhat bookish word apparently made the speaker append the tag "if you will," *as if the word's use needed to be sanctioned by the hearer.* Webster's (1961: 2617) gloss for the phrase is "if you wish to call it that." In Wimp English, however, the gloss has changed to "if I may be allowed to call it that." This interpretation is confirmed, for instance, by the example of its use by a cardiologist talking to some colleagues about the feasibility of a heart bypass operation while they jointly examine an angiogram: "This arterial blockage, if you will, could cause problems down the line" (*Borderline Medicine*, PBS Television, WNET, New York, December 17, 1990). *If you will* is a much more widespread locution than *so to speak* and has a peculiar semantic force, hence our concentration on it to the exclusion of the latter.[1]

The change in its meaning becomes obvious when one analyzes the frequent use of the phrase after tropes. Recently, we heard a guest (a U. S. Defense Department official) on a Sunday morning talk show append *if you will* to the phrase *walk on eggs*. Persons in the public eye are now habitually loath to utter something figurative for fear of departing from literal expression, as if a trope were a complication to be shunned, in the same way that anything verbally out of the ordinary is to be avoided. In some speakers the incidence of *if you will* has reached that of a verbal tic, akin to *you know* or *like*.

This is an example of Wimp English for the most fundamental reason. Any resort to tropological expression does something that literalness always avoids: it necessarily foregrounds the creativity involved in troping, the element of choice inherent in saying something figuratively rather than literally. The converse is not true. More importantly, the element of choice always highlights the subjectivity of the form of the utterance, hence of the *speaking subject*. What Wimp English wants to avoid at all costs, however, is just this kind of concentration on the speaking subject.

An interesting control on this analysis is the use of buzzwords or phraseological clichés. In Wimp English, these typically require no excuse, hence no *if you will* is heard after phrases like *down the pike, the ball's in their/his/her/your court*, etc. There is a sense of linguistic safety in using such locutions because of the (current) absence of unusualness. Sports metaphors may be complicated or indecipherable to someone lacking the appropriate knowledge of terminology, but the language of sports is an approved, even a correct means of semantic transference in ordinary American speech, which sustains an impersonal tenor while promoting bonding. As long as the utterer does not deem the linguistic material unusual, no prophylactic tag need be appended.

What accounts for the prevalence of Wimp English? The avoidance of individual responsibility and above all the need to be risk-free. Wimp English has found a home in advertising with the advent of consumer protection from exaggerated truth claims ("will not stick to most dental work," "good for *minor* aches and pains"). But TV is not any more to blame than the need to appease interest groups, governmental flip-flops, and national economic insecurity. What lies at the heart of Wimp English is *a failure of thought*.

Thought is always discriminatory, in the primary sense of the word: it makes distinctions. What binds together discourse strategies such as distancing by contrary-to-fact *(I would hope)*, defanging by adjectivization *(is appreciative of)* and concessive glossing by immediate demurral *(if you will)* is that they all seek to obliterate potential conflicts, oppositions, or even differences.

At bottom, Wimp English is a special manifestation of the strong tendency in American culture to level hierarchies. Grammatically, this tendency manifests itself in the preference for parataxis (coordination, comparison) over hypotaxis (subordination, differentiation), as in the currently ubiquitous but nonnormative use of *than* instead of *from* after *different/difference* (Shapiro 1988: 127–29). Nothing in grammar is more basic than the (asymmetric) rank relation between I and thou, between the speaking subject and the listener. Wimp English, in all of its manifestations, strives to subvert this hierarchization by insinuating a solidarity between Ego and Other which, in the final analysis, substitutes feeling for thought and submerges the referential in the phatic.

This trend can also be observed in a special sector of vocabulary, the designation of persons by sexual orientation. More and more in contemporary American English, particularly on signs carried by demonstrators, one sees male and female homosexuals differentiated by the designations *gay* and *lesbian*, respectively. These words are used more commonly than *homosexual* because the latter is perceived to be both too "clinical" (tending, therefore, toward a pejorative connotation; cf. the abbreviated version *homo*) and imposed on gays by straights. It is understandable, therefore, why gays have come to avoid the word *homosexual* as a self-designation.

What is peculiar, however, is the gravitation of *gay* toward the designation of male homosexuals, as in the binomial *gays and lesbians*. The second substantival constituent, *lesbian*, can only refer to a female, but *gay* is generic—as in *gay* rights, *gay* people, and the plural *gays* itself—so why the differentiation as to sex in the binomial? Cf. *lesbians and gay men.*

The distinction between *gay* and *lesbian* has been part of common usage since the early 1970s (Dynes 1985: 58). It is a linguistic sign of the change from the earlier movements of the '50s and '60s to gain public tolerance for homosexuals, as well as certain civil rights, to the movements of the '70s and '80s, including the feminist movement. It was the emergence of lesbians through the latter that forced the word into the *gay* rights movement. It is a tribute to the power of lesbians within the gay rights movement and also to the consciousness raising done among gay men that most major organizations now use these two terms. Be that as it may, it is still the case that terms used without suffixes that specifically indicate women are typically assumed to be male in the first instance.

The ensuing feeling of separatism between men and women homosexuals reflects divisions with regard to specific issues that affect them (including self-evaluation). From this point of view, it is natural, for instance, for women to insist on *lesbian* as a way of avoiding subsumption under a designation that is both generic and routinely appropriated by men. The use of *lesbian*, because of its restrictedness to females, has the effect of preventing (linguistically, at least) the dilution of the entire real-life congeries of meanings that attach to this word. Given the nature of sexual politics, particularism is just as much (if not more) a value as the need to make common cause with homosexuals of the opposite sex; hence the visibility of *lesbian* alongside *gay.*

Conversely, differentiation by sex can be equally a desideratum from the male point of view as from the female. Linguistically this tendency may be superseded by the need for a univerbal designation that is easier to use because of its brevity. Hence whether the word is *gay* or *lesbian*, it is better from the standpoint of linguistic economy than any phrasal compound such as *male/female homosexual*—whatever other drawbacks (such as particular evaluative connotations) these longer items might have. Beyond brevity, however, *gay* and *lesbian* have the important advantage of differentiating male from female referents, a function frequently made necessary by the communicative (social) context.

The social and semantic conditioning is not the entire answer to the question posed by the binomial *gays and lesbians*, however. In saying that *lesbian* is restricted in its referential scope to females, we are also recognizing a formal universal that attaches to all linguistic oppositions, namely that of *markedness*. Whereas the generic member of an opposition in semantics is relatively unrestricted in scope and hence unmarked (as is *man* in the opposition *man* vs. *woman*), the specific member is limited to a narrowed range of referential potential and hence marked (as is *woman*). The unmarked formal value of *gay* is reflected in its applicability to both men and women as a substantive and as an adjective.

Given the avowed goal of the gay rights movement of sexual equality between men and women, the persistence of *lesbian* and of the very opposition *gay* vs. *lesbian* in contemporary American English can be regarded as a sign of the power of traditional linguistic structure to reassert itself regardless of the ideological intent of its users. As represented linguistically, the male/female opposition comports a difference in valuation such that words designating the male are generic and unmarked, while the corresponding designations of females are specific and marked. In maintaining the distinction between the sexes, the widespread use of the binomial *gays and lesbians* is an adherence to general linguistic usage that not only undercuts some fundamental ideological positions but demonstrates the abidingly marked status of females in society regardless of sexual orientation.

A structurally analogous case of markedness with reference to Wimp English in American speech can be observed in the substitution of [ä] for [æ] in marked words.[2] The focus here, however, is on a specific form of avoidance, namely that of revealing one's linguistic ignorance.

Vacillation between [ä] ("broad" *A*) and [æ] ("flat" *A*) is a persistent feature of American speech, particularly in loan words or nomina propria, as in the twofold pronunciation of the stressed vowel of Colorado, Nevada, Iran, Iraq, Milan, etc. Whereas no Westerner would be caught dead saying *Color[ä]do* or *Nev[ä]da*, many of them, along with other Americans, do habitually say *Ir[ä]n, Ir[ä]q, and Mil[ä]n*, instead of the long-standing and traditional *Ir[æ]n, Ir[æ]q*, and *Mil[æ]n*. In the case of loan words, including designations of foreign places or things, even where initially there is vacillation between [ä] and [æ], as in *Viet Nam* (cf. the preference for [næm] over [näm] to render the slangy abbreviation *'Nam*), American speech in modern times seems to favor pronunciations that speakers likely construe as approximating the donor/original language's sounds, especially in the case of a smattering of knowledge of foreign (European?) languages. In this respect, American speech has tended to diverge from traditional British English—and the older American tradition (cf. Pyles 1952: 256–57)—in which anglicization has long been the norm (cf., for instance, the different rendering of names like *Kant* or *Dante*; or of words like *mafia).* Viewed from this perspective, pronunciations like *Ir[ä]n* simply conform to a current tendency.[3]

Recently, however, there has been a marked augmentation of the domain affected by the tendency—specifically, to include unfamiliar words, whether or not a particular word is ascertainably foreign and "known" to a speaker as such. In this new situation, the emphasis falls on unfamiliarity: the word in question is not part of a speaker's active vocabulary or is used sporadically. It may have been acquired from other speakers who are equally unfamiliar with it. In such cases, the pronunciation is likely to be at variance with the common or traditional pronunciation. Take the recently manifested vacillation in the stressed vowel of the journalistic buzz word (a Sanskrit borrowing) *mantra*: on two consecutive days (October 9 and 10, 1996) we heard *m[ä]ntra* instead of *m[æ]ntra* from Charlayne Hunter-Gault (PBS, *The News Hour)* and Mara Liasson (NPR, *Morning Edition)*. The foreign provenience of this word is clearly irrelevant as far as these speakers are concerned. Its new transferred meaning—i. e., anything repeated as a set piece, especially a political slogan, the dictionary meaning being a type of prayer—is the sense these journalists have evidently assimilated and foregrounded. But the traditional pronunciation *m[æ]ntra* is either unknown or eschewed. It is *the insecure knowledge of the word as such*, not its meaning, that induces [ä] for [æ].

This analysis is confirmed indirectly by cases where unfamiliarity cannot be invoked as the reason for [ä], but markedness can.[4] In a recent broadcast of his commentary, *The Nature of Things* (Vermont Public Radio), the naturalist Will Curtis several times pronounced the word *habitat* with [ä] for both of the relevant (stressed and unstressed) vowels. This untraditional pronunciation of a word in common use can be chalked up to its valorization as marked in the sense of "special" or "restricted." When a speaker accords salience or special status to a word that contains a vowel that can be rendered [ä] or [æ], [ä] may be utilized as a means of mirroring the marked value of the word *in context*. Mr. Curtis (whose topic was the disappearance of habitat for certain flora and fauna) evidently—and unconsciously—did this with *habitat*.[5]

This analysis joins hands with the earlier one, in that "unfamiliarity" is one of the concrete meanings of the abstract designation "marked." The foreignness of words lends itself typically to subsumption under the category of marked value, hence the special or restricted phonetic features commonly found in the pronunciation of foreign words unless and until they are nativized (if ever). This is especially true of names. Thus *Yasser*

Arafat is constantly pronounced with some combination of [ä]'s and [æ]'s, although the thoroughly anglicized version—all [æ]'s—is also extant. We recently heard a speaker wishing to dignify his ownership of the very expensive car called a *Lamborghini* pronouncing the first vowel [ä] instead of [æ]. The vowel [ä], through its occurrence in what is perceived as American "educated" speech in words like *rather*, as well as in British English (*tomato, banana*), has become associated with marked (foreign, formal, "high" style) pronunciation, whence its natural utilization as a phonetic mark of special status. Imitation of prestige dialects is likely to account for examples like the garden-variety word *pistachio* or the name *Andrea* being pronounced with [ä] rather than the plebeian [æ].[6]

All of this speaks in favor of the idea that the historically older urge of Americans to render foreign (European) words "correctly" at the expense of native phonetic norms has been subsumed, as but one specific manifestation, under the newer and more general drive for "authenticity." Truth is identified with the authentic. Thus, *K[ä]nt* and *D[ä]nte* persist as the only pronunciations in American speech, where the British norm has *K[æ]nt* and *D[æ]nte*,[7] not because of a desire to acknowledge the foreignness of the names but because nativizing their pronunciation might run the risk of making one's acquaintance with them seem less than authentic. Hence it is the avoidance of anything that, through speech, might be taken as a sign of inauthentic knowledge that seems to explain the proliferation of pronunciations like *m[ä]ntra, pist[ä]chio*, and even *h[ä]bit[ä]t*.

11

BOUNDARIES

Introduction

When I [Michael Shapiro] was growing up in Japan right after the war, I used to listen to recreations of major league baseball games over the Armed Forces Radio Network. My favorite team was the Boston Red Sox, and my hero was Ted Williams ("The Splendid Splinter"). Since the Red Sox are in the American League, they often played the Detroit Tigers (also in the AL), who had an outfielder named *Hoot Evers* (his real first name was Walter). Anyway, until I started reading the *Stars and Stripes* and the *Japan Times*, I thought this player's name was *Hoo Devers*. My mistake was based on interpreting the realization of /t/, i. e., the alveolar flap [D], as belonging to the last name rather than the first, having placed the word boundary before rather than after it. In linguistics the traditional designation for this phenomenon is *metanalysis*, by which is meant any boundary shift.

One very important thing about boundaries is that they are purely mental entities.[1] Physical boundaries, like lines in the sand, barriers, or any sort of markers, are dependent for their status on a stipulation of purpose (convention). This means that whatever we customarily regard to be "natural" boundaries are really dependent on a rule of interpretation. Aside from this and more generally, we perceive things as distinct partly because we implicitly or explicitly perceive their extent, their boundedness; that is what makes them distinct and differentiates them, whatever other features they may have. It is in this primitive sense that mathematicians speak of boundaries or limits, including the boundedness of space. The relation of biuniqueness or reciprocal implicature obtains between boundedness and distinctness. Anything that is distinct is necessarily bounded; conversely, anything bounded is necessarily distinct.

In language (and culture) we infer the existence of boundaries on the basis of the effects that can be attributed to them. In the case of a word boundary, the most general effect is, of course, that the word is rendered distinct as such, guaranteed its integrity as a unit. This idea or function is embodied, for instance, in the etymology of the word *definite* (from the Latin prefix *de* + *finis* [boundary, end]). In the case of my youthful aural mistake, the analysis comes down to saying that I relocated the boundary in such a way as to change the phonological composition of the words, misinterpreting *Hoot* as *Hoo* and *Evers* as *Devers*.

We mention this nonce example of metanalysis not only by way of introducing the topic of boundaries but as a clear example of what is involved semiotically in the subject. Our treatment of linguistic boundaries will demonstrate—at least implicitly— the structural isomorphism of all the levels of language, from the lowest phonological level to the highest level of syntax and discourse.

In early Middle English, for instance, the word *cheris* ('cherries') was used as a collective singular but came to be interpreted as a plural *cheri-s*, with a morpheme boundary between the stem and the -s, the latter now interpreted as the plural ending. This new segmentation, with its establishment of a constituent structure where none existed before, gave rise in turn to the creation of a new singular *cheri* ('cherry'), and *cheris* ('cherries') came to be used with plural verbs. Examples like this exist in the history of every language.

Let us mention one other general property of boundaries. Again, we will make a conceptual point by recurring to linguistic examples. In English, the word family *bind, band, bound, boundary, bond* presents an interesting set of meanings that—at the margins—seem to be at odds with each other. On one hand, there is the meaning of joining (or being joined) as in *bind, bound, band,* and *bond.* On the other hand, there is the antonymous sense of separating as in *bounded* and *boundary.* One is reminded of the notorious *cleave,* cf. *cleft palate* or *cloven hoof* with the biblical *cleave unto,* etc. (even though they turn out to be etymologically distinct in Old English). A similar case arises in comparing the meanings of *join* and *joint.* A joint is something that both separates and binds together.

What such extreme cases show is an important peculiarity of anything that is *unified* (like a structure, for instance). To be unified or structured—whatever else is true—means necessarily to have internal differentiation; in other words, a structure is a whole constituted by (disparate) parts. Unified entities such as structures are also *continuities.*

A continuity is a whole whose parts are interrelated, which is to say that a continuity is constituted by both part/part and part/whole relations. Something that is continuous but without parts is a mathematical and physical possibility but occurs in language and culture only at some incipient, preliminary, or undefined stage of semiotic development. It seems that the human cognitive capacity is unable to operate except by grading and ranking *continua.*

The most fundamental continuum in language is a gestalt called a *syntagm.* Syntagms are wholes consisting of parts organized hierarchically. There can be either sequential or simultaneous syntagms. In a sequential syntagm, the constituent parts are realized linearly—in time or in space. A sequential syntagm in language is any stretch of linguistic units (including words) connected with each other in relations of sub- or superordination. Thus, for example, any syllable is a sequential syntagm; any morpheme is a sequential syntagm; any coordinate construction, any adjectival phrase, any prepositional phrase is a sequential syntagm.

But besides sequential syntagms there are also simultaneous syntagms, a cardinal fact Saussure and many later structuralists failed to realize. These are gestalts constituted by parts that, rather than being arranged linearly, co-occur, so to speak, columnarly, in hierarchical continua; they are structured wholes or units that are internally differentiated.

Simultaneous syntagms are not limited to the level of *signantia* or phonological signs. *Signata* or meanings are also organized into gestalts or syntagms in which the constituents are hierarchically organized. With regard to grammatical meanings (like case, number, gender, tense, person, etc.), a signatum may have a unitary structure, i.e., be constituted by one and only one meaning, which is usually the grammatical feature value of the category in question. In the Indo-European pattern, for instance, the modern daughter languages typically display what is called syncretism, i.e., they incorporate several grammatical content forms (signata) in one expression form (signans). An ending that does this is called synthetic. Thus Latin *am-ō* ('I love') consists of a stem and an ending (*am-* and *-ō*) whereby the *-ō* expresses the categories of person and number simultaneously.

In the more familiar domain of lexical meaning, this simultaneous copresence of several meanings—several signata—within one simultaneous syntagm occurs practically without fail. Any dictionary entry reveals multiple senses that are listed in some order, usually starting with something like the primary or literal and proceeding through an array of secondary or trans-ferred meanings (connotations). Dictionaries tend to register fig-urative meanings only when these have been codified, leaving the tropological potential of a living language largely untouched.

Parenthetically, it is precisely the arena of semantic trans-ference that lends itself so neatly to illustrating the general prob-lem of simultaneous syntagms. In the two master tropes, metonymy and metaphor, the hierarchical relation between the literal and figurative signata of each is at the heart of the trans-ferred meaning that characterizes them.

Beyond the simple function of delimiting domains, includ-ing syntagms, is there something about the behavior of bound-aries that affects the character of semiosis? Staying with language structure for the moment, let us look at the more fa-miliar type of syntagm, the sequential or linear one. In a coordi-nate construction like *you and I/me*, the choice between subjective vs. objective case in the first person pronoun form de-pends on the syntactic position of the phrase. In formal English, it is *you and I* in subject position and *you and me* in all others. In colloquial English *you and me* can occur in subject position, with the marked form *I* being replaced by the unmarked *me*.

But increasingly in both spoken and written varieties of English, in America and the United Kingdom but not only, one hears the subjective case pronoun form replacing the standard objective case form in coordinate constructions. For example, a few years ago [May 24, 1993] we heard the following sentence from a commentator on the National Public Radio program *Morning Edition*, in a lame attempt at humor, admitting to the program's host his inability to predict the winners of the dou-bles competition in the French Open Tennis Championships: "I'm picking you and I."

This jarring solecism is more often to be found after prepo-sitions, eg., between *you and I*, etc. The substitution of *I* for *me* here is what is usually called a hyperurbanism (hypercorrection), meaning the use of the wrong form as a result of the speaker's wishing to sound educated. However, we would like to explore the possibility that there is a deeper reason for this substitution, and to propose a different interpretation, one that relies on an understanding of metanalysis or boundary shift.

First a short description of the grammatical facts. When grammatical government is involved, as it is in *between you and I/me*, the normal domain of the preposition extends to each constituent in the complement, as it does to the direct object of the verb in *picking you and me*. Thus whether there is a preposition preceding the coordinate phrase or not, the form of all constituents in the complement should be in the objective case. The second person pronoun *you* is syncretic; it does not differentiate the subjective from the objective form, but the first person does. Why do some speakers place the subjective form *I* in objective position?

The first thing to point out is the fact of a coordinate construction. We are dealing here not with a simple complement but a compound. Even in nonstandard American English there are no attested instances of sentences like *He picks I* or *She talks to I* (although some British dialects do have them). So the compound character of the complement is evidently a necessary precondition for the hyperurbanism to occur.

Now, one property of a unit, as we established earlier, is its boundedness. In a compound unit, the boundaries envelop all of the constituents; otherwise, the compound would lose its character as a unit. In other words, disregarding the conjunction, a coordinate phrase of the type *you and I* is bracketed *[you and I]* rather than *[you] and [I]*; it has only two major boundaries, at the two margins of the construction, rather than six minor boundaries—the number it would have if it were simply the additive product of two personal pronouns separated by a conjunction. In the solecistic construction, the individual constituents inside the brackets/ boundaries that enclose the compound seem to be insulated from case government. They undergo no change, even while being syntactically liable to it, apparently because compounds of this type are analyzed by speakers who utter these solecisms as being unitary, undifferentiated gestalts. Such speakers ignore the internal noun phrase boundaries, assigning case only to the whole compound noun phrase. In standard American English, by contrast, the boundaries are observed. The grammatical solecism can thus be understood as the effect of boundaries being suppressed, specifically the minor boundaries around the pronouns. (This might also explain why solecisms like *to he and I* are heard, but not *to him and I.*)

Not that the boundaries on either side of the individual constituents cease to exist just because the coordinate construction has boundaries enclosing it. Not at all. Here we have an example of the variable strengths of boundaries. In the hierarchy of boundaries involved in the phrase, the supervening compound boundary is the major or salient one, while the remaining minor ones are present but not germane.

The differential strength of linguistic boundaries is actually a well-known fact. Languages vary in the value they attach to particular boundaries, so that, for instance, common phenomena like phonetic assimilation may or may not take place at exactly the same boundaries in different (even related) languages.

We have touched upon the relative instability of boundaries indirectly with the introduction of metanalysis. Now we would like to offer some further examples of boundary shifts to show how the simultaneous syntagm and its boundary are interconnected, and also how a change in meaning can be attributed to a boundary shift. The sorts of changes we want to consider can all be put under the traditional category of *pleonasm*. This term, however, has never before been understood as involving metanalyses.

The meaning of the intransitive verb *continue* clearly involves the idea of duration beyond a given point. This can also be seen in the synonymous compound verb *go on*, in which the postposition *on* makes the semantics explicit. In the recent history of American English, *continue* has come increasingly to be used pleonastically, with the postposition *on*. A fairly routine analysis of something like this would make appeal to analogy, saying that the variant *continue on* has come into the language by analogy with *go on*, which has the same general meaning. But analogy does not explain the pleonasm. And here we have a case of metanalysis that is obscured by appealing to analogy.

The meaning represented by the postposition *on* is already contained in the simultaneous syntagm of *continue*. The neologism *continue on* results from altering the extent of the boundaries that define this syntagm: the syntagm is partly "unpacked," so to speak, with one element, namely *on*, moving from simultaneity to sequentiality. The linearization of the postposition is, in other words, concomitant with a boundary shift. Here the boundary has shifted rightwards, but it can also shift to the left. Take the fairly common solecism *equally as*, occurring in written as well as spoken American English instead of *as*. The meaning of semantic equivalence is already contained in the conjunction *as; equally as* pleonastically expresses this meaning by "unpacking" it from the simultaneous syntagm of *as* and linearizing it alongside *as*. Again, in the process, a boundary has shifted.

This kind of shift may also explain a bizarre syntactic phenomenon that is quite prevalent in spoken American English. We have in mind the reduplicative copula in *is that* constructions, e.g., *The problem is is that, The reason is is that*, etc.[2] Hillary Clinton, believe it or not, even used it in a speech to the American Hospital Association (excerpt televised by CNN on its *Early Prime* news broadcast, August 9, 1993): "The ratio is is that..." Could this be emphatic? Is it just a so-called hesitation phenomenon, a vagary of performance (not competence) in which the speaker is unsure what they will assert in the rest of the sentence?

Perhaps we should regard it as a pleonasm, which, of course, is a kind of (needless) repetition. But the advantage of changing perspectives becomes clear when we also adopt the corollary position of interpreting copula reduplication as a concomitant of a boundary shift. The situation is more complex than in our previous examples. Perhaps what we have here is the linearization of the redundant existential meaning that inheres in the simultaneous semantic syntagm of every topic word. The nouns *problem* and *reason* contain within their syntagms of signata the meaning of existing—albeit redundantly. The non-standard construction X *is is that* Y can be interpreted as being the product of the "unpacking" of the simultaneous syntagm of the topic word X: the once covert existential copula is linearized immediately following the topic word, a process accompanied by a shift in the boundary of the relevant syntagm.

But this interpretation also raises an important issue: why should boundaries shift at all? What is it about the content and/or the form of the linguistic material that would trigger metanalysis? To answer this question we have to remember the most fundamental fact about boundaries after their status as purely mental entities: their *instability*.

Ranking (hierarchization), which is also a purely mental operation, and segmentation are the two most unstable semiotic processes in both human learning strategies and human historical development. The content values of semiotic units are relatively easy to learn and to transmit, but learning and perpetuating how to rank them and where to draw the boundaries between these units is more difficult and hence more liable to error or misinterpretation.

Because both the establishment of rank relations and of boundaries are so prone to be misinterpreted, innovations with respect to these two types of semiotic processes can be understood as arising from their purely mental character and their resultant instability.

Effects of Boundaries

The most straightforward application of the boundary concept is in the observation that *boundaries have effects*. In the political life of nations, for instance, we know that a border is not merely a line on a map which demarcates the territory of a given state from contiguous ones. A border is also a barrier: it has the consequence of marking the line or limit beyond which persons and things cannot cross without license to do so; or lacking the latter, without incurring certain penalties. As a fact of political geography, a border must have physical properties in itself for it to be effective, including border guards and material installations which make trespass difficult and hazardous.

Such examples of boundaries, in which the stipulative aspect of a boundary's effect is materially incorporated in a physical object (like a fence or wall) that acts as a barrier, are actually in the minority. By far the most usual implementation of the boundary concept is the one embedded in the idea of penalties incurred by the violation of a boundary (transgression). This understanding is, of course, the one that is central to any system of norms, including ethics and jurisprudence.

The use of the word *penalty*, however, obscures an absolutely fundamental formal characteristic of situations involving boundaries: *the dominance of the negative*. To be sure, norms whose violation does not trigger penalties run the risk of being purely paper restrictions—and ultimately of becoming extinct. But whether normative statements are cast negatively or affirmatively, it is the negative that is fundamental both to the ontology of norms and to their practical consequences. (It is no accident that the Ten Commandments are predominantly of the form "Thou shalt not...").

The negative has, of course, been recognized for its definitional role in the history of logic, as epitomized, for example, in Spinoza's dictum *omnis determinatio est negatio*. A norm remains implicit until violated, until the boundary separating normative from non-normative behavior is crossed. The negative is thus at the foundation of all rules of conduct, and to the extent that conduct is a semiotic matter, the negative is thereby fundamental to semiosis.

In linguistic semiosis, however, the presence of boundaries is to be recognized not by instances of their violation but by their effects on linguistic form. The first such effect is simply the delimitation of a linguistic domain, which is to say that a linguistic rule always contains some reference to the context of its application, whether that context is sequential or simultaneous. The specification of the domain is essential to the form of both the rule and the linguistic result.

The boundary delimiting the domain of the rule is clearly essential to the rule's semiotic functioning. Indexing a phonological or syntactic domain cannot proceed without boundaries. From the semiotic point of view, rules have the function of promoting textual cohesion. However, the process of textual cohesion, as the word *cohesion* connotes, includes both the binding and the separating function of boundaries.

There are three aspects of cohesion that can be discriminated by the functions of rules and the varying strengths of boundaries included in their definitions. The three aspects or functions can be called *integrative, concatenative, and delimitative*. First, rules that apply within a domain irrespective of boundaries within this domain serve an integrative function. They produce signs of internal cohesion of the given domain. Second, rules that apply at boundaries may serve a concatenative function if they produce signs that link elements across the given boundary. Finally, they may have a delimitative function if they produce signs that do not link elements across boundaries.

Boundaries and Hierarchies

Because boundaries and hierarchies are both purely mental entities and have in common the property of instability, it is natural to ask the question whether boundaries play a role in the establishment or alteration of hierarchies. In sequential syntagms constituted by parts in rank relations to each other and to the syntagm as a whole, examining instances of change (rehierarchization) can perhaps clarify this question for us. For instance, in compounds like *boatswain* or *waistcoat* the traditional pronunciations [bóu̯sn] and [wéskɨt] reflect the fact that the constituent structure preserved in contemporary orthography refers to the compounds' origin; but more importantly, that this structure was superseded in the history of English by the words as wholes. Put another way, the whole acquired a phonetic realization that underscored its superordinate status vis-à-vis its parts. In the process—and this is what concerns us primarily—the boundaries separating the constituents (*boat + swain, waist + coat*) were erased, as a precondition or concomitant of the several reductions these compounds evidently underwent. (The traditional pronunciations of these items are being replaced by spelling pronunciations, which have the effect of reintroducing the etymological boundaries.)

The reverse directionality is observable in the folk etymologization of the word *asparagus* to *sparrow grass*: clearly, the latter involves a metanalysis—in this case, the establishment of a boundary where none existed before that accompanies the change from a word with no constituent structure to a compound (cf. Anttila 1985: 6ff.). Here, the parts are rendered equivalent to the whole as the boundary is established between them. Because it is a compound, of course, the whole is not equal to the sum of its parts, but that is not germane to the issue.

Both sets of examples involve a rehierarchization. And since both involve a change in boundaries, one is left with the idea that, at least provisionally, we should consider whether (re)hierarchization does not always proceed with an obligatory met-analysis.

And what about simultaneous syntagms? There ought to be a structural parallelism (isomorphism) between sequential and simultaneous syntagms with respect to the role of boundaries. Because of their simplicity, tropes are useful semantic structures to experiment with as diagnostics in trying to clarify this problem. A metonymy or a metaphor that is fresh (i.e., has not lost its figurative force) always involves the hierarchization of two signata in a simultaneous syntagm, the literal and the figural meanings. In fact, for the trope to exist as such the literal has to be subordinated to the figural meaning. In a metonymy like *pars pro toto* (synecdoche), say, Homer's *30 sails* for *ships*, there is an inclusion relation between tenor and vehicle. But beyond that, as with any trope, there has to be a negation involved in the meaning complex (the "figural situation"), a negative which assures that the literal not be taken literally but figuratively. In the case of a synecdoche, the negative has an attenuated force because of the inclusion relation: a sail is not a ship but is still a part of it. But in a case of pure metonymy (spatial or temporal contiguity rather than inclusion), the negational quotient is evident in full force. For instance, in the history of English the word *bead* (from Middle English *bede* ['prayer']) is the result of a metonymic shift associated with equivocal collocations like *counting one's beads*, meaning "prayers" or "tokens of prayers in a rosary." In the original change from "prayer" to "bead" the semantic permutation necessarily incorporates the meaning "not"—here "bead not prayer"—as long as the real-life connection between the two meanings is alive. (Once it has been collectively forgotten, the trope fades and loses its figurality.)

This "not" is the boundary in a simultaneous syntagm that is exactly parallel to the linear boundary necessarily present in a sequential syntagm. In a simultaneous syntagm the set of rank relations is always the cumulative result (gestalt, continuum) of pairwise comparisons; this is illustrated straightforwardly in the example of a trope, but any hypotactic syntagm will serve equally well.

The frequent mention of gestalts should alert one to the possibility that a field-theoretic view of structure is behind this concept.[3] Indeed, when it comes to simultaneous syntagms, we are clearly dealing with fields—in the case of the phoneme, with the ultimate field phenomenon of human semiosis. Hierarchical salience, for instance in the structure of tropes, is definitely a field phenomenon; its effects are best captured visually in a diagram using so-called peak notation (Anttila 1992: 35). The salient element here is the figural meaning, which can only appear against the background of the literal meaning. There is a kind of stereoscopic effect to such structures, in alignment with their simultaneousness, and corresponding to their semiotic depth.

Salience is a type of rank relation and, therefore, necessarily means the presence of hierarchy. But in language and culture the main type of relations is what Hjelmslev called "participative relations" (i.e., inclusive relations), in the sense that all oppositions in language are subject to the law of participation, there being no oppositions between A and non-A, but only between A on one hand and A + non-A on the other (Hjelmslev 1935: 102). For instance, it is because the reference potential or breadth of a word like goose includes both "gander" and "non-gander" that goose can be used to refer to "male goose," "female goose," and "goose regardless of sex." Participation is an inclusive relation inasmuch as the reference potential of one term includes that of the other.

Hjelmslev actually went beyond clarifying the difference between participative oppositions and the contradictory and contrary ones of traditional logic. He recognized that exclusion is merely a special case of participation, in which certain slots (Fr. cases) of the extensive (i.e., unmarked) term are empty

(1939/1970: 87). This crucially important insight cannot be documented here; suffice it to say there are linguistic data that confirm Hjelmslev's claim that inclusive relations are the superordinate type to which the diverse exclusive relations are subordinate. This is another way of saying that the main types of semantic oppositions all fall under the law of participation: contraries (e.g., "sweet" :: "bitter"), contradictories (e.g., "straight" :: "bent"), converses (e.g., "parent" :: "child"), directionalities (e.g., "up" :: "down"), and complementarities (e.g., "male" :: "female"). Logically diverse relations in meaning are conjoined in language with inclusive relations in value.

The relations between signata in the minimal semantic syntagm represented by a trope are analogous to the relations between figure and ground, except that the values of the terms are reversed. The figural signatum includes the literal, as the ground includes the figure. The two signata are, however, perceived as contradictories, again parallel to the figure/ground case. The way we can ascertain that there is a boundary separating the signata, apart from the fact of their distinctness, is to observe what happens when a trope fades and disappears. When ME *bede* changed from 'prayer' to 'bead', initially it was a metonymic shift, whereby both meanings coexisted. Once the meaning of 'prayer' faded, because Germanic *bede* was replaced by Romance *prayer*, there ceased to be the distinction between figural and literal, and *bead* was terminologized.

We can construe this process as being attended by a removal of the boundary between figural and literal when we identify it as a *neutralization*. A neutralization necessarily involves the suspension of the distinction between two opposed terms, with only one of the two appearing in the so-called position of neutralization as the representative of the opposition to the exclusion of the other term. When the domain is a hierarchy, neutralization means the collapse of rank distinctions; the outcome of this collapse as it affects the lexicon is one of two events or both: (1) the literal and the figural meanings go their separate ways, with the formerly figural meaning becoming independent, even terminologized; and (2) the formerly literal meaning fades and eventually drops out of the lexicon. The second outcome is what happened with *bede* ('prayer'). The first can be illustrated by a word like *hand*, in its sense of "worker." When the transferred meaning of this word first arose, it was clearly a trope, but today it is independent.

This sort of development argues for the presence of a boundary between the two copresent signata of a trope. The hierarchical relation that necessarily obtains between the figural and literal meanings is not merely a matter of valuation but of segmentation, too. As we argued earlier, the inherent negation in the structural relation between the two signata of a trope, the exclusive relation (figural, *not* literal) undergirding the inclusive one is tantamount to a boundary.

There is an interesting congruence between this way of thinking about simultaneous syntagms and the general characterization of continuity in Peirce. Speaking of topological space, Peirce qualifies it as continuous in the event it meets either of two conditions: it must return to itself or contain its own limits. If it is "unbroken," it must return to itself; if it has limits, such limits represent a breach of continuity, manifested as "topical singularities" of a lower dimensionality than that of the continuum itself. In two-dimensional space the limits can be either points or lines. In the case of a line, the topical singularity is itself continuous, but it is a continuum of a lower dimensionality than that of the space that contains it: "so space presents points, lines, surfaces, and solids, each generated by the motion of a place of lower dimensionality and the limit of a place of next higher dimensionality" *(CP* 1: 501).

In this manner a whole series of continua of varying dimensionalities can be envisaged, embedded within one another, with any continuum of N dimensions having as its limit, in the form of a topical singularity, a continuum of not more than N–1 dimensions. Dimensionality, then, is conceived as a topological characteristic of continua.

Applying these topological ideas to the analysis of the hierarchical structure of simultaneous syntagms in semiosis, we can identify syntagms with continua and rank relations with dimensionalities. The segmentation of the continuum into elements that are organized hierarchically is attended by boundaries between them, corresponding to the idea of limits in topological space.

Language and culture are organized into continua that illustrate Aristotle's conception of a continuum as containing its own limits. Every element of a syntagm is to varying extents both distinct (bounded) and conjoined with every other. In "The Law of Mind" (1892) Peirce uses the example of a surface that is part red and part blue and asks the question, "What, then, is the color of the boundary line between the red and the blue?" *(CP* 6: 126). His answer is "half red and half blue." With this understanding we are returned to the position enunciated at the outset that the wholes (continua, gestalts) of human semiosis are simultaneously differentiated and unified.

But perhaps the question we need to ask really is: what is simultaneity as such? And more precisely: does simultaneity have parts? We know that in visual perception the parts of a whole (gestalt) are presented simultaneously and can be apperceived totally, severally, or serially, depending on the particular focus prompted by interest and attention. But in non-spatial terms, again, is simultaneity as such stratifiable into levels or components?

One of the examples Peirce cites by way of exploring the relation between time and continuity suggests a positive answer. In "The Law of Mind" Peirce says: "what is present to the mind at any ordinary instant, is what is present during a moment in which that instant occurs. Thus, the present is half past and half to come" *(CP* 6: 126). This idea about time is congruent with his fundamentally Aristotelian position concerning the properties of a line, which for Peirce was any line, not necessarily a straight line, and for Aristotle an irreducible geometrical object. Thus if a line is divided into two halves, called line intervals, then the endpoints of both segments are loci; and "a line interval by the mere fact of existing as a line interval 'defines,' as it were, its endpoints. They are abstract properties of the line interval itself, and the notion of a line interval with no endpoints is senseless" (Ketner & Putnam in Peirce 1992: 40). When the original line is reconstituted, the two middle endpoints once again coincide at the point of division as one point. This point which is capable of splitting into two corresponds exactly to the moment of the present that is simultaneously half past and half future.

We can perhaps get a firmer grasp on the nature of simultaneity by looking at the continuum from a slightly different point of view, suggested by another of Peirce's examples (from his eighth and final Cambridge Conferences Lecture of 1898, "The Logic of Continuity"), which deserves to be cited in full (Peirce 1992: 261–62):

> Let the clean blackboard be a sort of Diagram of the original vague potentiality, or at any rate of some early stage of its determination. This is something more than a figure of speech; for after all continuity is generality. This blackboard is a continuum of two dimensions, while that which it stands for is a continuum of some indefinite multitude of dimensions. This blackboard is a continuum of possible points; while there is a continuum of possible dimensions of quality, or is a continuum of possible dimensions of a continuum of possible dimensions of quality or something of that sort. There are no points on this blackboard. There are no dimensions in that continuum. I draw a chalk line

on the board. This discontinuity is one of those brute acts by which alone the original vagueness could have made a step toward definiteness. There is a certain element of continuity in this line. Where did this continuity come from? It is everything upon it continuous. What I have really drawn there is an oval line. For this white chalkmark is not a *line*, it is a plane figure in Euclid's sense,—a *surface*, and the only line [that] is there is the line which forms the *limit* between the black surface and the white surface. Thus discontinuity can only be produced upon that blackboard by the reaction between two continuous surfaces into which it is separated, the white surface and the black surface. But the boundary between the black and white is neither black, nor white, nor neither, nor both. It is the pairedness of the two.

In this image of blackboard and chalk mark we have the perfect visual analog of the simultaneous syntagm in human semiosis, which is a continuum ramified by discontinuities that are themselves continua. In this structure, the boundary is not only necessarily present but plays the crucial role of binding and separating simultaneously.

NOTES

Chapter 1

1. A curiosity of the history of scholarship on this subject is two articles by B. F. Skinner (1939, 1941). Skinner's conclusion regarding alliteration in the first of these, that "Shakespeare might as well have drawn his words out of a hat" (1939: 191), was countered in detail by Goldsmith (1950). See also Pirkhofer (1963: 3–14). Hymes 1960 is a good example of a more ramified approach to the problem of the sound–meaning nexus in 20 sonnets (10 each) by Words-worth and Keats which utilizes the concept of the "summative word," i.e., reckons the repetition of certain sounds to be anagrammatically related to a particularly significant ("dominant") word in a given poem. A recent book on the general problem of sound–meaning correspondences that includes some analysis of Shakespeare's poetry is Tsur 1992.

2. The discussion in this section is based on common knowledge about universal linguistic phonetics—to be found, with specific reference to English, for instance, in Laver (1994: 503ff.). It is noteworthy that this distinction is not "theory-laden," to use the terminology of the philosophy of science: however else they may analyze language, with all the attendant differences depending on doctrine (the "conceptual

framework"), phoneticians and philologists are uniformly in agreement that the basic division in the sound structure of all known human languages is the distinction between vowels and consonants, i.e., between vocalic sounds (sonorants) and consonantal sounds (obstruents).

3. Since the analysis of sonority in Shakespeare's sonnets does not deal with vowels, all further reference to sonorants is meant to include only nasals, liquids, and glides.

4. The syllable as the gestalt domain of phonetic context in poetry is matched at the metrical level by the foot, which is the context for ictuses (stresses).

5. This conception of the sound structure of poetry as fundamentally dependent on sonority and obstruency was first advanced in Shapiro and Shapiro 1993. One might well ask: why count SUs and OUs rather than sonorants and obstruents? The answer is twofold. First, because the context of verse is based on the syllable (cf. n. 4), and the syllable is defined as a phonic *domain*—a molecular concept—in which the atoms (sounds) are formed into gestalts. Second, the atomistic conception of sound–meaning correspondences never counts the same sound twice—hence its fundamental impotence—whereas the structural conception being advanced herein recognizes the *relevance of one and the same sound to more than one unit*, given contiguous sounds. It should be noted that vowel chains (i.e., sequences of vowels), bordered on either side by sonorants, do not count as sonorant units, since they deviate from the optimal syllabic pattern in English of CVC [consonant(s) + vowel + consonant(s)].

6. Line ends are assumed to be immune to ligature with line beginnings (despite enjambment), so there is no OU here; ditto between lines 10 and 11, in which an SU would otherwise appear ("room/Even in" [to be read with a contracted form of *even*]). Cf. lines 7–8 in sonnet 4 below.

7. All texts of the Sonnets are cited from the *New Penguin Shakespeare* edition (Shakespeare 1986), of which the general editor is T. J. B. Spencer and the associate editor is Stanley Wells. This edition is in the series of Shakespeare texts now used—and recommended as authoritative—by the Royal Shakespeare Company. The *New Cambridge Shakespeare* edition of the Sonnets (1996), published under the editorship of G. Blakemore Evans, does not in any way supersede the Penguin Shakespeare; in fact, Evans specifically acknowledges his debt to it and to its editor, John Kerrigan (ix), as does the editor of the new Arden–Third Series entry, Katherine Duncan-Jones (Shakespeare 1997). The most detailed commentary is still that of Booth 1977; but see now Vendler 1997. In determining sonorant and obstruent units, Shakespeare's speech is presupposed on the basis of Kökeritz 1953 and Cercignani 1981. One major assumption is that the speech of poetry in Shakespeare's time did not drop *r*s before consonants or in auslaut (even though there is plenty of evidence that *r*-less dialects already existed in Early Modern English). Another is that diphthongs were phonological units—as generally analyzed in contemporary English—not combinations of vowel + off-glide. Word boundaries are routinely disregarded when no pause between contiguous words is obligatory in an allegro tempo (conversational) reading of the lines.

8. Strictly speaking, there are 140 metrical positions (MPs), which are equivalent to the number of vowels that are actually pronounced. A word like "powerful" in this poem counts as disyllabic, not trisyllabic, reflecting the pronunciation with syncope of the medial vowel; similarly syncopated are "oblivious" (3 MPs) and "Even" (1 MP). In compiling the statistical profiles of the sonnets, only MPs were considered relevant. The main thrust of the argument is in fact unaffected by the asymmetries between MPs and syllables; hence for

the purposes of this study they and any related local problems of pronunciation are ignored as immaterial. It should be noted that of the 154 sonnets, there are seven with something other than 140 syllables: #3 (142), #99 (150), #118 (144), #121 (142), #126 (120), #145 (112), and #146 (138).

9. This follows from the phonotactics and syllable structure of English, a language abundant in both sonorant and obstruent clusters. Where both sonority and nonobstruency are possible measures of sonority, it is primarily the sonorant units that determine poetic sonority—for the simple reason that (ontologically) the positive realization of the category by which something is measured is by definition its primary realization, the realization of its negated opposite being secondary. But in languages like French or Italian that contain few obstruent clusters, the reverse is true, and it is the OQ that is the prime indicator of poetic sonority via nonobstruency. For example, a Baudelaire sonnet like the famous "Correspondances" (La Nature est un temple où de vivant piliers) has only 12 obstruent clusters over its 168-syllable span, yielding an OQ of .071 (its SQ is .125—only 21 SUs). Mallarmé's "Sonnet" (Sur les bois oublié quand passe l'hiver sombre), with 27 SUs and a resultant SQ of .161, has only 5 obstruent clusters, hence an OQ of .030! Petrarch's sonnets typically have OQs going as low as the .058 range.

10. A different sense of this term—essentially the repetitions and reversals characteristic of the design of classical music rather than tonality—is used by Kenneth Burke (1957) to examine the sound structure of Coleridge's poem.

11. Since Kerrigan's commentary is relied on in more than one instance, perhaps it ought to be mentioned that there is nothing exceptionable in what is attributed to him. The interpretations supplied in this paper tally with those of numerous other sources besides Kerrigan, of which for obvious reasons only a representative few can actually be cited here.

12. Among eminent critics who have crossed swords over this poem are William Empson and John Crowe Ransom.

13. Kerrigan remarks (Shakespeare 1986: 290): "The section of the book within which 94 falls is peculiarly connective: 92 follows 91 with *But*, and 93 picks up with *So;* 95 is essentially a development from the couplet of 94, and 96 continues to worry at the *faults* discussed in all these poems. If it is read in this light, 94 looks like an intense meditation on the issues raised in 92 and confronted in 93."

14. As the data of appendices 2 and 3 show, there are 8 sonnets (5 percent) with SQs in the .300s, with an average OQ of .172, and 91 sonnets (59 percent) with OQs in the .200s, with an average SQ of .197. Sonnet 91 appears in these respects to be indeterminate as to the function of low sonority.

15. Leishman (1996, 187–88) compares Petrarch, Ronsard, and Shakespeare in this respect.

16. Admittedly, this may be less than the optimal way of defining "same numerical range," since, for example, .501 and .599 are much further apart than are .499 and .501 or .599 and .601.

17. Sonnet 16 shares with 71 the OQ .136, but only 72 has a lower obstruency (.100).

18. These statistics may have a bearing on the old question of Shakespeare scholarship as to whether the order of the Sonnets in the so-called Quarto edition of 1609 (the *editio princeps*—abbreviated Q—underlying all modern editions) is correct. Two modern books which argue anew for a reordering of the poems are Stirling 1968 and Padel 1981. But their analyses (like earlier ones) ought to be scrutinized in the light of the present one, specifically as concerns the statistical data presented herein, which, together with the evidence of the linked poems analyzed earlier, tend to substantiate the authoritativeness of the order in Q.

19. When the 77 sonnets in the .100–.199 SQ range are com-

bined with the lone sonnet (#4) in the .086–.099 range, the combined average OQ is .242.

20. Kerrigan, Introduction (Shakespeare 1986: 12–13).

21. The range goes beyond 140 syllables because the principle of counting used was 140 syllables + number of syllables to the end of the sentence. See appendix 5.

22. It follows (a) that we might think of a high ratio of OUs to syllables as the opposite of sonority but (b) that sonority as measured by 1/SQ is not the same as sonority as measured by OQ.

Chapter 2

1. "Тут анатомия всех русских отношений к начальству" (*PSS* 1: 432, from an 1861–1862 manuscript sketch of a projected revised version of his "tale"). The abbreviation *PSS* refers hereinafter—by volume (and book, in the sole case of vol. 28) and page number—to the Soviet-era edition of Dostoevsky's complete works (Dostoevskii 1972–1990). Here as throughout, except when bibliographical accuracy requires proper transliteration or an alternate spelling, we use the form "Dostoevsky."

2. English translation in Frank and Goldstein 1987: 36.

3. Vinogradov (1976: 104) reviews a few representative reactions, such as that of Annenkov ("madness for madness' sake"), and from the periodical *Finnish Messenger*, "a tale boring to the point of exhaustion;" "a breach of decency intolerable to the circle of educated readers" (these English translations from an abridged version = Vinogradov 1979: 220; Russian original first published in Iskoz 1922). For greater ease of access, all further references to this essay will be to the English translation, as will those below to the articles by Bem and by Chizhevsky; likewise the book on Dostoevsky's poetics by Bakhtin.

4. Wasiolek 1973: 5; Belinskii's views are in his "Vzgliad na

russkuiu literaturu 1846 goda" *(PSS* 10: 7).

5. Mochulski 1967: 47. There is now a handy survey of Gogolianisms in Dilaktorskaia 1999: 186–203.

6. This view recurs, unattributed but almost verbatim, in Ronald Hingley's introduction to a trade paperback translation by George Bird (Hingley 1968: ix): "the faults of the story are sufficiently obvious, for it is long-winded, repetitive and in parts obscure."

7. Wasiolek, 6. The original is Belinskii's "[Review of] *Peterburgskii sbornik,* izdannyi N. Nekrasovym," February 28, 1846 (= his *PSS* 9: 543).

8. Wasiolek, 5. The original is in Belkin 1956: 364.

9. See Terras 1998: 22. The Shklovskian interpretation is in Shklovskii 1957: 60–61.

10. Letter to his brother Mikhail, dated October 1, 1859 *(PSS* 28/1: 340).

11. All Russian references are to *PSS* 1 by page number, the English to the Bird translation (see n. 6). We have silently corrected the translation in the few cases where it misrepresents the original. All unattributed translations, here and throughout, are our own.

12. Cf. Neuhäuser 1979, cit. Wöll 1999: 148: "Tragödie des Individuums, das von einer verkehrten gesellschaftlichen Ordnung bis zum Wahnsinn getrieben wird" (apt—but, we think, not in the way that Wöll means).

13. The locus classicus is Bem 1979: 246.

14. Bem, 235. Also: "Dostoevsky altered this character [Kovalëv] in a way which intensified the tragic impression of his tale.... Senselessness and randomness are replaced here by meaningfulness and necessity" (239). According to Bem, Goliadkin's distant kinship with Gogol's madman Poprishchin is signaled by the episode with the dog. In "The Nose" Kovalëv "wanted to take a look [in the mirror] at the pimple which had popped up on his nose the evening before"; cf. Goliad-

kin: "вот бы шутка была ... если б вышло, наприпер, что–нибудь не так,—прыщик там какой–нибудь" (110) ("A fine thing if something untoward had happened, and a strange pimple had come up" [3–4]). Bem also refers, among other comparisons, to the physical resemblance between the doctors in the stories (238) and to the use of correspondence as a vehicle in the subplots (242).

15. A happy exception is Rice 1985: 240–52.

16. See Vinogradov, 227-228; also Gasperetti 1989: 217; and the latter's citations where GS alludes to "certain nasty German poets" as false models for Klara and to "some sort of novel" (230).

17. Or what Chizhevsky (1962: 129) calls the "who."

18. For an analysis that explores a character's "being spoken through"—in this case, the famous protagonist Archie Bunker of the American TV sitcom, *All in the Family*—see Marianne Shapiro 1980b.

19. Actually, he's got *no* part.

20. This is reminiscent of the Gogolian "You all know me, gentlemen."

21. Terras makes the comparison (1998: 23).

22. Mr. Goliadkin is seminal in a line of literary descendancy that will include, for example, Bulgakov's Ivan Bezdomnyii and Nabokov's Pnin.

23. Cf. the discussion of similar gambits based on recurrence in the analysis of the television character referred to in n. 18 above.

24. This kind of move generally trivializes the uncanny, but it is essential that this very triviality is itself uncanny. As a clue to our thinking, it is hyperreal.

25. Bakhtin (1984) seems to touch on that possibility—but does not fall for it—when he remarks that Goliadkin sometimes seems to be telling his own adventures.

26. There are two of nearly everyone in the hierarchy of fathers:

Andrei Filippovich and Olsufii Ivanovich Berendeev; two women in GS's life, Klara Olsuf'evna and Karolina Ivanovna; GS's first Petersburg encounter is with two colleagues; at Olsufii Ivanovich's house there are two servants, and the guests appear in pairs. See Wöll (1999:182) for some of these. Wöll goes so far as to posit a doubling of all other figures in the story.

27. On the mirror in general, see David Patterson 1988; also the following observations specifically: Lacan's "'moi'...seeks the recognition of the other through identification" (61). With regard to looking in the mirror, "already, in Goliadkin's attraction to the mirror, we discover the elements of 'paranoiac alienation'. Already we encounter the division of self marked by the double: here is the man and there the mirror image that displaces him" (63). Again: "In the case of the madman," Lacan writes, "the absence of the Word manifests itself through the stereotypes of a discourse in which the subject, one might say, is spoken rather than speaking" (65). Note also (68–69) when it comes to Judgment and the Word generally, Goliadkin "meets with silence among his colleagues" and "even fears the silence of his servant" (68). The doctor and His Excellency "are the two main authorities of truth in the novel." Having failed with the doctor, Goliadkin's "struggle to regain himself culminates in a frustrated return to the Other, which comes in the form of an attempt to regain a relationship with His Excellency," but "this attempt also meets with silence" (70). Peace (1998: 108) finds this "suspended confrontation" a "typically Gogolian device."

28. "We see what happens when a person is driven to extreme defensive efforts" (Breger 1989: 123).

29. See Chizhevsky (1962), who is good on the "'fixity' of an ethical being," lacking in GS, but relies too much on GS as a "passive bearer of the rational principle," and his analysis leans excessively on the thought pattern that reads from the

great works back into the early ones. Apropos, see also
Sherry 1975: 265.

30. This is noted briefly in passing by Rosenthal (1982: 81):
"Throughout the story he will experience shame rather than
guilt about his behavior."

31. Frank (1987: 307) upgrades Goliadkin's values in the effort to
wedge him into the ethical individual-versus-society role,
describing him as "at least *believ*[ing] in the pious official
morality" and moving to "subvert the values presumably
shared by his official superiors."

32. A keen analysis of the story points to the primal terror, then
to the evolution of the early tenderness GS experiences vis-
à-vis his double, as an expression of how "le thème de la dé-
mence s'accompagne chez [Dostoievski] de la nécessité de
lier l'échec ... à la réussite" (Arban 1981: 39).

33. Here shame is "outside," where the sharer is *known*, and guilt
"inside," where conscience is a *secret* sharer.

34. Bahktin, 216. The original is: "с самой ядовитой и далеко
намекающей улыбкой" (167).

35. Ayers (1988: 290–91) links Goliadkin's downfall to the fate of
urban man, adducing the scene in which Goliadkin stages
the "social masquerade" of going to a shop and ordering several items "destined for a lady" without giving an address, an
impulse "born of Goliadkin's deep-seated wish to be someone"; and going to a money changer and taking satisfaction,
while losing in the exchange, in the very transaction itself
(294). "In the heart of the metropolis the individual is utterly
anonymous" (289); and again: "The nakedness of Goliadkin
[whose name encompasses the root of the word for nakedness—MS] is in his very typicality, a typicality arrived at by
stripping urban man to a core of anxiety" (290). This over-
generalized assessment nonetheless contains one of the few
potential explanations of why this is a poem of Petersburg.

36. If as Chizhevsky says (124), GS is the "passive bearer of the

rational principle" of overweening self-interest, then surely GJ, making full use of externals and creating new opportunities, is the active one, the actualization of GS's dream of doing the rational and sensible thing. Chizhevsky argues powerfully that it is above all GS's shame that leads to his detachment from concrete individual being. Note how Chizhevsky's conception of the story as representing stasis or conflict within the ethical sphere assigns the blame for Goliadkin's calamity to the society, and therefore works as part of a Hegelian historical idealism. Doubles challenge sanity because they attack humanist assumptions that identity has a core.

37. *PSS* 28/1: 113 (translation in Bakhtin 1984: 211).
38. The term as far as we know is coined by Arban (1981: 33).
39. Nabokov (1981: 104), cit. Galina Patterson (1998: 107). The latter article consists of a close comparison of *The Double* with Nabokov's *Despair* (see also Foster 1993). But it encapsulates the need to distinguish between Nabokov's opinion of Dostoevsky himself and his contempt for "Dostoevshchina" (108, n. 6). Patterson also surveys several Gogolisms (122–23), such as the episode of the small dog that haunts Goliadkin in the street, drawn from "Diary of a Madman."

Chapter 3

1. "The work of the poet or novelist is not so utterly different from that of the scientific man. The artist introduces a fiction; but it is not an arbitrary one; it exhibits affinities to which the mind accords a certain approval...which if it is not exactly the same as saying that the synthesis is true, is something of the same general kind." These words were written ca. 1890 by America's greatest philosopher-scientist, Charles Sanders Peirce, who was also the modern founder of semiotics, the theory of signs. The locus of Peirce's discussion is

an article entitled "A Guess at the Riddle" (Peirce in Houser & Kloesel 1992: 261), perhaps Peirce's most original contribution to speculative philosophy. In mentioning poets and novelists he certainly could not have had Dostoevsky in mind. But Peirce's ideas about the highest kind of synthesis that the mind is compelled to make, as he put it, "in the interest of intelligibility, that is, in the interest of the synthesising 'I think' itself," can be shown to apply with particular force to Dostoevsky. A demonstration that includes a discussion of Dostoevsky's particular artistic manner of synthesizing thought is at the heart of this chapter.

2. All Dostoevsky passages are given in English translation; pages refer to the Norton Critical editions followed by references to the volume, page, and line number(s) of Dostoevskii 1972–90 (= *PSS*).

3. The great achievement of Dostoevsky the novelist rests in part on his ability to incorporate what Peirce would call Secondness into the ideological novel. Miguel de Unamuno—Spain's Dostoevsky, as Ortega y Gasset is its Turgenev—begins his masterwork *Tragic Sense of Life* (*Il sentimiento tragico de la vida*) with the following words, to which very little would need to be added in order to fashion an adequate formulaic summary of what Dostoevsky is about: "'Homo sum; nihil humani a me alienum puto,' said the Latin playwright. And I would rather say: no other man do I deem a stranger. For to me the adjective *humanus* is no less suspect than its abstract substantive *humanitas*, humanity. Neither 'the human' nor 'humanity,' neither the simple adjective nor the substantivized adjective, but the concrete substantive man. The man of flesh and bone; the man who is born, suffers, and dies—above all who dies; the man who eats and drinks and plays and sleeps and thinks and wills; the man who is seen and heard; the brother, the real brother" (Unamuno 1954: 1).

Chapter 4

1. Likhachev (1973: 75) states: "Позволительно говорить не о Возрождении в России, а лишь об отдельных его элементах, об отдельных явлениях гуманистического и возрожденческого характера и о реформационных и гуманистических движениях" [One may legitimately speak not of the Renaissance in Russia but only of some of its elements, some phenomena of a humanistic and renaissance character, as well as of reformational and humanistic movements]. Unless indicated otherwise, all translations are ours.

2. This section relies on Miłosz 1969: 27–28. Cf. Strzetelski 1977: part 1; also Ulewicz 1984.

3. For a discussion of Gogol's "tropological vision," see Shapiro and Shapiro 1988: 179–90.

Chapter 5

1. Among the astute critics who have documented this lack of fit is Williams (1990: 235): "Any study leads to the discovery of discrepancies"; cf. now Rosenshield 1997. A handy bibliography spanning much of the secondary literature is available in Milne 1990; see also Terry 1991 and more recently Weeks 1996. On balance, despite its occasional lapses of logic and judgment, the best single treatment remains Barratt 1987.

2. Page references are to the Ardis reprint (1980) of the text of the novel as first published in Mikhail Bulgakov, *Romany*, ed. Anna Saakiants (Moscow: Khudozhestvennaia literatura, 1973), as this version is still the most widely circulated one. The translation utilized here is Mirra Ginsburg's (New York: Grove Weidenfeld, 1987).

3. Here is a sampling of opinion which takes implicit account of the fact that this statement does not compute (all page references are to Weeks 1996). Haber (170): "And indeed, as a spiritual phenomenon, the manuscript, the work of art, is

indestructible, whatever its material fate might be"; Barratt (89) takes Krugovoy to task for discounting the statement as a vagary of the devil's; Lakshin (73) uses it as a pretext for the praise of Bulgakov's courage: "Mikhail Bulgakov died believing in the stubborn, indestructible power of art...these words served the author as an incantation against the destructive work of time." The last of these statements is actually most apropos, although most dependent on encomiastic rhetoric: it catches the incantatory force of the counterfactual.

4. For a relentless theologizing of the text—but with diametrically opposed conclusions—see Krugovoy 1991 and Ericson 1991.

5. A good survey is contained in the editor's Introduction to Weeks (3–67). Her own advocacy of history and apocalypticism as the key to a unified reading is unconvincing. The claim of a Masonic layer is made by Belobrovtseva and Kul'ius 1993. The sort of scavenger hunt that tends to level Bulgakov's achievement and gives source studies a bad name is exemplified by Sokolov 1991.

6. A curious exception is Krugovoy's otherwise learned study, which relies on branding Woland simply the "representative of universal evil" (77), with all the attendant simplifications of his role. Krugovoy also insists, counter to the facts of the plot, that Woland's power is "limited and held in check by the 'department' of metaphysical good, the department of Yeshua" (97). Why, then, would Yeshua appeal on the Master's behalf to Woland? Krugovoy's explanation is that "Yeshua recognizes the juridical validity of Woland's claim [on the souls of the Master and Margarita]" and "therefore, he 'asks' Woland to free both of them not on the basis of the impersonal letter of the law, but by the strength of forgiving and liberating mercy, as Margarita does by asking Woland to forgive Frieda" (219). But firstly, the latter is an example of

a genuine and necessary appeal; secondly, one might question the necessity for such a demonstration at all: the unmotivated argumentational switch from within the narrative to a putative external necessity is unconvincing.

7. Weeks' arguments (1996: 28–30)—and those of the critical companions on whom she leans—for Ivan Bezdomnyi's authorship of both of the novel's main narratives are weak.

8. Weeks 1984. Latterly, Weeks (1996: 64) says that she tends to think of her own earlier view as an oversimplification.

9. "Что бы делало твое добро, если не существовало зла, и как бы выглядела твоя земля, если бы с нее исчезли тени?"(356).

10. For instance by Weeks and Haber in Weeks 1996.

11. See Barratt's pointed criticism of both Ericson and Krugovoy in Weeks 1996: 86–87. The two epitomize monistic approaches, and (as indicated earlier) come to opposite conclusions about Woland's status in the scheme of providence, Krugovoy "find[ing] signs of Woland's insidious intent everywhere, Ericson say[ing] of Bulgakov's devil that he has 'little, if anything' of the tempter about him."

12. "А не надо никаких точек зрения!—ответил странный профессор,—просто он существовал, и больше ничего" (50).

13. "А я действительно похож на галлюцинацию. Обратите внимание на мой профиль в лунном свете,—кот полез в лунный столб и хотел что-то еще говорить, но его попросили замолчатъ, и он, ответив:—Хорошо, хорошо, готов молчатъ. Я буду молчаливой галлюцинацией,— замолчал" (282).

14. Our entire discussion of the Trinity is indebted to Rahner's fundamental work.

15. See, e. g., Krugovoy 1991: 46.

16. For a compact discussion, see Curtis 1987: 75–108.

17. "Почему-то мучил вездесущий оркестр, под аккомпане-

мент которого тяжелый бас пел о своей любви к Татьяне" (15).

18. "Никанор Иванович до своего сна соверершенно не знал произведений поэта Пушкина, но самого его знал прекрасно и ежедневно по несколько раз произносил фразы вроде: 'А за квартиру Пушкин платить будет?' или 'Лампочку на лестнице, стало быть, Пушкин вывинтил?', 'Нефть, стало быть, Пушкин покупать будет?'" (163).

19. In a letter to us concerning this chapter, April 19, 1995.

20. *The Economist*, October 12, 1996, p. 88.

Chapter 6

1. Sologub 1962: 117 [X, 161]. All quotations are from this translation; the bracketed material refers to chapter and page numbers in the original from the Forsyth edition (Sologub 1966), which is a reprint of the first Soviet edition (Moscow, 1933) that includes a foreword by Orest Tsekhnovitser. It should be noted that Field often takes liberties with the original in order to render it into idiomatic English, and where the disparity is significant we have cited the exact Russian text in brackets. For a more recent translation that has an appendix of critical articles, see Sologub 1983.

2. "Sologub's...*Melkii bes*...may be recognized as the most perfect Russian novel since the death of Dostoevsky... . Peredonov has become...the most famous and memorable character of Russian fiction since *The Brothers Karamazov*" (1966: 444–45). These words were, of course, written in the 1920s.

3. There are now several book-length studies of Sologub, including one devoted to *The Petty Demon* (Greene). For a bibliography of the secondary literature on Sologub up to 1984, see Lauer and Steltner 1984. Besides Ivanits 1976, native influences on Sologub's entire oeuvre have been discussed by Rabinowitz 1978, foreign ones and Pushkin's by Brodsky

1974. For a better treatment of the Gogolian strain in Sologub, see Snyder 1986.

4. See Debreczeny 1983: 209–11 for a discussion of the shifts
    of viewpoint in *The Queen of Spades*.

5. Peredonov's treatment of this servant suggests a non-
    Russian parallel which is interesting enough to note *en pas-
    sant*. Klavdiia is falsely accused of stealing raisins and forced
    to compensate the Peredonovs; cf. Rousseau, *Confessions 1*,
    in which Jean-Jacques steals a ribbon from his hostess and
    sees to it that blame falls on a maid, who is dismissed. We
    would suggest that further and deeper parallels exist be-
    tween Rousseauism in general and *The Petty Demon*.
    Rousseau's arguments for harmony between man and na-
    ture, for a more liberal education, and for a certain freedom
    of the spirit are clearly congenial to Sologub's outlook.

6. See the foreword to the second edition of *The Petty Demon*,
    reproduced in Field's translation (Sologub 1962: 353 [32]).

7. Our use of the phrase "boundary shifts" does not mean to
    imply that in Pushkin the lines between the real and the su-
    pernatural are ever unclear; they are not. But the narrative
    contexts do alternate, even though we always know what
    realm we are in. For a perspicacious assessment of Dosto-
    evsky's view of Pushkin, see Terras 1983.

8. The original reads as follows (Sologub 1975: 271):

> Я сжечь ее хотел, колдунью злую.
> Но у нее нашлись проклятые слова,—
> Я увидал ее опять живую,
> Вся в пламени и искрах голова.
>
> И говорит она: "Я не сгорела,—
> Восстановил огонь мою красу.
> Огнем упитанное тело
> Я от костра к волшебству унесу.

Перебегая, гаснет пламя в складках
Моих магических одежд.
Безумен ты! В моих загадках
Ты не найдешь своих надежд."

Note that the poem's date (1902) coincides with the novel's completion.

9. Not counting the two short paragraphs Koz'menko devotes to *The Queen of Spades* in his commentary to the 1988 Moscow edition (Sologub 1988: 291), Ivanits 1976 remains the only discussion prior to ours to take account of the parallels between *The Petty Demon* and *The Queen of Spades* but terms them merely "literary references" and limits them to narrow resemblances between the Princess and Pushkin's Countess. Greene (1986: 87–88) briefly mentions Pushkin as "an important presence" in the novel but only with reference to *Eugene Onegin*, citing *EO* VII.26.6, where the phrase *melkii bes* occurs in Tat'iana's description of Pykhtin.

10. Peredonov's lack of religion should not be conflated with opinions concerning Sologub's own attitude. Although Sologub was accused of being an irreligious by some fellow Symbolists, he was attracted to the religious wing of the movement. Most of *The Petty Demon* originally appeared in *Voprory Zhizni* [*Questions of Life*], the religious-philosophical journal founded by the Merezhkovskys. See Pachmuss 1971: 116–30.

11. Some scholars have interpreted *The Petty Demon* as depicting a Symbolist neo-Platonic universe divided into essences and reflections; see Kalbouss 1983, for example. The image cited here could pertain to his interpretation.

12. Forsyth (Sologub 1966: viii), in the introduction to his edition of the original (which he translates as *Shabby Demon*), echoing the description of Peredonov in XIV, 141, in which he is described as walking "под отчуждением с неба."

13. The original passage from which this phrase is taken (with

its idiosyncratic punctuation preserved) runs as follows: "'*Мелкий бес*' Сологуба воспроизвел иные черты стиля Гоголя, створяя их с воздержанностью квази-пушкинской прозы; 'гоголизм' Сологуба имеет тенденцию перекрасить себя в пушкинизм; и Пушкин, и Гоголь условны у С. не менее: интересен симптом: ход на Гоголя, минуя Толстого и Достоевского."

Chapter 7

1. All subsequent references to this work will be given in the body of the text as *DI*.

2. All subsequent references to this work will be given in the body of the text as SG. The Bakhtin bibliography has grown to such proportions as to be susceptible of no convenient summary. However, a concise list to 1990 is available in Holquist 1990, which, along with Morson and Emerson 1990 and Danow 1991b, are among the latest book-length treatments of the critic's life and works. The articles in Morson 1986 and Morson and Emerson 1989 give a good idea of the interest his ideas have aroused; Todorov 1984: 92 contains a handy list of Bakhtin originals and translations. The most far-ranging insider's view of Bakhtin as a semiotician is in Ivanov 1974: 310–67. See also Danow 1984: 79–97.

3. For a good survey of the "stylistic" meaning of punctuation (among other features of written language), see Vachek 1979.

4. The factual material in this section is drawn from Kahn 1979: 64–65, 195–200, 324–26, in which all the philological arguments for this particular version of the fragment are scrupulously laid out (superseding, we believe, those of Dirk and Raven 1971, to cite one accessible commentary).

5. As Dunkel 1979 makes clear, the best evidence on this topic is contained in the second century A.D. text called the *Certamen*.

6. To the best of our knowledge, the explanation that follows

has not been launched before. Kahn 1979: 200–01 explains *palintropos* by reference to the "allusive nature of Heraclitus' style and his systematic use of resonance," echoing the Homeric *palintonos* (a variant reading in the fragment itself), "which is the clue to the significance of the whole fragment as description of cosmic structure and unity" (200). The whole phrase in Kahn's view (201) is an illustration of the way Heraclitus goes about forging a link between his doctrine of opposites and his cosmology. Our explanation and Kahn's do not, of course, exclude each other.

7. We owe a fundamental debt to Miner 1979—henceforth designated in parentheses as *JLP*—for our understanding of the structure, interpretation, and history of *renga* and *haikai*, as well as for the texts and translations cited. A concise summary of all the most important aspects of these two Japanese verse forms can be gotten from Miner 1983.

8. The absence of one or both of these prerequisites seems (in our opinion) to account for the lack of success of the Western imitations of *renga* in Paz et al. 1972.

9. Provençal poems are cited from Hill and Bergin 1973 (abbreviated *APT)*, to which the page numbers in the text refer. The translations are by Marianne Shapiro. Extensive discussions of rivalry as a topic in the poetry are to be found in Paterson 1975, which emphasizes the importance of the practitioners of *trobar clus* ("closed" poetics). Actual poetic competitions were not unknown in medieval Japan (called *utawase* or *rengaawase*, depending on the kind of poem), but they seem not to have had much viability. See Carter 1984.

10. For an account of competing explanations of the Old Provençal [OP] term *midons* ("my lord") as applied to a lady, from models of Arabic poetry to the adaptation of feudal vassalage to play with gender, see Hackett 1971.

11. The earliest OP lyrics in which the lover/lady relationship is compared with the love of God are analyzed by Denomy

1947. Paradoxes of courtly love are discussed by Topsfield 1974 and in works on specific poets and lyrics (e.g., Spitzer 1944 and Dragonetti 1977).

12. Comparison of the *tenso* with the *conflictus* can be found in Jones 1934: 66–68. Another OP genre, which may be considered a specialized kind of *tenso*, the *pastorela*, enjoyed a wide literary influence but in OP meant a spirited dialogue of seduction and resistance between a knight and a shepherdess.

13. The classic accounts of Dante's palinodic trajectory are those of Singleton 1958 and Freccero 1986.

14. W refers to Peirce 1982, the multivolume chronological edition now in progress that will eventually supersede Peirce 1965-66. The enormous potential of Peirce's philosophy for the study of literature has yet to be tapped (some sustained efforts in that direction are Winsheimer 1983, Overing 1987, and especially Haley 1988). As pointed out by Singer 1984: 79, the significance of Peirce's conception of sign and semiosis as systematically dialogical has not been generally recognized (but see Brock 1975). Although the compass of this chapter does not allow more than a cursory reference to Peirce's ideas, we have incorporated a juxtaposition of Peirce and Bakhtin in order to indicate at very least the potential richness of a Peircean approach to the study of verbal art. Cf. Kent 1989.

15. The standard way of referring to Peirce 1961–65 is by volume and paragraph number separated by a dot. Two other relevant passages are 5.506 and 6.338.

Chapter 8

1. See especially Blagoi 1941: 117–18, 131–32; Pumpianskii 1939; and Koplan 1930.

2. Koplan 1930: 121, n. 2 has a comprehensive list of these citations.

3. All quotations from Pushkin's works in the original are from Pushkin 1977 (which is based on the multivolume Academy

of Sciences edition). Further citation in the body of this chapter will be in the form *PSS* x: xxx, i.e., by volume and page number. References to Lomonosov's poetry are made without specific page citations and are to Lomonosov 1986.

4. Unless indicated otherwise, all prose translations of Pushkin are cited from Wolff 1986. Further references to this item will appear in the body of the paper in the form *POL:* 147, which is the locus of this excerpt.

5. "Нет сомнения в том, что Пушкин хорошо помнил основные поэтические произведения Ломоносова и мог свободно цитировать их по памяти" (Gorodetskii 1962: 26). Koplan (1930: 118, n. 2) mentions the existence of a three-volume edition of Lomonosov's works dated 1803 in Pushkin's library, which does not limit the scope of Pushkin's acquaintance with Lomonosov's poetry to this edition (as Koplan acknowledges). It is interesting that Pushkin took the time and effort to copy out Lomonosov's blasphemous poem "Гимн бороде (Hymn to a/the Beard)" sometime in the 1830s; see Tsiavlovskii et al. 1935: 563 ff.

6. Beside the Koplan and Pumpianskii articles mentioned in n. 1, see Blagoi 1972/I: 254-67. Cf. Gukovskii 1957: 101-05

7. Blagoi 1972/I: 267 points out that Pushkin's version contains a last stanza that makes distinct textual reference to Lomonosov's imitation of Horace (rather than to Derzhavin's).

8. Lebedev 1987: 309–10 mediates Pushkin's reception of the theme from Lomonosov via Batiushkov's "Переход через Рейн (Crossing the Rhine)" (1816–17).

9. See Tomashevskii 1956: 527-28. The six-foot iamb was introduced into Russian verse by Lomonosov; see Bondi 1986.

10. Koplan 1930: 121, which also quotes Pushkin as having called Lomonosov "истинно классический" (truly classical) to the exclusion of all other Russian eighteenth-century writers; but we could not find the exact locus from among Koplan's textual listing (n. 2).

11. "Pushkin sanctions Lomonosov's *method*, the method of constructive combination of heterogeneous linguistic series, the method of stylistic merging of extremes" (Vinogradov 1935: 36).

12. Pumpianskii 1939: 123. The linking of Lomonosov with Peter goes back to Batiushkov and was endorsed later in the century by Belinskii; see Blagoi 1972/1: 256 and his gloss (1972 11: 265, n. 1) of the line from *Медный всадник* /*The Bronze Horseman*/, "Полнощных стран краса и диво" (The beauty and miracle of the northern countries), as a reminiscence from Pushkin's own verses dedicated to Zhukovskii in 1816.

13. Grigor'eva 1981: 143-44 calls attention to the fact that the designation *студеное море* for the White Sea (i.e., instead of Белое море) was widespread at one time, particularly in northern Russia. But the likelihood is that Pushkin simply meant *студеный* as a synonym for *холодный* 'cold' in this context.

14. "As if the petty honors of a modish writer were necessary to the glory of the great Lomonosov!" (*PSS* 7: 22).

15. Vinogradov 1935: 35 quotes Shevyrev's 1841 memoir as follows: "We remember the reverence with which Pushkin spoke of him [Lomonosov] as of the creator of the language: he didn't even allow anyone to say anything against the memory of our great master in his presence."

16. Gasparov 1983 is only the latest in a series of studies that attempts to trace "reminiscences" of Dante in Pushkin.

17. The one exception is Rozanov 1930, whose enumeration of the Petrarch *loci* in Pushkin we follow here.

18. Petrarch poems are cited from the Contini edition (Petrarca 1964), English translations from Durling 1976, and Pushkin texts from the seventeen-volume Academy edition (1939–59).

19. "There, beneath days cloudy and brief, is born a people… whom dying does not pain." Pushkin mistakenly omits the

grave accent over *là* and uses a spelling of *cui il morir* which accurately reflects the pronunciation but differs from the standard edition in omitting the elided vowel. The appropriateness of these lines to the subject matter of the chapter, specifically to the duel between Onegin and Lenskii, transpires from the fourth stanza of the *canzone*, for which the Crusade of 1333 served as an occasion for dedicating this poem to Giacomo Colonna.

20. The spelling *Madona* is consistent in Pushkin (Vinogradov et al. 1956–61) and doubtless reflects the typical degeminated Muscovite colloquial pronunciation of the time. It is interesting to note that the painting referred to is one attributed to Pietro Perugino (1445?–1523).

21. The circumstances surrounding these marginalia are of some interest in themselves. The copy of Batiushkov's *Opyty* was in the possession of Pushkin's oldest son, Aleksandr, when it was examined by the critic Leonid Maikov, who copied out all the comments and published excerpts from them in an article, "Pushkin o Batiushkove" ("Pushkin on Batiushkov") (Maikov 1895: 190–222). Pushkin's copy of the *Opyty* has since been lost. In any event there is no certain way of dating his marginalia, which seem to have been written at different times. Although Maikov himself (1895: 196–97) puts the date somewhere between 1825 and the second half of 1826 and no later than 1828, the commonly accepted dating in modern editions is 1830 (Lebedev et al. 1978: 630); but cf. Semenko (1977: 190-92), who offers a rather convincing argument for a later date, namely 1834. Our references are to the pages of Lebedev 1978. All of the Batiushkov excerpts cited in the latter have been checked against the 1977 edition of the *Opyty*.

22. In the number (6, also from 1816) of *Vestnik Evropy* preceding the one containing his "Petrarka," Batiushkov had published an essay entitled 'Ariost i Tass [Ariosto and Tasso].'

Both were reprinted in the *Opyty*.

23. There is some question as to the extent of Pushkin's knowledge of Italian (see the list of studies on this topic in Gasparov 1983: 350, n. 30). We believe it reasonable to assume that his reading knowledge was serviceable but depended almost exclusively on French translations as a crutch.

24. When Turgenev excitedly translated some Pushkin lines to Flaubert, the latter's reaction was: "Mais il est plat, votre poète!"

25. Gasparov 1983: 145ff. thinks the source is Ovid, and it is possible that Ovid provides a common provenance of the desert image for both Petrarch and Pushkin, but the diction is certainly closer to Petrarch.

26. The figures in the table are derived from the first 14 lines of poems chosen at random from two anthologies, Stepanov 1972 and Obolensky 1962.

27. In Russian, including that of the historical period at issue here, the sonorants are (ignoring the distinction between palatalized and non-palatalized) *m, n, r, 1, v,* and *j.* All other consonants are obstruents, except that within a word *v* is a sonorant only when followed by a sonorant, and an obstruent otherwise. In Italian (cf. Agard and Di Pietro 1965: 13–20 et passim), of the sounds corresponding to the Russian system, all but *v* (which is uniformly an obstruent) are sonorants as well.

28. As Rozanov points out (1930: 126), the manuscript contains an error. Where Petrarch wrote "S'amor non è, che dunque è quel ch'io sento?," Pushkin (doubtless relying on a faulty memory of the original) has "Se amor non è, che dunche?..." This is the mistake that gave rise to Korsh's surmise (1908), disputed by other investigators, about Pushkin's poor Italian. All modern editions correct the error.

29. It could even be argued that the relative absence of sonority units (only 14 for 96 syllables, hence the quotient .146) sup-

ports both the poem's teleology and the overtly privative conclusion ("Тебе ж нет отзыва" ["But to you there is no response"]) this drift leads to.

Chapter 9

1. For a recent discussion of this episode, see Shishkin 1983 (with further references therein). Our account here relies also on Gukovskii 1928, from which the quotations are taken. The translations were completed in 1743 and published the following year in a separate brochure.

2. As his antecedents, Gasparov (1976) cites Tynianov [1924] 1965, Tomashevskii 1958, and especially Taranovskii 1963. On the importance of Tynianov (overestimated, to our mind), cf. also Gasparov 1984. An extension of Tomashevskii's pioneering treatment of Pushkin's stanzas is now in Lotman and Shakhverdov 1979. As Vickery (Eekman and Worth 1983: 466, 478–79) points out, the attempt to link metrical variants with themes goes back in Russia to Andrei Bely, to whose approach (in *Simvolizm* [1910]) an important corrective is provided by Zhirmunskii 1925: 41. Gasparov acknowledges (1979: 282) that there is reason to be skeptical about Taranovskii's claims and singles out the criticism of Vishnevskii 1977 (esp. 149–51) as preeminently objective and well argued. Cf. now Vishnevskii 1985 for an even more serious demurral, specifically from Taranovskii's characterization of the Russian trochaic pentameter. Even after a thorough study of much of Gasparov's output we cannot escape the feeling that Timofeev's objections (1982: 151–59) to Gasparov's whole enterprise are largely valid. Despite its evident improvement over the first steps of its predecessors, Gasparov's approach remains open to the charge that it is mired in what has been referred to as "rampant empiricism" (Jakobson *SW* 5: 574).

3. For a study of this poetic form "which will influence for decades to come the way we think about poetic technique"

(Wesling and Bollobás 1983: 53), see Marianne Shapiro 1980a. This book is to our knowledge the first to show conclusively and in great detail how poetic form mirrors poetic content while being, moreover, systematically part of the latter. (Sestinas were also written by Russian poets, particularly in modern times by Symbolists like Bal'mont.)

4. Taranovskii (1963: 320) goes beyond observations of rhythmic coloring of metrical variants to the more vulnerable claim of a "synaesthetic connection between the rhythmic movement of the Russian five-foot trochee and the rhythm of human footsteps," which echoes Jakobson's remark (SW 5: 465) that "Russian trochaic pentameter [with its] sharp asymmetry, [its] brokenness of the rhythmical step,…renders the meter especially appropriate for the theme of agitated walking."

5. His definitions have been subjected to renewed scrutiny by Kholshevnikov (1984: 168–73) and Gasparov (Kholshevnikov 1984: 174–78). Trubetskoi explicitly assumes the systematic relevance of metric feet to the structure of Russian syllabotonic verse (as do we, following his lead), but Kholshevnikov (1984: 58–66) has attempted to mount another assault against this position. We find his argumentation unconvincing and prefer the cogent reasoning of Laferriere (1979: 90–93, n. 4; not cited by Kholhsevnikov), Cf. Rancour-Laferriere 1989.

6. Trubetskoi does not return to the matter of privative oppositions in this article after their first mention. Even more puzzling is Jakobson's avoidance of markedness in his many examinations of the Russian verse system spanning almost the entirety of his long scholarly career.

7. Markedness is a formal semiotic universal affecting the valorization of terms of oppositions throughout grammar, from phonology to stylistics and discourse. Markedness is always context-sensitive and applies wherever there is a choice. The

so-called marked term is more narrowly defined—is of more restricted scope—vis-à-vis its unmarked, less narrowly defined counterpart. For more on the larger topic, see now Battistella 1996.

8. Trubetskoi (1975: 301) expresses his view that iamb is unmarked but supports it with a statistical basis that we would judge to be the exact converse of the real directionality between verse design and verse instance.

9. We have to state this principle without adducing the usual array of corroborative references for the simple reason that we can find no discussion of it. However, it is a principle well known (albeit in other terms) to musicians and music theorists, who treat the onsets of musical material (as opposed to codas) as possessing special properties. Note that the principle of marked beginnings does not apply to defective cases, most prominent among which for our purposes is that of units in parallel. In paired units there is no middle (third) element, hence no real opposition between beginnings and ends, only first and second. That is why the second of two cola in Biblical *parallelismus membrorum* is marked rather than the first. Cf. n. 19.

10. Laferriere also correctly disparages (1979: 96–97, n. 6) the various alternative terms for hypermetrical stressing that refer to this phenomenon variously as "nonmetrical stressing," "iambic substitutions [in trochaic lines and vice versa]," "metrical/foot inversions," etc. It would be well to keep distinct legitimate cases of hypermetrical stress from the episodic intrusion of metrical "inversions." Cf. Laferriere 1980: 429-34 and Rancour-Laferriere 1981.

11. A more extensive discussion of the respects in which this distinction affects the systematic analysis of Russian accentuation is in Shapiro 1986.

12. Laferriere (1979: 98ff.) offers a different explanation of hypermetrical stressing (which disagrees with that of Jakobson

1973; but cf. a bit of waffling at Laferriere 1980: 429), along with a devastating critique of the Halle-Keyser theories of meter (110–12).

13. In the light of this new formulation some of the ambiguities and differences between Trubetskoi's and Jakobson's earlier statements of the rule that are discussed by Gasparov (1974: 126–28, 190–92) could be reanalyzed with profit.

14. The statistical regularities referred to are, of course, not "laws," and only a tin ear would render the Russian original literally as "fulfilled" in English instead of "realized." Here Laferriere is not to blame, for he is only reproducing the solecisms of his source.

15. Laferriere (1979: 115) also equates this with Gasparov's "law of ascending onset" (Gasparov 1974: 77).

16. We have stated this quotation in corrected form (the source has the two parenthesized glosses reversed); cf. Gasparov 1974: 77 and Zhirmunskii 1922: 121.

17. This is a good illustration of the invariably context-sensitive nature of markedness.

18. See the theoretical agenda with practical applications of Shapiro 1976 (and Eekman and Worth 1983: 353–69). Further work along these lines that involves significant extensions of the theory is now available in Michael Shapiro 1980a (of which Shapiro and Shapiro 1988: chapter 4 is a revision). Marianne Shapiro's (1980a) espousal of this agenda is "a wide generalizing of [its] claims [that makes] asymmetry into the crucial feature of poetic language and the history of poetic influence. …[t]his working hypothesis enables her to reveal many powerfully significant facts about her chosen poetic tradition. The sestina's main feature is rhyme on the same end-word in a different sentence and a different position. Same word in new position equals different meaning, necessarily. Contiguity and nonsynonymy of terms become structuring principles in sestinas that must rhyme by repe-

tition, and these are principles of asymmetry of elements" (Welling and Bollobás 1983: 58). Cf. also Kovtunova 1986, which relies in part on Grigor'ev (1979: 185–86) and his call for the extension of Karcevskij's ideas about the asymmetry of the sign to poetic structure.

19. Kugel's (1981) analysis of the cola of Biblical *parallelismus membrorum* as involving a semantic structure that he casts in the shorthand form "A, what's more B" is a good illustration of the implications of Shapiro 1976 (not cited by Kugel).

Chapter 10

1. The corresponding phrase in British English is *if you like*. It seems to be used even more promiscuously by speakers in the United Kingdom than in American English.

2. In order to avoid needless confusion over phonological differences between varieties of American English, we have chosen to stick to phonetic transcription and to follow the practice of *Webster's Third New International Dictionary of the English Language, Unabridged* in using [ä] as a sign to cover all of the varieties that occur as the stressed vowel or vowel nucleus in words like *llama*. For a discussion of the contemporary distribution of these sounds, see the forematter in Cassidy 1985. A concise historical characterization of broad and flat *A* in American English occurs in Robertson 1954: 392–94; cf. Mencken 1957: 334ff.

3. There are clearly plenty of exceptions, including words from Amerindian languages and Spanish, particularly in the Southwest and California.

4. In the case under discussion, the association of [ä] with foreign lexemes and [æ] with native ones has resulted in the former being valorized as marked and the latter as unmarked.

5. It might seem a plausible alternative to attribute this pronunciation of *habitat* to something like a subliminal aware-

ness of the Latin source. But familiarity with Curtis' marked Eastern New England speech provides a convincing riposte to any such suggestion.

6. The recent appearance of the spelling *Ondrea* to render the name among status-seeking speech communities bears this out. Jones 1984 (s.v.) gives the alternate *D[a:]nte* but only *K[æ]nt*. We suspect that the truer picture of present-day British English, with its wholesale importation of Americanisms of all kinds, would include *K[a:]nt*.

Chapter 11

1. The characterization "purely mental" needs to be qualified somewhat. What needs to be emphasized here for a proper understanding is that in human semiosis units of any kind are in varying degree dependent on interpretation, including stipulative convention, when the units are fully coded. A phoneme or morpheme, for instance, typically has a material shape consisting in speech of sound waves. Rules of selection and combination in a language determine what is to be counted as a phoneme or morpheme. But in the case of boundaries the only physical clue we have as to a boundary's presence is via its effects on contiguous units. Hence the designation "purely mental" for boundaries as for ranking.

2. For more on this construction, see Shapiro and Haley 2002.

3. The pioneer in adapting gestalt psychology and field theory to linguistics, particularly the theory of change in language, is the Indo-Europeanist and theoretician Raimo Anttila. See esp. Anttila 1977, 1985, and 1992.

References

Agard, Frederick B., and Robert J. Di Pietro. 1965. *The Sounds of English and Italian.* Chicago: University of Chicago Press.

Alter, Robert. 1965. *The Art of Biblical Poetry.* New York: Basic Books.

Annenkov, P. V. 1934. *Literaturnye vospominaniia.* Moscow: Academia.

Anttila, Raimo. 1977. "Dynamic Fields and Linguistic Structure: A Proposal for a Gestalt Linguistics." *Die Sprache* 23: 1–10.

_____. 1985. "Dynamics in Morphology." *Acta Linguistica Academiae Scientiarum Hungaricae* 35: 3-30.

_____. 1992. "Field Theory of Meaning and Semantic Change," in *Diachrony within Synchrony: Language History and Cognition*, ed. G. Kellermann & M. D. Morrissey, 23–83. Frankfurt am Main: Peter Lang.

Arban, Dominique. 1981. "Le Statut de la Folie dans les oeuvres de jeunesse de Dostoïevski," *Dostoevsky Studies* 2: 27–41.

Aristotle. 1941. *The Basic Works of Aristotle*, ed. R. McKeon. New York: Random House.

Ayers, David. 1988. "Two Bald Men: Eliot and Dostoevsky," *Forum for Modern Language Studies* 24: 287–300.

Bacon, Francis. 1958. *The Advancement of Learning*, ed. G. W. Kitchin. London: Dent.

Bakhtin, M. M. 1972. *Problemy poètiki Dostoevskogo*, 3rd ed. Moscow: Khudozhestvennaia literatura.

_____. 1981. *The Dialogic Imagination: Four Essays*, ed. M. Holquist, trans. C. Emerson & M. Holquist. Austin: University of Texas Press.

_____. 1984. *Problems of Dostoevsky's Poetics*, ed. and trans. C. Emerson. Minneapolis: University of Minnesota Press.

_____. 1986. *Speech Genres and Other Late Essays*, ed. C. Emerson & M. Holquist, trans. V. W. McGee. Austin: University of Texas Press.

Barnfield, Richard. 1990. *The Complete Poems*, ed. G. Klawitter. Selinsgrove, Penn.: Susquehanna University Press.

Barratt, Andrew. 1987. *Between Two Worlds: A Critical Introduction to 'The Master and Margarita'*. Oxford: Clarendon Press.

Batiushkov, K. N. 1886. *Sochineniia*, III, ed. P. N. Batiushkov. St. Petersburg: Tipografiia Kotomina.

_____. 1977. *Opyty v stikhakh i proze*, ed. I. M. Semenko. Moscow: Nauka.

Battistella, Edwin L. 1996. *The Logic of Markedness*. New York: Oxford University Press.

Beker, Miroslav (ed.). 1981. *Comparative Studies in Croatian Literature*. Zagreb: Zavod za znanost i književnost Filozofskog fakulteta u Zagrebu.

Belinksii, V. G. 1953-1959. *Polnoe sobranie sochinenii*, I-XIII. Moscow: AN SSSR.

Belkin, A. A. (ed.). 1956. *F. M. Dostoevskii v russkoi kritike: Sbornik statei*. Moscow: GIKHL.

Belknap, Robert L. 1990. *The Genesis of* The Brothers Karamazov: *The Aesthetics, Ideology, and Psychology of Making a Text*. Evanston, Ill.: Northwestern University Press.

Belobrovtseva, I., and S. Kul'ius. 1993. "Roman M. Bulgakova 'Master i Margarita' kak èzotericheskii tekst: 'masonskii' sloi romana," in *Bulgakovskii sbornik*, I, ed. I. Belobrovtseva & S.

Kul'ius, 30–39. Tallinn: Tallinnskii pedagogicheskii universitet.

Belyi, Andrei. 1934. *Masterstvo Gogolia: Issledovanie.* Moscow: Ogiz.

Bem, A. L. (ed.). 1929. *O Dostoevskom: Sbornik statei,* I. Prague: F. Svoboda.

_____. 1936. "'Nos' i 'Dvoinik'," in *O Dostoevskom: Sbornik statei,* III, 139–163. Prague: F. Svoboda.

_____. 1979. "'The Nose'" and 'The Double'," in Meyer & Rudy 1979: 229–248.

Bethea, David M. 1991. "Bulgakov and Nabokov: Toward a Comparative Perspective." *Zapiski russkoi akademicheskoi gruppy v S. Sh. A.* 24: 187–209.

Blagoi, D. D. 1941. "Pushkin i russkaia literatura XVIII veka," in *Pushkin— Rodonachal'nik novoi russkoi literatury,* ed. D. D. Blagoi & V. Ia. Kirpotin, 101–66. Moscow: AN SSSR. [expanded version in Blagoi's *Literatura i deistvitel'nost',* 201–300. Moscow: GIKHL, 1959]

_____. 1972. *Ot Kantemira do nashikh dnei,* I-II. Moscow: Khudozhestvennaia literatura.

Bogatyrev, P. G. 1956. "Zagovory," in *Russkoe narodnoepoèticheskoe tvorchestvo,* ed. P. G. Bogatyrev, 2nd ed., 255–64. Moscow: GIMP.

Bondi, S. M. 1986. "Shestistopnyi iamb Pushkina." *Pushkin: Issledovaniia i materialy* 12: 5–27.

Booth, Stephen. 1969. *An Essay on Shakespeare's Sonnets.* New Haven: Yale University Press.

_____ (ed.). 1977. *Shakespeare's Sonnets.* New Haven: Yale University Press.

Breger, Louis. 1989. *Dostoevsky: The Author as Psychoanalyst.* New York: New York University Press.

Brock, Jarrett. 1975. "Peirce's Conception of Semiotic." *Semiotica* 14: 124–141.

Brodsky, Patricia Pollock. 1974. "Fertile Fields and Poison Gardens: Sologub's Debt to Hoffman, Pushkin, and Hawthorne." *Essays in Literature* 1: 96–108.

Burke, Kenneth. 1957. "On Musicality in Verse," in his *The Philosophy of Literary Form: Studies in Symbolic Action*, 2nd ed., 294–304. New York: Vintage Books.

Cadet, Michel. 1993. "Les lectures stratifiées de Dostoïevski par André Gide," in *Dostoevsky and the Twentieth Century: The Ljubljana Papers*, ed. M. V. Jones, 197-208. Nottingham: Astra Press.

Carter, Steven D. 1984. "A Lesson in Failure: Linked-Verse Contests in Medieval Japan." *Journal of the American Oriental Society* 104: 727–37.

Cassidy, Frederic G. (ed.). 1985. *Dictionary of American Regional English, I: Introduction and A–C*. Cambridge, Mass.: Harvard University Press.

Cercignani, Fausto. 1981. *Shakespeare's Works and Elizabethan Pronunciation*. Oxford: Clarendon Press.

Chizhevskii, Dmitrii. 1929. "K probleme dvoinika (Iz knigi o formalizme v ètike)," in Bem 1929: 9–38.

Chizhevsky, Dmitri. 1962. "The Theme of the Double in Dostoevsky," in *Dostoevsky: A Collection of Critical Essays*, ed. R. Wellek, 112–129. Englewood Cliffs, N.J.: Prentice-Hall [= Chizhevskii 1929].

Čiževskij, Dmitrij. 1971. *Comparative History of Slavic Literatures*, trans. R. N. Porter, ed. M. P. Rice. Nashville: Vanderbilt University Press.

Coetzee, J. M. 1985. "Confession and Double Thoughts: Tolstoy, Rousseau, Dostoevsky." *Comparative Literature* 37: 193–232.

Colapietro, Vincent. 1989. *Peirce's Approach to the Self: A Semiotic Perspective on Human Subjectivity*. Albany: State University of New York Press.

Contini, Gianfranco. 1964. "Preliminari sulla lingua del Petrarca," in Petrarca 1964: vii–xxviii.

Curtis, J. A. E. 1987. *Bulgakov's Last Decade: The Writer as Hero.* Cambridge: Cambridge University Press.

Daniel, Samuel. 1963. *The Complete Works in Verse and Prose*, I, ed. A. B. Grosart. New York: Russell & Russell.

Danow, David K. 1984. "M. M. Bakhtin's Concept of the Word." *American Journal of Semiotics* 3: 79–97.

_____. 1991a. *The Dialogic Sign: Essays on the Major Novels of Dostoevsky.* New York: Peter Lang.

_____. 1991b. *The Thought of Mikhail Bakhtin: From Word to Culture.* New York: St. Martin's Press.

_____. 1997. "Dostoevskij's *Dvojnik* and Its (Anti-)Poetic Ambiance. *Russian Literature* 41:19–36.

Debreczeny, Paul. 1983. *The Other Pushkin: A Study of Alexander Pushkin's Prose Fiction.* Stanford, Calif.: Stanford University Press.

Denomy, A. J. 1947. *The Heresy of Courtly Love.* New York: Macmillan.

Dilaktorskaia, O. G. 1999. *Peterburgskaia povest' Dostoevskogo.* St. Petersburg: Dmitrii Bulanin.

Dirk, G. S., and J. E. Raven. 1971. *The Presocratic Philosophers: A Critical History with a Selection of Texts.* Cambridge: Cambridge University Press.

Dolinin, A. 1968. "Estranged: Toward a Psychology of Sologub's Work," in *The Noise of Change: Russian Literature and the Critics (1891-1917)*, ed. and trans. S. J. Rabinowitz, 124–48. Ann Arbor: Ardis. [original in *Zavety* 7 (1913): 55–85]

Dostoevskii, F. M. 1959. *Pis'ma*, IV. Moscow: Goslitizdat.

_____. 1972-1990. *Polnoe sobranie sochinenii v tridtsati tomakh*, I–XXX, ed. V. G. Bazanov et al. Leningrad: Nauka.

_____ [= Dostoyevsky, Fyodor]. 1976. *The Brothers Karamazov*, trans. C.Garnett, ed. and rev. R. E. Matlaw. New York: Norton.

_____ [= Dostoyevsky, Fyodor]. 1989. *Notes from Underground*, trans. and ed. M. R. Katz. New York: Norton.

Dragonetti, Roger. 1977. "The Double Play of Arnaut Daniel's Sestina and Dante's *Divine Comedy.*" *Yale French Studies* 15: 227–52.

Driver, Sam. 1989. *Pushkin: Literature and Social Ideas.* New York: Columbia University Press.

Dunkel, George. 1979. "Fighting Words: Alcman *Partheneion 63 Maxontai.*" *The Journal of Indo-European Studies* 7: 249–72.

Durling, Robert M. 1976. *Petrarch's Lyric Poems: The Rime sparse and Other Lyrics.* Cambridge, Mass.: Harvard University Press.

Dynes, Wayne. 1985. *Homolexis: A Historical and Cultural Lexicon of Homosexuality.* New York: Gai Saber Press.

Eco, Umberto. 1976. *A Theory of Semiotics.* Bloomington: Indiana University Press.

Eekman, Thomas, and Dean S. Worth (eds.). 1983. *Russian Poetics.* Columbus, Oh.: Slavica.

Èikhenbaum, B. M. 1923. "Put' Pushkina k proze." *Pushkinist* 4: 59–74 [rpt. in his *O proze, O poèzii,* 29-45. Leningrad: Khudozhestvennaia literatura, 1986]

Ericson, Jr., Edward E. 1991. *The Apocalyptic Vision of Mikhail Bulgakov's* The Master and Margarita. Lewiston, Me.: Edward Mellen.

Erofeev, Viktor V. 1985. "Na grani razryva ('Melkiy bes' F. Sologuba na fone russkoi realisticheskoi traditsii)." *Voprosy literatury* 2: 140–158.

Fanger, Donald. 1967. *Dostoevsky and Romantic Realism: A Study of Dostoevsky in Relation to Balzac, Dickens, and Gogol.* Cambridge, Mass.: Harvard University Press.

Felperin, Howard. 1985. *Beyond Deconstruction: The Uses and Abuses of Literary Theory.* Oxford: Clarendon.

Fletcher, Giles, the Elder. 1964. *The English Works,* ed. L. E. Berry. Madison: University of Wisconsin Press.

Florenskii, Pavel. 1914. *Stolp i utverzhdenie istiny.* Moscow: Put'.

Foster, John. 1993. *Nabokov's Art of Memory and European Mod-*

ernism. Princeton, N. J.: Princeton University Press.

Frank, Joseph. 1976. *Dostoevsky: The Seeds of Revolt, 1821–1849*. Princeton, N.J.: Princeton University Press.

_____, and David I. Goldstein (eds.). 1987. *Selected Letters of Fyodor Dostoyevsky*, trans. A. R. MacAndrew. New Brunswick, N.J.: Rutgers University Press.

Freccero, John. 1986. *Dante: The Poetics of Conversion*, ed. R. Jacoff. Cambridge, Mass.: Harvard University Press.

Gasparov, Boris. 1983. "Funktsii reministsentsii iz Dante v poèzii Pushkina (stat'ia pervaiia)." *Russian Literature* 14: 317–350.

_____. 1985. "Encounter of Two Poets in the Desert: Pushkin's Myth," in *Myth in Literature*, ed. A. Kodjak et al., 124–153. Columbus, Oh.: Slavica.

Gasparov, M. L. 1973a. "K semantike daktilicheskoi rifmy v russkom khoree," in *Slavic Poetics: Essays in Honor of Kiril Taranovsky*, ed. R. Jakobson et al., 143–150. The Hague: Mouton.

_____. 1973b. "Russkii iamb i angliiskii iamb," in *Philologica: Issledovaniia po iazyku i literature. Pamiati akademika Viktora Maksimovicha Zhirmunskogo*, ed. V. N. Iartseva, 408–15. Leningrad: Nauka.

_____. 1974. *Sovremennyi russkii stikh: Metrika i ritmika*. Moscow: Nauka.

_____. 1976. "Metr i smysl: k semantike russkogo trekhstopnogo khoreiia." *Izvestiia AN SSSR, Seriia literatury i iazyka* 35: 357–366.

_____. 1979. "Semanticheskii oreol metra: k semantike russkogo trekhstopnogo iamba," in *Lingvistika i poètika*, ed. V. P. Grigor'ev, 282–308. Moscow: Nauka.

_____. 1982. "Semanticheskii oreol trekhstopnogo amfibrakhiia," in *Problemy strukturnoi lingvistiki 1980*, ed. V. P. Grigor'ev, 174–192. Moscow: Nauka.

_____. 1984. "Tynianov i problema semantiki metra," in *Tynianovskii sbornik* [Riga] 1: 105–113.

_____. 1984. *Ocherk istorii russkogo stikha: Metrika, ritmika, rifima, strofika*. Moscow: Nauka.

Gasperetti, David. 1989. "*The Double*: Dostoevsky's Self-Effacing Narrative," *Slavic and East European Journal* 33: 217–234.

Gerbstman, A. I. 1968. "O zvukovom stroenii narodnoi zagadki," *Russkii fol'klor* 11: 185-97.

Gide, André. 1923. *Dostoïevski: Articles et causeries*. Paris: Plon.

_____. 1952. *Dostoevsky*. London: Secker & Warburg.

Ginguéné, Pierre Louis. 1824. *Histoire littéraire d'Italie*, II, 2nd ed. Paris: Michaud. [Pushkin owned the first ed.]

Girard, René, 1963. *Dostoïevski du double à l'unité*. Paris: Plon.

_____. 1997. *Resurrection from the Underground: Feodor Dostoevsky*, ed. and trans. J. H. Williams. New York: Crossroad.

Gogol', N. V. 1940. *Sobranie sochinenii*, X. Moscow: AN SSSR.

_____. 1961. "The Inspector General," in *An Anthology of Russian Plays*, I, ed. and trans. F. D. Reeve. New York: Random House.

Goldsmith, Ulrich K. 1950. "Words out of a Hat? Alliteration and Assonance in Shakespeare's Sonnets." *Journal of English and Germanic Philology* 50: 33-48. [rpt. in his *Studies in Comparison*, ed. H. E. Barnes et al., 11–30. New York: Peter Lang, 1989]

Gorodetskii, B. P. 1962. *Lirika Pushkina*. Leningrad: AN SSSR.

Greene, Diana. 1986. *Insidious Intent: An Interpretation of Fedor Sologub's* The Petty Demon. Columbus, Oh.: Slavica.

Greene, Thomas. 1968. "The Flexibility of the Self in Renaissance Literature," in *The Disciplines of Criticism: Essays in Literary Theory, Interpretation, and History*, ed. P. Demetz et al., 241–264. New Haven: Yale University Press.

Grigor'ev, V. P. 1979. *Poètika slova*. Moscow: Nauka.

Grigor'eva, A. D. 1981. "Iazyk liriki Pushkina 30-kh godov," in *Iazyk liriki XIX v.: Pushkin, Nekrasov*, ed. A. D. Grigor'eva & N. N. Ivanova, 3–219. Moscow: Nauka.

Gukovskii, G. A. 1928. "K voprosu o russkom klassitsizme: sostiazaniia i perevody." *Poetika* 4: 126–148.

_____. 1957. *Pushkin i problemy realisticheskogo stilia*. Moscow: GIKHL.

Hackett, W. M. 1971. "Le problème de 'midons'," in *Mélanges de philologie romane dédiées à la memoire de Jean Boutière*, ed. I. M. Cluzel & F. Pirot, 285–94. Liege: Soledi.

Haley, Michael Cabot. 1988. *The Semeiosis of Poetic Metaphor*. Bloomington: Indiana University Press.

Hamp, Eric P. 1988. "Of SUPPORTIVE OF" *American Speech* 63: 95–96.

Hardwick, Charles S. (ed.). 1977. *Semiotic and Significs: The Correspondence between Charles S. Peirce and Victoria Lady Welby*. Bloomington: Indiana University Press.

Hascall, Dudley. 1971. "Trochaic Meter." *College English* 33: 217–26.

Hill, R. T., and T. G. Bergin. 1973. *Anthology of the Provençal Troubadours*, I, 2nd ed., rev. T. G. Bergin, with the collaboration of S. Olson et al. New Haven: Yale University Press.

Hingley, Ronald. 1968. "Introduction," in *Great Short Works of Fyodor Dostoevsky*, trans. G. Bird, xvii–xiii. New York: Perennial Library.

Hjelmslev, Louis. 1935. *La catégorie des cas: Etude de grammaire générale*. Aarhus: Universitetsforlaget.

_____. [1939] 1970. "Notes sur les oppositions supprimables," in his *Essais linguistiques*, 2nd ed., 82–88. Copenhagen: Nordisk Sprog-og Kulturforlag.

Hollander, John. 1959. "The Metrical Problem." *Kenyon Review* 21: 279–296.

Holquist, Michael. 1990. *Dialogism: Bakhtin and His World*. London: Routledge.

Houser, Nathan, and Christian Kloesel (eds.). 1992. *The Essential Peirce*, I (1867-1893). Bloomington: Indiana University Press.

Hymes, Dell. 1960. "Phonological Aspects of Style: Some English

Sonnets," in Sebeok 1960: 109–131.

Il'inskaia, I. S. 1970. *Leksika stikhotvornoi rechi Pushkina: "Vysokie" i poèticheskie slavianizmy.* Moscow: Nauka.

Iskoz [= Dolinin], A. S. (ed.). 1922. *F. M. Dostoevskii: Stat'i i mater'ialy,* I. St. Petersburg: Mysl'.

Ivanits, Linda. 1976. "The Grotesque in Fedor Sologub's Novel, *The Petty Demon,*" in *Russian and Slavic Literature,* ed. R. Freeborn et al., 137–174. Cambridge, Mass.: Slavica.

Ivanov, Viach. Vs. 1974. "The Significance of M. M. Bakhtin's Ideas on Sign, Utterance, and Dialogue for Modern Semiotics," in *Semiotics and Structuralism,* ed. H. Baran, 310–367. New York: International Arts and Sciences.

Jackson, Robert Louis. 1966. *Dostoevsky's Quest for Form: A Study of His Philosophy of Art.* New Haven, Conn.: Yale University Press.

Jakobson, Roman. 1960. "Closing Statement: Linguistics and Poetics," in Sebeok 1960: 350–377. [rpt. *SW* 3: 18–51].

_____. 1961-85. *Selected Writings,* I–VII. The Hague: Mouton. [Cited as *SW* vol. no: page(s)]

_____. [1923] 1969. *O cheshskom stikhe preimushchestvenno v sopostavlenii s russkim.* Providence: Brown University Press [rpt. in *SW* 5: 3–130].

_____. 1973. "Ob odnoslozhnykh slovakh v russkom stikhe," in *Slavic Poetics: Essays in Honor of Kiril Taranovsky,* ed. R. Jakobson et al., 239–52. The Hague: Mouton [rpt. *SW* 5: 201–14]

_____. 1980. *The Framework of Language.* Ann Arbor: Michigan Studies in the Humanities.

Jones, Daniel (comp.). 1984. *Everyman's English Pronouncing Dictionary,* 14th ed., rev. and ed. A. C. Gimson. London: Dent & Sons.

Jones, David. 1934. *La tenson provençale.* Paris: Droz.

Kahn, Charles H. 1979. *The Art and Thought of Heraclitus: An Edition of the Fragments with Translation and Commentary.*

Cambridge: Cambridge University Press.

Kalbouss, George. 1983. "Sologub and Myth." *Slavic and East European Journal* 27: 440–451.

Kent, Thomas. 1989. "Dialogic Semiotics." *American Journal of Semiotics* 6: 221–237.

Ketner, Kenneth Laine, and Hilary Putnam. 1992. "Introduction: The Consequences of Mathematics," in Peirce 1992: 1–54.

Kholshevnikov, V. E. (ed.). 1984. *Problemy teorii stikha.* Leningrad: Nauka.

Kökeritz, Helge. 1953. *Shakespeare's Pronunciation.* New Haven: Yale University Press.

Koplan, B. 1930. "'Poltavskii boi' Pushkina i ody Lomonosova." *Pushkin i ego sovremenniki* 38-39: 113–121.

Korsh, F. E. 1908. "Znal li Pushkin po-ital'ianski?" *Pushkin i ego sovremenniki* 7: 54–56.

Kovtunova, I. I. 1986. "Simmetricheskii dualizm iazykovogo znaka v poèticheskoi rechi," in *Problemy strukturnoi lingvistiki 1983*, ed. V. P. Grigor'ev, 87–108. Moscow: Nauka.

Krugovoy, George. 1991. *The Gnostic Novel of Mikhail Bulgakov: Sources and Exegesis.* Lanham, Md.: University Press of America.

Kugel, James. 1981. *The Idea of Biblical Poetry.* New Haven: Yale University Press.

Laferriere, Daniel [= Rancour-Laferriere]. 1979. "Iambic versus Trochaic: The Case of Russian." *International Review of Slavic Linguistics* 4: 81–136.

_____. 1980. "The Teleology of Rhythm in Poetry, with Examples Primarily from the Russian Syllabotonic Meters." *PTL* 4: 411–450.

Lauer, Bernhard, and Ulrich Steltner (eds.). 1984. *Fedor Sologub, 1884–1984: Texte, Aufsätze, Bibliographie.* Munich: Sagner.

Laver, John. 1994. *Principles of Phonetics.* Cambridge: Cambridge University Press.

Lebedev, E. N. 1987. "M. V. Lomonosov i russkie poety XIX v.," in *Lomonosov i russkaia literatura*, ed. A. S. Kurilov, 296–339. Moscow: AN SSSR.

Lebedev, E. N. et al. (comps). 1978. *A. S. Pushkin-kritik*. Moscow: Sovetskaiia Rossia.

Leishman, J. B. 1966. *Themes and Variations in Shakespeare's Sonnets*, 2nd ed. New York: Harper & Row.

Likhachev, D. S. 1973. *Razvitie russkoi literatury X–XVII vekov: Èpochi i stili*. Leningrad: Nauka.

Linche, Richard. 1877. "Poems," in *Occasional Issues of Unique and Very Rare Books*, IV, ed. A. B. Grosart. Manchester: Charles E. Simms.

Linnér, Sven. 1962. *Dostoevskij on Realism*. Stockholm: Almqvist & Wiksell.

Lodge, Thomas. 1963. *Complete Works*, II. New York: Russell & Russell.

Lomonosov, M. V. 1986. *Izbrannye proizvedeniia*, 3rd ed. Leningrad: Sovetskii pisatel'.

Lotman, M. Ju., and S. A. Shakhverdov. 1979. "Metrika i strofika A. S. Pushkina," in *Russkoe stikhoslozhenie XIX v.: Material po metrike i strofike russkix poètov*, ed. M. L. Gasparov, 145–257. Moscow: Nauka.

Maikov, L. 1895. *Istoriko-literaturnye ocherki*. St. Petersburg: Panteleev.

Masson, David I. 1954. "Free Phonetic Patterns in Shakespeare's Sonnets." *Neophilologus* 38: 277–289.

Medvedev, P. N., and M. M. Bakhtin. 1979. *The Formal Method in Literary Scholarship: A Critical Introduction to Sociological Poetics*, trans. A. J. Wehrle. Baltimore: The Johns Hopkins University Press.

Mencken, H. L. 1957. *The American Language: An Inquiry into the Development of English in the United States*, 4th ed. New York: Alfred A. Knopf.

Meyer, Priscilla, and Stephen Rudy (eds.). 1979. *Dostoevsky and Gogol: Texts and Criticism*. Ann Arbor: Ardis.

Milne, Lesley. 1990. *Mikhail Bulgakov: A Critical Biography.* Cambridge: Cambridge University Press.

Miłosz, Czesław. 1969. *The History of Polish Literature.* The Hague: Mouton.

Miner, Earl. 1979. *Japanese Linked Poetry: An Account with Translations of Renga and Haikai Sequences.* Princeton, N.J.: Princeton University Press.

_____. 1981. "Some Theoretical Implications of Japanese Linked Poetry." *Comparative Literature Studies* 18: 368–378.

_____. 1983. "Renga and Haikai," in *Kodansha Encyclopedia of Japan*, VI, 296–300. Tokyo: Kodansha.

Mirsky, D. S. 1966. *A History of Russian Literature.* New York: Random House.

Mochulski, K. 1967. *Dostoevsky: His Life and Work*, trans. M. A. Minihan. Princeton, N. J.: Princeton University Press.

Modzalevskii, B. L. 1910. *Biblioteka A. S. Pushkina (Bibliograficheskoe opisanie).* St. Petersburg: Tipografiia Imperatorskoi Akademii Nauk [rpt. Moscow: Nauka, 1988]

Morson, Gary Saul (ed.). 1986. *Bakhtin: Essays and Dialogues on His Work.* Chicago: University of Chicago Press.

Morson, Gary Saul, and Caryl Emerson. 1990. *Mikhail Bakhtin: Creation of a Prosaics.* Stanford, Calif.: Stanford University Press.

Nabokov, Vladimir. 1944. *Nikolai Gogol.* New York: New Directions.

_____. 1981. "Fyodor Dostoevski," in his *Lectures on Russian Literature*, ed. F. Bowers, 97–136. New York: Harcourt Brace Jovanovich.

Neuhäuser, Rudolf. 1979. *Das Frühwerk Dostojevskis: Literarische Tradition und gesellschaftlicher Anspruch.* Heidelberg: Winter.

Newton, Robert P. 1975. "Trochaic and Iambic." *Language and Style* 8: 127–56.

Obolensky, Dimitri (ed.). 1962. *The Penguin Book of Russian Verse.* Baltimore: Penguin Books.

Overing, Gillian. 1987. "Swords and Signs: A Semeiotic Perspective on *Beowulf.*" *American Journal of Semiotics* 51: 35–57.

Pachmuss, Temira. 1971. *Zinaida Hippius: An Intellectual Profile.* Carbondale: Southern Illinois University Press.

Padel, John. 1981. *New Poems by Shakespeare: Order and Meaning Restored to the Sonnets.* London: Herbert Press.

Paterson, Linda M. 1975. *Troubadours and Eloquence.* Oxford: Clarendon Press.

Patterson, David. 1988. "Dostoevsky's *Dvoinik* per Lacan's *Parole,*" in his *The Affirming Flame: Religion, Language, Literature,* 58–76. Norman: University of Oklahoma Press.

Patterson, Galina. 1998. "Nabokov's Use of Dostoevskii: Developing Goliadkin's 'Symptoms' in Hermann as a Sign of the Artist's End." *Canadian Slavonic Papers* 40: 107–124.

Paz, Octavio et al. 1972. *Renga: A Chain of Poems by Octavio Paz, Jacques Roubaud, Edoardo Sanguinetti, Charles Tomlinson,* trans. C. Tomlinson. New York: George Braziller.

Peace, Richard. 1998. "Gogol and Dostoevsky's *The Double,*" in *Polyfunktion und Metaparodie: Aufsätze zum 175. Geburtstag von Fedor Michailovich Dostoevskij,* ed. Rudolf Neuhäuser, 103–114. Dresden: Dresden University Press.

Peirce, Charles Sanders. 1965-66. *Collected Papers,* 2nd printing, 8 vols. in 4, ed. C. Hartshorne, P. Weiss & A. Burks. Cambridge, Mass.: Harvard University Press.

_____. 1976. *The New Elements of Mathematics,* I–IV., ed. C. Eisele. The Hague: Mouton.

_____. 1982–2000. *Writings of Charles S. Peirce: A Chronological Edition,* I–VI, ed. M. H. Fisch et al. Bloomington: Indiana University Press.

_____.1992. *Reasoning and the Logic of Things,* ed. K. L. Ketner & H. Putnam. Cambridge, Mass.: Harvard University Press.

Perlina, Nina. 1985. *Varieties of Poetic Utterance: Quotation in The Brothers Karamazov.* Lanham, Md.: University Press of America.

Petrarca, Francesco. 1964. *Canzoniere*, ed. G. Contini. Turin: Einaudi.

Pirkhofer, Anton M. 1963. "'A pretty pleasing pricket'—On the Use of Alliteration in Shakespeare's Sonnets." *Shakespeare Quarterly* 14: 3–14.

Pooler, C. Knox. 1918. "Introduction," in *The Works of Shakespeare* [= The Arden Shakespeare]: *Sonnets*, ed. C. K. Pooler, vii–xxxviii. London: Methuen.

Pumpianskii, L. V. 1939. "'Mednyi vsadnik' i poèticheskaiia traditsiia XVIII veka." *Pushkin: Vremennik Pushkinskoi komissii* 4–5: 117–124.

Pushkin, A. S. 1939–1959. *Polnoe sobranie sochinenii*, I–XVII. Leningrad: AN SSSR.

Pyles, Thomas. 1952. *Words and Ways of American English*. New York: Random House.

Rabinowitz, Stanley J. 1978. "Fedor Sologub and His Nineteenth-Century Russian Antecedents." *Slavic and East European Journal* 22: 324–335.

_____. 1980. *Sologub's Literary Children: Keys to a Symbolist's Prose*. Columbus, Oh.: Slavica.

Rahner, Karl. 1974. *The Trinity*, trans. J. Donceel. New York: Seabury Press.

Rancour-Laferriere [= Laferriere], Daniel. 1981. "Stress Shifts Induced by Syllabotonic Rhythm: Exploring an Intersection of Russian Poetics and Experimental Psychology." *Russian Literature* 10: 31–48.

_____. 1989. "Further Remarks on the Teleology of Metrical Rhythm," in *Russian Verse Theory*, ed. by B. P. Scherr and D. S. Worth, 275–285. Columbus, Oh.: Slavica.

Rank, Otto. 1971. *The Double: A Psychoanalytic Study*, ed. and trans. H. Tucker, Jr. Chapel Hill: University of North Carolina Press.

Rice, James. L. 1985. *Dostoevsky and the Healing Art: An Essay in Literary and Medical History*. Ann Arbor: Ardis.

Robertson, Stuart. 1954. *The Development of Modern English,* 2nd ed., rev. F. G. Cassidy. Englewood Cliffs, N.J.: Prentice-Hall.

Robinson, T. M. 1987. *Heraclitus: Fragments.* Toronto: University of Toronto Press.

Rosenshield, Gary. 1997. "*The Master and Margarita* and the Poetics of Aporia: A Polemical Article." *Slavic Review* 56: 187–211.

Rosenthal, Richard J. 1982. "Dostoevsky's Use of Projection: Psychic Mechanism as Literary Form in *The Double.*" *Dostoevsky Studies* 3: 79–86.

Rozanov, M. N. 1930. "Pushkin i Petrarka." *Moskovskii pushkinist* 2: 116–154.

Rozanov, V. V. 1970. *Legenda o Velikom Inkvizitore F. M. Dostoevskogo: Opyt kriticheskogo kommentariia s prilozheniem dvukh ètiudov o Gogole.* Munich: Fink.

Sebeok, Thomas A. (ed.). 1960. *Style in Language.* Cambridge, Mass.: M. I. T Press.

Semenko, I. M. 1977. "Batiuskov i ego *Opyty,*" in Batiushkov 1977: 433–492.

Senderovich, Savely. 1980. "On Puskin's Mythology: The Shade Myth," in *Alexander Pushkin Symposium II,* ed. A. Kodjak et al., 103–115. Columbus, Oh.: Slavica.

Serman, I. Z. 1966. *Poèticheskii stil' Lomonosova.* Moscow: Nauka.

Shakespeare, William. 1986. *The Sonnets and A Lover's Complaint,* ed. J. Kerrigan. London: Penguin.

_____. 1996. *The Sonnets,* ed. G. B. Evans. Cambridge: Cambridge University Press.

_____. 1997. *Shakespeare's Sonnets* [= The Arden Shakespeare—Third Series], ed. K. Duncan-Jones. Ehrhardt: Thomas Nelson & Sons.

Shapiro, Marianne. 1980a. *Hieroglyph of Time: The Petrarchan Sestina.* Minneapolis: University of Minnesota Press.

_____. 1980b. "The Semiotics of Archie Bunker," *Ars Semeiotica* 3:159–180 [revised version in Shapiro and Shapiro 1988: ch. 11]

Shapiro, Marianne, and Michael Shapiro. 1993. "Pushkin and Petrarch," in *American Contributions to the Eleventh International Congress of Slavists*, ed. R. A. Maguire and A. Timberlake, 154–69. Columbus, Oh.: Slavica.

Shapiro, Michael. 1976. *Asymmetry: An Inquiry into the Linguistic Structure of Poetry*. Amsterdam: North-Holland.

_____. 1978. "Inexact Rhyme in Russian Proverbs and Riddles," in *Studia linguistica A. V. Issatschenko oblata*, ed. H. Birnbaum et al., 359–368. Lisse: Peter de Ridder.

_____. 1980a. "Poetry and Language, 'Considered as Semeiotic.'" *Transactions of the Charles S. Peirce Society* 16: 97–117.

_____. 1980b. "Russian Conjugation: Theory and Hermeneutic." *Language* 56: 67–93.

_____. 1982. "Remarks on the Nature of the Autotelic Sign," in *Georgetown University Round Table on Languages and Linguistics 1982*, ed. H. Byrnes, 101–111. Washington, D.C.: Georgetown University Press.

_____. 1983. *The Sense of Grammar: Language as Semeiotic*. Bloomington: Indiana University Press.

_____. 1985. "Teleology, Semeiosis, and Linguistic Change." *Diachronica* 2: 1–34

_____. 1986. "The Russian System of Stress." *Russian Linguistics* 10: 183–204.

_____. 1988. "Dynamic Interpretants and Grammar." *Transactions of the Charles S. Peirce Society* 24: 123-30.

_____. 1991. *The Sense of Change: Language as History*. Bloomington: Indiana University Press.

Shapiro, Michael, and Marianne Shapiro. 1988. *Figuration in Verbal Art*. Princeton, N. J.: Princeton University Press.

Shapiro, Michael, and Michael C. Haley. 2002. "The Reduplicative Copula IS IS," *American Speech* 77: 305–312.

Sherry, Charles. 1975. "Folie à deux: Gogol and Dostoevsky,"

Texas Studies in Literature and Language 17: 257–273.

Shishkin, A. B. 1983. "Poèticheskoe sostiazanie Trediakovskogo, Lomonosova i Sumarokova." *XVIII vek* 14: 232–246.

Shklovskii, Viktor. 1957. *Za i protiv: Zametki o Dostoevskom.* Moscow: Sovetskii pisatel'.

Short, T. L. 1981. "Semeiosis and Intentionality." *Transactions of the Charles S. Peirce Society* 17: 197–223.

Singer, Milton. 1984. *Man's Glassy Essence: Explorations in Semiotic Anthropology.* Bloomington: Indiana University Press.

Singleton, Charles S. 1958. *Journey to Beatrice.* Cambridge, Mass.: Harvard University Press.

Sismondi, Jean Charles-Leonard de. 1829. *De la littérature du midi de l'Europe*, I, 3rd ed. Paris: Treuttel & Würtz.

Skinner, B. F. 1939. "The Alliteration in Shakespeare's Sonnets: A Study in Literary Behavior." *The Psychological Record* 3: 186–192.

_____.1941. "A Quantitative Estimate of Certain Types of Sound-Patterning in Poetry." *American Journal of Psychology* 54: 64–79.

Smith, Hallett. 1981. *The Tension of the Lyre: Poetry in Shakespeare's Sonnets.* San Marino, Calif.: Huntington Library.

Snyder, Harry. 1986. "The Gogolian Echoes in Sologub's *The Petty Demon*: Are They Imitative of or Organic to Gogol's *Dead Souls*?" *Modern Language Studies* 16: 189–205.

Sokolov, B. V. 1991. *Roman M. Bulgakova 'Master i Margarita': Ocherk tvorcheskoi istorii.* Moscow: Nauka.

Sologub, Fedor. 1962. *The Petty Demon*, trans. A. Field. New York: Random House.

_____. 1966. *Melkii bes*, ed. J. Forsyth. Letchworth: Bradda Books.

_____. 1975. *Stikhotvoreniia*, ed. M. Dikman. Leningrad: Sovetskii pisatel'.

_____. 1983. *The Petty Demon*, trans. S. D. Cioran., ed. M. Barker.

Ann Arbor: Ardis.

_____. 1988. *Melkii bes*, ed. M. V. Koz'menko. Moscow: Khudozhestvennaia literatura.

Spenser, Edmund. 1947. *Works: A Variorum Edition: The Minor Poems*, II, ed. C. G. Osgood et al. Baltimore: The Johns Hopkins University Press.

Spitzer, Leo. 1944. *L'amour lointain de Jaufre Rudel et le sens de la poésie des troubadours*. Chapel Hill: University of North Carolina Press.

Stepanov, N. L. (comp.). 1972. *Poèty pushkinskoi pory: Antologiia*. Moscow: Khudozhestvennaia literatura.

Stirling, Brents. 1968. *The Shakespeare Sonnet Order: Poems and Groups*. Berkeley: University of California Press.

Strzetelski, Jerzy. 1977. *An Introduction to Polish Literature*. Cracow: Nakładem Uniwersytetu Jagiellońskiego.

Taranovskii, Kirill. 1963. "O vzaimootnoshenii stikhotvornogo ritma i tematiki." *American Contributions to the Fifth International Congress of Slavists, I: Linguistic Contributions*, 287–322. The Hague: Mouton.

Tarlinskaja, Marina. 1993. *Strict Stress-Meter in English Poetry Compared with German and Russian*. Calgary: University of Calgary Press.

Terras, Victor. 1981. *A Karamazov Companion: Commentary on the Genesis, Language, and Style of Dostoevsky's Novel*. Madison: University of Wisconsin Press.

_____. 1983. "Kritische Betrachtungen zu Dostoevskijs Pushkinbild," in *Dostoevskij und die Literatur*, ed. H. Rothe, 74–81. Cologne: Böhlau.

_____. 1998. *Reading Dostoevsky*. Madison: University of Wisconsin Press.

Terry, Garth. 1991. *Mikhail Bulgakov in English: A Bibliography, 1891–1991*. Nottingham: Astra Press.

Timofeev. L. I. 1982. *Slovo v stikhe*. Moscow: Sovetskii pisatel'.

Todorov, Tzvetan. 1984. *Mikhail Bakhtin: The Dialogical Prin-*

ciple, trans. W. Godzich. Minneapolis: University of Minnesota Press.

_____. 1990. *Genres in Discourse*, trans. C. Porter. Cambridge: Cambridge University Press.

Tomashevskii, B. V. 1956. *Pushkin: Kniga pervaia (1813–1824)*. Moscow: AN SSSR.

_____. 1958. "Strofika Pushkina." *Pushkin: Issledovaniia i materialy* 2: 49–184.

Tomasović, Mirko. 1981. "Croatian Renaissance Literature in the European Context," in Beker 1981: 95–123.

Toporov, V. N. 1969. "K rekonstruktstii indoevropeiskogo rituala i ritual'no-poèticheskikh formul (na materiale zagovorov)." *Trudy po znakovym sistemam* 4: 9–43.

Topsfield, Leslie M. 1974. *Troubadours and Love*. Cambridge: Cambridge University Press.

Trubetskoi, N. S. 1923-1924. Review of Jakobson [1923] 1969. *Slavia* 2: 452–460.

_____. [1937] 1963. "K voprosu o stikhe 'Pesen zapadnykh slavian' Pushkina," in his *Three Philological Studies*, 55–67. Ann Arbor: Department of Slavic Languages and Literatures, University of Michigan. [rpt. Trubetskoi 1987: 359–70]

_____.1975. *Letters and Notes*, ed. R. Jakobson. The Hague: Mouton.

_____. 1987. *Izbrannye trudy po filologii*. Moscow: Progress.

Tsiavlovskii, M. A., et al. (eds.). 1935. *Rukoiu Pushkina: Nesobrannye i neopublikovannye teksty*. Moscow: Academia.

Tsur, Reuven. 1992. *What Makes Sound Patterns Expressive?: The Poetic Mode of Speech Perception*. Durham, N.C.: Duke University Press.

Tynianov, Ju. N. 1929. *Arkhaisty i novatory*. Leningrad: Priboi.

_____. [1924] 1965. *Problema stikhotvornogo iazyka: Stat'i*. Moscow: Sovetskii pisatel'.

Ulewicz, Tadeusz. 1984. "The European Significance of Jan Kochanowski from the Renaissance to the Romantics," in

Cross Currents: A Yearbook of Central European Culture, III, eds. L. Matejka & B. Stolz, 151–175. Ann Arbor: Department of Slavic Languages, University of Michigan.

Unamuno, Miguel de. 1954. *Tragic Sense of Life*, trans. J. E. C. Flitch. New York: Dover.

Vachek, Josef. 1979. "Some Remarks on the Stylistics of Written Language," in *Function and Context in Linguistic Analysis: A Festschrift for William Haas*, ed. D. J. Allerton et al., 206–221. Cambridge: Cambridge University Press.

Vendler, Helen. 1997. *The Art of Shakespeare's Sonnets*. Cambridge, Mass.: Harvard University Press.

Vinogradov, V. V. 1935. *Iazyk Pushkina: Pushkin i istoriia russkogo literaturnogo iazyka*. Moscow: Academia.

_____. 1936. "Stil' 'Pikovoi damy.'" *Vremennik Pushkinskoi komissii* 2: 74–147. [rpt. in his *Izbrannye trudy: O iazyke khudozhestvennoi prozy*, 176–239. Moscow: Nauka, 1980]

_____. 1941. *Stil' Pushkina*. Moscow: GIKHL.

_____.1959. *O iazyke khudozhestvennoi literatury*. Moscow: Goslitizdat.

_____. 1976. "K morfologii natural'nogo stilia: Opyt lingvisticheskogo analiza peterburgskoi poèmy 'Dvoinik,'" in his *Izbrannye trudy: Poètika russkoi literatury*, 101–140. Moscow: Nauka.

_____. 1979. "Toward a Morphology of the Naturalist Style," in Meyer & Rudy 1979: 217–228 [= abridged translation of Vinogradov 1976].

Vishnevskii, K. D. 1977. "K voprosu ob ispol'zovanii kolichestvennykh metodov v stikhovedenii," in *Kontekst 1976: Literaturno-teoreticheskie issledovaniia*, ed. A. S. Miasnikov, 130–160. Moscow: Nauka.

_____. 1985. "Èkspressivnyi oreol piatistopnogo khoreiia," in *Russkoe stikhoslozhenie: Traditsii i problemy*, ed. L. I. Timofeev, 93–113. Moscow: Nauka.

Ward, Dennis.1975. "Pushkin's Èxo—Sound, Grammar, Meaning." *Studia Slavica Hungarica* 21: 377–386.

Wasiolek, Edward. 1973. *Dostoevsky: The Major Fiction.* Cambridge, Mass.: M.I.T. Press.

Webster, Noah. 1961. *Websters Third New International Dictionary of the English Language, Unabridged,* ed. P. B. Gove et al. Springfield, Mass.: G. & C. Merriam.

Weeks, Laura D. 1984. "Hebraic Antecedents in *The Master and Margarita*: Woland and Company Revisited." *Slavic Review* 43: 224–241.

———— (ed.). 1996. *The Master and Margarita: A Critical Companion.* Evanston, Ill.: Northwestern University Press.

Wellek, René. 1963. *Essays on Czech Literature.* The Hague: Mouton.

Wells, Rulon. 1960. "Nominal and Verbal Style," in Sebeok 1960: 213–220.

Wesling, Donald, and Enikö Bollobás. 1983. "Verse Form: Recent Studies." *Modern Philology* 81: 53–60.

Wierzbicki, Jan. 1981. "Miroslav Krleža in the European Spiritual Context," in Beker 1981: 563–580.

Williams, Gareth. 1990. "Some Difficulties in the Interpretation of Bulgakov's *The Master and Margarita* and the Advantages of a Manichaean Approach, with Some Notes on Tolstoi's Influence on the Novel." *The Slavonic and East European Review* 68: 234–256.

Winsheimer, Joel. 1983. "The Realism of C. S. Peirce, or How Homer and Nature Can Be the Same." *American Journal of Semiotics* 2: 225–263.

Wolff, Tatiana (ed. and trans.). 1986. *Pushkin on Literature,* rev. ed. London: Athlone Press.

Wöll, Alexander. 1999. *Doppelgänger: Steinmonument, Spiegelschrift und Usurpation in der russischen Literatur.* Frankfurt: Peter Lang.

Wright, George T. 1985. "Shakespeare's Poetic Technique," in *William Shakespeare: His World, His Work, His Influence, II:*

His Work, ed. J. F. Andrews, 363-87. New York: Charles Scribner's Sons.

Zernov, Nicholas. 1961. *Eastern Christendom.* New York: Putnam.

Zhirmunskii, V. M. 1922. "Melodika stikha (Po povodu knigi B. M. Èikhenbauma 'Melodika stikha', SPb., 1922)." *Mysl'* 3: 109–139. [rpt. in Zhirmunskii 1977: 56–93]

_____. 1925. *Vvedenie v metriku: Teoriia stikha.* Leningrad: Academia. [rpt. in Zhirmunskii 1975: 5–232].

_____. 1975. *Teoriia stikha.* Leningrad: Sovetskii pisatel'.

_____. 1977. *Teoriia literatury, poètika, stilistika.* Leningrad: Nauka.

Index